THE
BROKEN
CIRCLE

THE
BROKEN
CIRCLE

A MEMOIR OF ESCAPING AFGHANISTAN

ENJEELA AHMADI-MILLER

The events expressed in this book, while true, were composed from the author's memory. Some of the names and identities of people in this book have been altered or composited for the sake of simplicity and to protect privacy.

Poems by Hafiz translated into English by the author

Published by Little A, New York

www.apub.com

Amazon, the Amazon logo, and Little A are trademarks of Amazon.com, Inc., or its affiliates.

ISBN-13: 9781503903784 (hardcover)
ISBN-10: 1503903788 (hardcover)
ISBN-13: 9781503903760 (paperback)
ISBN-10: 1503903761 (paperback)

Cover design by Faceout Studio, Jeff Miller

Cover illustration by Christina Chung

Interior map by Mapping Specialists, Ltd.

Printed in the United States of America

First edition

It was the birth of my beautiful son, Alexander Miller,
that inspired me to write my memories of Afghanistan,
the country of my birth.

HOW BIRDS FLY

Once in the past, I asked a bird
"In what way do you fly
in this gravity of wickedness?"
She responded,
"Love lifts my wings."
—*Hafiz*

CONTENTS

Prologue

A Tapestry of Time and Place

I had not thought about Afghanistan in years. I had forgotten, buried the images of death and war under the busyness of an American life.

There was the party to prepare for; five hundred invitations were in the mail to local fashionistas for the introduction of my new line at a posh gallery downtown. Everyone who is anyone in Dallas, even my husband's, Henry's, influential real estate friends, will be there.

We arrive at the party, Henry and I, celebrities on this night. Beautiful people greet us, coiffed, dressed to dazzle, each of them elegant and striking. The gallery is brilliant with light; the modern art pieces hang like illuminated gems on the white panels. Waiters with trays of appetizers and flutes of champagne serve the guests. Anticipation builds as we mingle, hugs and kisses all around. I look around in wonder—this is perfect, the apex of my dreams. Even if I had climbed the highest mountain and stood on top of the world breathing in the heady air, I could not have been more elated. All these movers and shakers here to see my designs, the work of my imagination.

The music takes on a new beat, thrumming and dramatic, and the first model sashays in. There are twelve in all—gorgeous, thin, leggy, high-cheeked blondes, brunettes, and redheads. They strut, they pose, they turn, and the smoothness of the fabric along their slender roundness accents every curve, every undulating movement of their bodies. They look like a million bucks; the jeans I have designed look like a million bucks. My face burns with pride.

Then an unstoppable wave of memory, of that Cinderella moment in Kabul when my sister Shahnaz, bedecked in gold jewelry and flowing green wedding dress, every bit as gorgeous as any of these models, promenaded into the grand ballroom of the stately Serena Hotel on the arm of her husband, Saleem. One of the happiest memories of my life. As the crowd oohs and aahs at the fashion show, they flash me glances of congratulations and admiration, but I'm transported. A child in a world falling apart around me. I think of my sister's wedding, and the day my mother left Kabul, and the rumble of invading Soviet tanks.

I glance around. *Where is my son?* And I remember Alexander is at home.

Once the models have finished walking, I step away from the party to make a call.

"Bring him to me," I tell the nanny. "Come to the party with him."

When he arrives, I hold him in my arms, and as people congratulate me, I am not thinking of jeans, or models, or accolades, or even sales and the comforts that would bring. I'm thinking only of him, and us, and how I will never leave him like she left me. I will never make him question my love for him. I will never make him search for me.

I know now who I am. I am Afghan, and I am American. I am one fabric of existence: a tapestry of past and present.

I am safe, happy, prosperous, and enjoying every moment of my life. But I am sad for the ones left behind, those who could not escape.

My son is only three, but he should know this story. He must know where I come from. The delicate fabric of our lives here, woven by a young refugee fleeing a country that she loved.

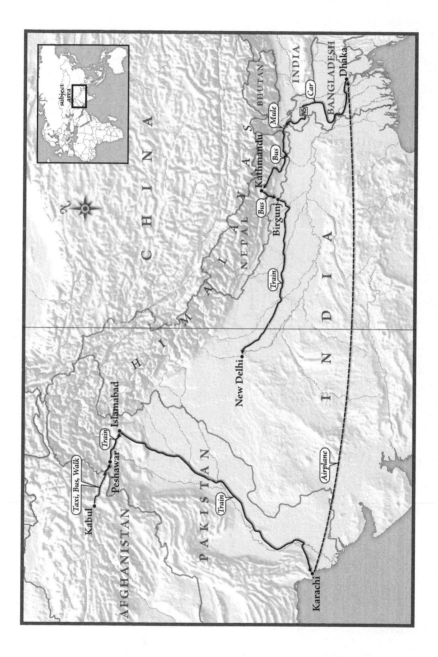

1

ENGAGEMENT PARTY

The Rigveda, a sacred text, speaks of Kabul as a vision of paradise set in the mountains. For me it was many things—my birthplace, my playfield, my home, the crucible of my soul. But I like the description of paradise best.

Outside the gates of my house, Kabul stretched out along the sloping plains and into rocky foothills, a city both modern and ancient. High-rise office buildings were neighbors to the bazaar that had stood since the time of Babur the Conqueror, who made the city his capital. Now a modern electric trolley ran along every major road and most streets, carrying Kabuli from the suburbs to their work or shopping. The paved streets of the city were a slice of a larger world—men in turbans and men in suits; women in burkas and girls in miniskirts. There were mosques, synagogues, and churches, and in 1975, the year of my birth, it was a city of peace.

I remember most vividly the turn of the seasons. When the buttercups and lilies bloomed, their petals unfolding in a carpet of whiteness across the field in front our home, I knew springtime had arrived. They lifted a delicious odor into the cool breeze, as sweet as *jalebi*, my favorite dessert. The fruit trees in our orchard would ripen soon—peaches, pears, pomegranates, and later in the year there would be apples and oranges. New green shoots of grass sprouted around the trees, and to the north, the Hindu Kush mountains were snowcapped and shrouded in sporadic clouds. Cherry trees blossomed along the roads, roses came to life in gardens, and a new season emerged from the winter darkness.

I played soccer in the tree-lined streets, paved and clean, with my friends and sisters. I rode bikes and played volleyball and watched my brothers fly kites when the winds blew off the plains. I ran and played until I heard the *azan*—the song of the mullah. From my yard, I could look up and see the minarets of our mosque. It was five o'clock and time to return home for dinner.

Winter in Kabul came in December, and the snow would pile up high on the sides of the house, soft as giant pillows. Zia, my brother, often dared the three of us girls to climb on the roof with him and jump off. Zulaikha would have nothing to do with it. She would never get on the roof. Laila would come up only if Zia coaxed her. Zia had only to dare me, and I'd climb up. I'd walk right up to the edge of the roof, stare down for a moment at the white mound, and then lift off into space, yelling all the way, flailing my arms until landing in the white softness.

We did this until the maid came out and spotted me in midair. She ran and told Mother, who put a stop to our fun with a strong word of warning: I had to stop acting like a tomboy. She had a way of letting me know she disapproved of me. She then would call Shapairi, my second oldest sister, and have her clean me up. Shahnaz, my oldest sister, was far too busy with her makeup and clothes and her job to have any time to help dress us or clean us up.

My childhood was filled with fun and camaraderie. I was the second youngest of eight children of a prominent Kabul family, and we lived behind the whitewashed walls surrounding the house Padar had built for us in the Karte Seh neighborhood. I grew up during one of the most prosperous periods in the history of Afghanistan. My neighborhood was full of mansions of every size, and it was situated not far from the downtown district, where new government buildings were being constructed. At one end of my street was the large building where the National Assembly of Afghanistan met. Our national *loya jirgas* were convened here. From time to time, a line of big cars would stream down our street, bringing delegates from all over the nation to meet.

When driving through town with Padar, we often passed by the tree-filled campus of Kabul University. It was crowded with students, men and women strolling the manicured grounds between buildings, talking and enjoying life. This was a place where prosperity and tradition intersected, each in appreciation for the other's place in its citizens' hearts. Shahnaz, my oldest sister, and Shapairi, who was a year younger, were in high school and were the most beautiful girls in town, or at least I thought so. Shahnaz had an elegant way to her that reminded me of royalty, with a demureness that added to her mystery. Her lips were always bright red with fresh lipstick that made her clear light skin almost shine. Shapairi was an outspoken tomboy who was as bold as Shahnaz was shy and refined. They both dressed in the highest fashion and were intensely sought after by young men.

But a boy could never approach Shahnaz and Shapairi just to chat and be friends. Such things were never done. Our traditions did not allow a boy to talk to a girl in public without risking great disdain from those in the neighborhood. It would be shameful and full of bitter consequences for a girl to be seen alone with a boy. She would gain a certain reputation. Still, there were ways that a girl could know who was interested in her.

Boys often followed Shahnaz and Shapairi home from school—always at a distance, always in a group, always without speaking directly to them. Boys followed them when they walked to the bazaar to shop for the fine material they desired for their dresses and skirts, or to the ice cream shop, or to the mall.

———

I would wait by our front door for them to return from school. They both wore their uniforms: black dresses, black hose, high heels, and white scarves around their necks. One day, Shapairi, full of exasperation and fluster, tore through the door, reciting the names of boys who had been trailing behind her, none of whom had a chance of ever catching her eye. Shahnaz strolled in quietly behind Shapairi as if she had not noticed anyone following them at all. To her it was just another beautiful day in Kabul.

After Shahnaz graduated from high school, she began working at Ariana Airlines. At the airport where she worked, a tall, handsome pilot took immediate notice of her. If she ever did anything to encourage him, it would not have been more than a well-timed smile or suggestive glance from her green eyes, heavy with smoky makeup. They could chat only in passing. He would stop and offer some pleasantry, and she would smile in her way. Shahnaz always looked her best at work, in her high-fashion tight skirts, elegant silk blouses, and her expensive jewelry—ready to greet a prime minister or royalty or a president when they stepped off their planes.

She and the pilot could never touch each other. And they would never be in a room alone until his parents talked to my parents and the courtship was approved.

They learned about love from a distance. This is the truest love of all, when two people must wait and build up great ideas about each other until the passion becomes so unbearable and deeply rooted that they must have each other. That is how love becomes the most desirable and lasting. I wanted this love more than anything. I wanted the traditions to work for me. I wanted my life to end up like the romance stories that Shahnaz would read to me and three of my other siblings—Laila and Zulaikha, and my brother Zia, my closest friend and playmate.

Shahnaz used to gather us together in our living room and tell us about a story she had just read. She was always reading, mostly novels, and the one she had just completed was even more astonishing than the one before. We sat raptly at her feet in our living room of expensive Italian furniture and listened intently to the tales of women falling in love with noble men who were courageous and dashing and handsome. We would laugh and blush in wonder. I remember gazing into her face that glowed with passion as she recounted each story, hinting that she knew these happy endings to be true. After she finished reading, Shahnaz had this way of looking through us with a far-off look, as if she could see something in the distance, something possible that we couldn't see. I wanted to be like her and know about this world beyond the white stuccoed walls of our compound, beyond the streets of our neighborhood and the trolleyed streets of the city.

There came a day when this man who followed her did call, or rather his mother called Mommy, who then spoke to Padar.

It was not always possible in my large family at my young age to figure out how events were coloring my future, what they would mean to me when I grew older. Yet it was simple to know something important was taking place.

We lived in a spacious home with sitting rooms, a formal dining room, and a large living room, where my parents greeted distinguished guests. Every room had crystal chandeliers imported from Europe. We had maids' quarters and a guesthouse. In one of the side yards, we had a volleyball court, a badminton court, a playground, and over an acre of fruit trees surrounded by a high white stucco wall that divided all the properties of the wealthy Karte Seh neighborhood.

Padar, Abdullah Ahmadi, was tall with jet-black hair and a broad forehead and a manliness that always held my admiration. Besides being my father, Padar was many things: a businessman, a property owner, a communications engineer employed by the American embassy, fluent in seven languages, a man of great bravery, and, to our great family shame, an alcoholic. But before he was any of these things, he was a poet. He had memorized most of Rumi's and Hafiz's poems. The other passion in his life was his total devotion to his wife, our mother, Miriam, who took that dedication with a dram of insouciance that could be at times subversively hostile.

Padar's habit after dinner was to recite his favorite poem from Hafiz, and halfway through he would stop. Mommy would then take up and finish as we sat raptly at their feet, listening to them speak of love and courage and dedication, and the words of the great Hafiz washed over us.

One night they spoke alone. After dinner we were asked to go to our rooms. I asked Laila, who was five years older and much smarter about these things, about all of this. She explained that Shahnaz had a suitor, and Padar, from what she knew, liked him, but Mommy thought Shahnaz could do better, a wealthy businessman or a diplomat.

When Laila said "diplomat," it filled all my thoughts with the American man who often came to our home for Padar's parties. Padar had worked at the embassy since he and Mommy were first married, and so he had friendships with many Americans, including the ambassador. He had many other diplomatic friends and acquaintances.

Several times a year, my father would host parties for his friends. All of us had to dress in our best clothes because the prime minister and ambassadors and politicians would be there. Diplomats from embassies all over Kabul would drive through our gates in their long black cars, and the men in handsome suits and elegant ladies in dresses that glittered would be welcomed into our home. Noor, our family's longtime housekeeper, and the household staff prepared for days at Mommy's meticulous direction. If the party was large, she'd hire a caterer, who would take over the side yard and prepare mounds of food. Everything had to be perfect—the music, the food, the house, and of course her children.

At the party, men and women mingled, the men drinking while the women smoked up the whole house. There were so many flashy, well-dressed men, but one man stood out: the American diplomat—tall and handsome beyond anything in Shahnaz's storytelling. We heard he had his eye on her. If he had, Mommy would have been very happy. But the American never called and spoke to Padar.

In time, Mommy agreed to the courtship of Shahnaz and the pilot, Saleem Rodwal. Saleem's father was an important general in the army, and Saleem was allowed to visit our home, and he and Shahnaz could sit on the Italian sofas and sip chai tea and talk. I had no idea what else they would do. Yet wasn't that the greatest part of love, to talk? I imagined they spoke poetry to each other, like Padar and Mommy, and her man would get that dreamy look in his eye the way Padar did for Mommy when he recited Hafiz.

Shahnaz's engagement party was the biggest party Padar had ever thrown. It was an event of great happiness and celebration. Family and friends of the groom, Mommy's family and relatives, Padar's family, and all of his diplomatic friends from the embassy attended in force. It seemed the entirety of Kabul wanted to celebrate the engagement of Shahnaz and Saleem.

A caterer set up a huge white tent in the side yard and brought in his stoves and utensils. Kitchen workers prepared mounds of chicken and beef and lamb and fish kabobs, and brown and white and green rice, and every flavor of tea, along with desserts and breads and hors d'oeuvres.

Mommy dressed me in new yellow pants and a top. And when the crowd began gathering outside the tent, I climbed the pear tree by the gate to watch the waiters and waitresses bustle around the guests stretched out in our ample yard. Padar greeted everyone, pride evident in his smile, with kisses and hugs.

And Shahnaz, elegant with her long black hair pulled to the side like a princess, dazzled in the afternoon sun in her emerald-green pencil skirt with silver stripes. Her high cheekbones were highlighted by her bright-red lipstick and smoky eye shadow. She hugged Padar repeatedly and told him how thankful she was for such a grand party. She floated from person to person, from the tent to the house, hugging and shaking hands, receiving the best wishes of her guests and family in the honor of the moment till she burst with a radiant glow as if she had absorbed all of the happiness in Kabul.

Her eyes turned to the gates when a chain of big black cars pulled up, and men in suits hustled to open the doors. A barrel-chested man, General Rodwal, Saleem's father, stepped out of one of the cars. With his bodyguards and his sons around, the general walked up the drive, and Padar went to him and greeted him with kisses on the cheek, the way men do, and hugs. Beside the General strode Saleem, tall and handsome with a definite swagger that caught my sister's eye.

While I watched Shahnaz and Saleem greet each other, Padar called to me.

"Enjeela, come down from there." His face upturned, he peered at me through the branches of the tree. "Come help me."

Before climbing down from the tree, I glanced around. It was evening now, and down my street I could see the dim city lights and hear the faint rumble of traffic. To me, Kabul was the busiest and most wonderful place in the world.

"Enjeela, come down now," Mommy said as she regarded me. Her mouth was set and her arms were folded across her chest.

I stepped from limb to limb until I touched the last branch and jumped the few feet to the ground.

Mommy had a heated look to her eyes. "Look at you." I followed her gaze to the large black spot on my new yellow blouse. She took my hand and nearly dragged me to a table under the tent, where my two aunts sat smoking. Mommy slumped in a chair and dabbed at my blouse with the corner of a wet napkin.

Mommy's two cousins came over, both in dark suits, with drinks in hand and stood nearby, somber-faced, watching Mommy work on my stain. Everyone had drinking glasses, and they would pretend they were sipping sodas, mentioning names of different soft drinks, but the smell of alcohol was heavy in the air. There was some chatting between them, but it was brief and staccato, as if they all had something else on their minds. My aunts smoked one cigarette after another, stubbing out one, then lighting another, as they scanned the crowd.

Somewhere behind me I heard Shahnaz laughing, her world so full of happiness. I couldn't see her, but I imagined she was smiling and beautiful and everyone around her was enjoying themselves.

One of my aunts nodded toward the gate. "Look who's here."

Mommy turned and stared, her hand frozen in midair over my blouse. "Damn Parchamis. What're they doing here?" She turned back to me, and she didn't seem angry at me any longer. "I didn't invite them."

"They're friends of the groom," one of my aunts said.

Squinting as they watched the group of men stroll up the driveway, Mommy's two cousins seemed to tense—their thin and angular faces turned pale, and their fingers twitched on the outside of their drink glasses. I knew that Mommy's cousins worked in government, but I didn't know what they did. Sometimes Mommy talked about them at dinner, and I knew she had long conversations with them over the phone.

Mommy gave up on my blouse and dropped the napkin on the table. She tightened her mouth the way she did when she grew angry. Her gaze turned to the crowd. My aunts smoked, and their eyes became bullets as they stared at the Parcham men. My cousins stood stiffly, as if they wanted to disappear.

Behind me, I heard Shahnaz thanking a guest for coming, her voice filled with enthusiasm and love. I turned and found her. Padar was nearby, greeting someone with his enthusiastic salaam that made you feel especially glad to know him. I worked my way to him and took his hand, and he gripped it tightly. Even with unwelcome invaders, there was love and hope on this night.

2

ABDULLAH

My padar, Abdullah, had a motorcycle and a degree in engineering from Kabul University and not much else when he met my mother. Part of the modernization under King Zahir Shah in the fifties and sixties was that anyone who qualified academically could find their way to the university, either through private or public scholarships. Under King Zahir Shah and then under President Daoud Khan, the economy was opening up with investment money from both the United States and Russia. Roads, secondary and primary schools, universities, hospitals, dams, and agricultural projects had been planned and built. New businesses were springing up, and Padar stepped right into this opportunity. Educated men and women were slowly replacing the traditional leaders and businessmen in the country, gradually implementing progressive changes in everyday Afghan life.

Padar had graduated from the university and begun working at the American embassy when he met Mommy. He had spotted Mommy when she was out with her sisters, probably in one of the bazaars or new shopping malls springing up in the best neighborhoods. After making inquiries, he found her family. Soon his mother, my paternal grandmother, approached her mother, and the courting began.

Mommy said he was sharply handsome when they met, a bit wild in that he drove a motorcycle, and definitely a tough guy, someone who knew how to take care of himself and get things done. We had no doubt, when she told us these stories, that she had been attracted to him.

When Padar first met her, she used to dye her short, lush hair blond. When she was on the back of his motorcycle, tooling through the streets of Kabul, she'd hold him tight around the waist and let her hair stream behind her in the wind. She thought he was cool and tough and handsome. He had been captured by her beauty and cultured ways. You didn't have to be around Padar and Mommy for very long to realize he was deeply in love with her.

Had she loved him? If I had asked her that question directly, she probably would have brushed me off. Her stepmother, who had come into her home after her mother died, had wanted to marry off her husband's three daughters, and here was an eligible, handsome suitor, who was intent on pursuing my mother. What my father may have lacked in money and possessions, he made up for in confidence and determination. He knew what he wanted, and he wanted Miriam Siddiqui. Her stepmother approved of this brash suitor and pushed for her marriage, and her father approved. Mother definitely had a say in the matter, and she often said she had found him overwhelmingly attractive but was a little bothered that he didn't come from a family of successful businessmen. So Padar began to court her. Mommy was seventeen and was just finishing high school.

They were married in 1956, and true to tradition, Padar's family threw an elaborate engagement party, at least what was elaborate for their time and place. The Ahmadis were by no means wealthy, not like Mommy's family, but they weren't poor. And so, to the question of love, Mommy more than likely went into the relationship knowing that she would have to learn to love her husband over time. And she did in her way.

Padar never lost the sparkle in his eye for Mommy. He worked hard to please her, holding down two jobs for most of his working life in Afghanistan, both at the American embassy and as a landowner.

By the time I was born in 1975, Padar had become a prosperous owner of both homes and farmland, which he owned in partnership with his brother. They hired farmers, who became like family, and his warehouse in Kabul, which I went to with him often as a little girl, was stacked to the rafters with potatoes, corn, and other foodstuffs that were sold to local markets.

For his large family of eight children and his fashionable wife, he built the single-story rambling house in the prestigious Karte Seh neighborhood. The home sat on several acres, with a gated courtyard in front, and grass and flowers beside the driveway. Mother was proud of her home, and while it wasn't the biggest or most elaborate in the area, she had decorated it beautifully, with taste and a sense of fashion. Padar's contacts at the embassy used to allow employees to order furniture from America several times a year. Every room of our house was furnished with American and Italian goods. The gourmet kitchen, where Noor, our family cook of many years, held court, playing his favorite Indian music while he cooked, connected to the dining room, for which Mommy had purchased an elaborate cherry wood table. We each had our own bedrooms with American mattresses and beds from Italy. And Padar had a study filled with books.

It was in this house on Shura Street where all of my happiest memories of Afghanistan were nurtured. It was a home filled with beauty and fun and love that I held close to me as a promise of my future. The life I lived there has never left me—it's planted so deep in my soul, it's as much a part of me as the blood in my veins. I learned to dream there. I also learned that not all the good dreams come true. My search for love and hope would be a long one.

Padar was a proud man, a strong man, a brave man who loved his family and built us a beautiful life because he believed it was his duty as a husband and as a Muslim. I also think he did all of this out of his love for Mommy because he knew she wouldn't be happy without the finest things. I learned from him in those days that it was possible to be a man of duty and of love. His Islamic faith required him to be as generous as he was exacting. And I observed him on many occasions practicing the generosity that was central to his religion. All of his children attended school, and there was never a question whether we would be able to go. We were required to wear uniforms and purchase books and supplies. While schools were open to everyone in those days, not everyone could afford the cost of attendance. He was a most generous man, and he often helped children of relatives or of household servants attend school. He was as fastidious as my mother was fashionable. He always wore a dark suit, white shirt, and tie. On nearly every occasion, even if he took us to the carnival during Eid al-Fitr, he dressed up, if not in a coat and tie, in slacks and a shirt.

Padar was my first teacher. At dinner he would tell us stories from the Quran. When I drove with him in the car on errands, he would always tell me how we were to treat others as Muslims.

"Never do anything to hurt your neighbor," he said to me. It was the way he conducted his business, treated his tenants, and treated us. He told me often that Muslims don't hurt other people, either in business or their bodies. He taught me to practice my religion in action—not just in thought. He was adamant that a true Muslim didn't kill other people in order to force their religion on them or hurt other people in a business or personal dispute.

Mommy taught us how to say our prayers, how to celebrate the Muslim holidays, how to fast and pray, how to dress and behave as Muslim women. But Padar taught me how to treat people correctly—never harm your neighbor.

———

I didn't think much about college or the fact that my parents told me that I could study anything I wanted: the terms "doctor," "lawyer," and "teacher" were always mentioned, but I had no idea at my age what those people even did. If I had any ideas at all, I wanted to be like Padar, a businessman. Mother talked a lot about her sisters' successful business, how they traveled the world looking for rugs, and about their trips through Europe. I could easily understand business—selling rugs like my aunts or owning houses and land like Padar. Every time I drove through town with him to collect rents from his tenants, I enjoyed watching through the window all the shops full of expensive clothes and goods, the busy bazaars, and restaurants filled with Kabuli eating and talking and enjoying themselves. People were busy; Kabul was exciting. I wanted to be part of this wonderful life, and running a shop or a restaurant or buying houses and land didn't at all seem out of reach for me. It all seemed possible.

I could become anything I desired. This was freedom.

———

At day's end, when Padar came home from the embassy with snacks or treats or gifts, he would settle into the family room with a drink and a cigarette and call my sisters and brothers in. They would have to read their homework to him. If they didn't have it finished or if they couldn't answer his questions, he'd get very impatient. I hadn't started school yet, but when I did I had no intention of being embarrassed like this. Learning was a part of growing up, and I intended to give a lot of attention to it.

3

Modern Woman

My mother, Miriam, was a Muslim, and she was a modern woman. Her wealthy family had used the decade of democratic reforms in the late sixties and early seventies to help build a prosperous and free country. Though she was a Siddiqui—an ancient family that traced its ancestors back to a relative of Muhammad, Abu Bakr—she had stopped wearing the veil when she was a young girl after Queen Humaira appeared in public without one in 1959. She had taken this courageous act to encourage Afghan women to modernize. Women were unveiling, stepping out of the home, and taking part in society, though they were still Muslim in spirit and practice. The years between 1965 and 1978 were the times of the greatest democratic and modern reforms in the history of Afghanistan. Mother always talked about the freedom we had under King Zahir Shah and then President Daoud Khan. She took up with the times and thrived in so many ways. She wore leather pants to prove it. She also wore silk blouses and high heels and curled her black hair every day.

She kept a beautiful house while raising eight children. She taught us about our faith, constantly telling us stories of the Prophet, of the end of the world according to the Quran, and of how we were to behave as Muslim women. But she also told us that we were free to have the lives we wanted to have.

"You don't have to marry if you don't want to," she said to me and my sisters one day.

"What?" my sister Laila said. "We don't need husbands?"

"No, you don't. You can do things for yourselves. Look at your aunts."

Both of Mommy's sisters were busy entrepreneurs. They operated a rug business in Kabul and traveled the world. They owned their own homes, drove their own cars, and roamed wherever and with whomever they wished. Her brother, my uncle, was the most urbane and sophisticated man I'd ever met. A successful banker, he was always kind and thoughtful. Mommy's whole family was very successful, both in business and in government. She lived her life with an expectation of success, the way she walked and talked and dressed. Shahnaz and Shapairi even took to calling her a princess, but never to her face.

My mother demanded order. She assigned Shahnaz to check the younger children's homework each evening, and my sister learned her duties well. She was very strict and wasn't afraid to hit any of us if our work wasn't done correctly or neatly enough.

I wouldn't start first grade until I was six, but Mommy prepared me for that day with constant reminders. "Education is like eating," she said. If we weren't learning, we weren't growing. She had high expectations for all of us.

If my sisters and brothers weren't doing well in school, she wasn't happy. Attending school and then going off to college was an expectation for all of us—girls and boys—without distinction. Education was such a preoccupation of hers that I never gave a thought to the idea that in other parts of Afghanistan, children didn't go to school or even have access to learning.

She often talked about college regretfully. She had wanted to get a degree in fashion design after high school, but then she married

Padar and that opportunity closed to her because it was traditional that women didn't work outside the home. Still she kept up her sewing, making dresses and shirts and blouses for all of us. Beautiful things for Shahnaz and Shapairi, who were older and could wear more fashionable skirts and blouses. She made dresses for me and Laila and Zulaikha.

One year she even sewed uniforms for my brother Ahmad Shah's neighborhood volleyball team. He loved playing volleyball with his friends from school. So he talked Mommy into sewing uniforms for the guys who came over to play on our backyard court. They were fancy colored jerseys with numbers on the back. He was so proud of them that he decreed that anyone who came over had to be dressed in uniform to play.

While Mommy cared for the house and saw to the household staff and constantly monitored what Noor was cooking for the family meals, I was busy. My brother Zia, who was six years older than me, my sisters Zulaikha and Laila, and I were always together out in our yard or at our neighbor's house. Zia and I were especially close. Vida, my younger sister, was too small to run and play in the games, so she stayed inside where the maids and Mommy could watch her. Outside I climbed trees in our orchard. I ran along the top of the wall that coursed between the expansive yards of our neighbors. I was fast, zigging and zagging at full speed as the wall made its way from one side of our neighborhood to the other. No one could catch me.

On occasion I did fall, bruising my knees, dirtying my clothes, and making a mess of myself. When I went home, Mommy would turn up her nose at me. "Look at you," she'd say, and then huff a bit. Hands on her hips, she'd call Shapairi to come and take me away to the bath.

If Mommy kept an eye on how I cared for my clothes, part of her concern most likely came from the fact that she made almost everything I wore with her own hands. More so than any of my siblings, I loved to shop with her for fabric she would use to make my pajamas, dresses, and blouses. She taught me how to select fabrics for colors and patterns, and then at home I would stand beside her as she worked at her sewing machine. She taught me to thread the needle on the machine and how to hold the cloth as the machine stitched the material. Most of all, I enjoyed just standing next to her, which gave me comfort and assurance I needed. Those sessions with Mommy nurtured my sense of fashion, which grew, years later, into an entrepreneurial spirit to make a living owning clothing stores.

During Ramadan, when we fasted, Mommy was busy with Noor, making sure the large meals that we would eat each evening to break our fast were prepared properly. We fasted all day, only drinking some water or tea. In the evening we gathered around the family table and waited as Noor brought out the plates of rice and kebabs, and baklava for dessert.

Then there was Eid al-Fitr after Ramadan. Padar would give Shapairi money to buy us all outfits—three each. Each day of Eids, we'd wear a new one. A carnival set up not far from our house with rides and entertainment. My parents would take us, giving us money to buy tickets for rides. We'd always come home exhausted and dirty, our new outfits so filthy, Mother was appalled. The very next day, we'd do the same thing. The three-day holiday was one of my greatest memories.

———

Within months after their engagement party, Shahnaz and Saleem were married in a dazzling ceremony and celebration that took place at the Kabul Serena Hotel, with more than five hundred guests in attendance. Shahnaz moved in with Saleem's parents. It's the custom that sons don't leave their parents' house until they're married for one year. They bring their new brides home to live for the first year.

After the wedding, the tone of our family dinners changed. It was as if Shahnaz leaving our home had caused a shift in the entire city of Kabul. Padar and Mother talked about the troubles with the government and about the protests in the countryside. It was concerning because Padar owned lots of farmland outside Kabul, and Mommy spoke often to the cousins that had attended Shahnaz's engagement party, both of whom were far up in government. I overheard her many times speaking to them on the phone. She always had a sense of unease in her speech, as if something drastic was taking place. Both Shahnaz and Shapairi said Mommy could be so dramatic at times. I didn't know what to make of it.

One day I asked Zia and Laila, who were smart about these things, what Mother was upset about. Laila explained that just before Shahnaz was married, the government had changed. The people who took over from President Daoud Khan didn't like democracy. The new president was a communist. I had no idea what that meant, but my sisters' schools had new books they wanted the students to read, so I knew it was different from the way things had been up till then.

"It means they don't like freedom," Zia told me one night.

Later, Ahmad Shah, my oldest brother, who had a real taste for gory stories, told us that when President Taraki took over, all of Daoud Khan's family were shot: his wife, his children, his sister, his brother, and his grandchildren. They even killed his little baby granddaughter. Eighteen people, shot right in the Arg-e-Shahi, the presidential palace, the big one where the kings of Afghanistan have lived for centuries.

That sent shivers down my spine. The palace wasn't far from our home. Padar had driven us by it many times on our way to the American embassy, where he worked. So many people killed, and little kids. Who would shoot little kids?

My mother loved Daoud Khan. She talked about him all the time. He had brought so much prosperity to the country, and now he was gone. No wonder she was sad all the time.

Dinners around Mother's long Italian table were usually very talkative. Padar would tell us interesting things that were going on in the world. But after the government changed, so did the tone of our mealtimes. I heard more about the fighting taking place in the countryside and cities to the south. I didn't know what all of this meant or how it could change my life. Laila often tried to explain things to me later, but it only brought up more questions. She did tell me that the communists were kicking teachers out of the schools who wouldn't teach their ideas. University students were protesting, and Padar didn't want us going near the campus. The army was beginning to draft more soldiers, and they talked about what Ahmad Shah would do as he neared graduation from high school. Padar didn't want him to join the army. Mother was even more determined that he wouldn't fight for the communists. Bits of fear slowly crept into our home through every conversation, but to me, danger had to be far away. Behind the whitewashed walls of our home on Shura Street, our life went on in the same patterns of school and play and friends. If life was changing outside the walls, I didn't believe it could ever reach inside our home.

Along with the other changes, strange men began coming to our house to speak to Padar about business. I used to stand in the hall just outside the visitors' reception room until Noor came along and shooed me away. It was a room solely for entertaining guests. They smoked cigars, drank from small glasses, and talked business and about the fighting in the cities and about the army being called out to shoot their fellow Afghans.

A shift was happening faster than I could process. I thought that if I just kept doing the things I always did that life would return to normal, so on clear days I would escape to my favorite pear tree at the end of the driveway beside the gate. I sat up there, where I could see over the entire city. The government buildings down the street were large and new. The sky stretched out forever, a tight blue sheet that ran up to the tips of the snowcapped Hindu Kush mountains in the distance.

4

Gravity of Darkness

These pleasant days of my childhood in Kabul came to an end with a phone call from the countryside. I was in my sister Laila's room with Zulaikha, sitting on the floor talking, when I heard Mommy lift the receiver in the coolness of the hallway and give her greeting, "Salaam."

This afternoon, her voice didn't have her usual confidence and command. Her hello cracked with hesitation, as if she had expected this call, and because it had finally come, it was unbearable to hear. She listened in silence for a long beat.

"What?" she said, her voice frantic. "Don't do it. Don't do it." She kept screaming over and over again.

That Mommy would cry like that was a great shock. But that she had finally raised her anguished voice was not unexpected.

Laila and Zulaikha had just come home from school, and they were both dressed in their volleyball uniforms. The three of us were talking about Laila's ambition to play volleyball in the Olympics. She was good, and she was motivated to practice hard. I believed every word of her dream. Women and girls were doing the most amazing things in those days in Kabul, opening businesses, becoming doctors and lawyers and other professionals, traveling on their own. Women were no longer cloistered behind the veil.

Our chattering stopped when Mommy shouted, "Don't do it!"

Do what? My sisters and I looked at each other with mouths open.

"It's her cousins," Laila said. She knew them by name. I had seen them many times before, the last time at my sister's engagement party. I recalled they had both had a petrified look when those Parcham men strutted into the party.

Ahmad Shah had explained to me that Parcham was a communist party that believed Afghanistan should have a socialist revolution in the same way Russia had their revolution. From the way Padar and Mommy spoke about them, I knew they were opposed to their socialist revolution, like so many others in Afghanistan. When the Parcham began their revolution, there had even been a great uprising in the city of Herat, where thousands of people had been killed by the army.

The receiver hit the marble floor with a hard thud. Laila, Zulaikha, and I rushed into the hall. We found Mommy on her knees with her hands covering her face, weeping. We had never seen this before. She was always so composed and self-assured. We never saw her without her hair neatly brushed and a fashionable outfit. But now her shoulders were heaving, and a cry of anguish seeped through her fingers.

Laila elbowed me. "Enjeela, go find Shapairi."

Shapairi was our eldest sister now that Shahnaz had moved out. She would know what to do. I stared down at Mommy in frozen disbelief that she was capable of such emotion and anguish.

"Enjeela, go!" my sister shouted.

By the time I returned with Shapairi, Mommy was sitting up against the wall. She had wiped her tears and composed herself, but she wasn't speaking to any of us. My older sisters pushed me out of the way as they talked to her in sympathetic whispers. Shapairi helped her up, and they both went into her room and closed the door. They didn't come out the rest of the day or that evening for dinner.

When Padar arrived home from work, Shapairi told him what happened, and he disappeared into their bedroom. At dinner, Padar said only that she wasn't feeling well. No one spoke about her crying earlier or the phone call. We carried on as we usually did, following all the same behaviors and rituals as on any other evening, just without Mommy. After dinner, we adhered to the custom of reciting a poem by heart. Padar gathered us. He knew almost all of Rumi and Hafiz by heart, and he pushed us to memorize them too. My sisters Laila and Zulaikha and Shapairi, and my brothers, Zia and Ahmad Shah, sometimes spoke out the lines in half-hearted ways, depending on their moods. But I loved poetry, and even though I was very young at the time, I had many of the poems completely memorized. Poems had this way of touching the deepest parts of me that gave me comfort. My favorite poem was written by the great poet Hafiz. Though I was the youngest to contribute to this family ritual (Vida was only three and couldn't participate), I restlessly waited my turn to recite. It wouldn't do for me to be half-hearted; I wanted more than ever to please Padar.

"Enjeela, recite," Padar finally said to me, waving his hand. Padar had a most discerning and intelligent glare. He expected me to do well.

I stood erect before him and smoothed down my blouse. I took a breath, notched up my chin, and called it forth:

> Within the Circle
> The moon is most delighted when it is round
> And the sun is the vision of a pure circle of gold
> That had been refined and surfaced in flight by
>   the creator's lighthearted kiss
>
> And the different kinds of fruits rounded to
>   swing freely within the circle
> From the branches, it appears the origin of a
>   sculptor's hands

And the pregnant belly curved and shaped by ex-
cellent of its kind by the soul within
And the plants and the round surface of the universe and Mother Earth itself

I have gotten the creator's hint
There is something within the circle the creator loves
Within the circle of a perfect one

There is the Beloved's endless community
Of Light

I understood that this circle encompassed the entire universe, which was far too large for me to comprehend. But this poem made it small enough for me to understand my place in it. God had put me in the wonderful city of Kabul, part of a nation of good people, and this was only a fragment of the giant circle of the Beloved. And inside that larger circle were spaces of kindness and love and hope with my brothers and sisters and parents. I was part of the circle of life, and I could rest in the gentle arms of the Beloved. I believed every word of that poem, that good things enveloped me as they had my parents and Shahnaz and her happy marriage. My life in Kabul wrapped around me, a full circle of love and hope.

Padar's grin widened as I spoke, and a gleam of pleasure rose in his eyes. I knew he was pleased. He slouched in his wing chair, his legs crossed, his hand clutching a sweaty glass of Scotch and water. He nodded at my words, his searching gray eyes never leaving me as he took a sip. He wore a neatly trimmed mustache, and his lips twitched imperceptibly as he kept the rhythm of the words, as if he could feel their pulse.

Still in his suit, his tie barely loosened, he prodded us late into the evening to recite more poems while he drank his Scotch, only leaving the room to pour himself more. From the smell of it, he was drinking it straight now. Something had transpired that made him drink until his eyes were so glassy he wasn't even aware of our presence, as if he were trying to forget something. Days later, Laila told me what she had learned from Shapairi about what had happened, what Mommy had heard on the other end of that phone call. Mommy's favorite cousins had committed suicide. They had shot themselves shortly after the call with Mommy. The phone call had been their farewell. In my country, even in death, there is a certain courtesy family members maintain. It had been their choice to take their own lives rather than live without freedom.

They must have faced being arrested and tortured like so many others who defied the new government. Now my cousins were gone, and with them, the days of freedom and hope for the future of my country. This freedom that Zia described must be a great thing if people so willingly sealed it with their own blood.

5

PRISONER OF LOVE

Mommy was different after that call. The sadness over the death of her cousins never seemed to lift from her mind. It was during this time of grieving that she began to tell us stories from the Quran.

The one she spent the most time on was the story of Moses. After school, she would gather us around in the family room, all the kids except Shapairi and Ahmad Shah. Only later did I understand why she gathered the four of us and not my older siblings.

"A woman in Egypt had a little baby. But Pharaoh had made a new law that the firstborn of every slave family had to die. The woman couldn't let her child die, so she made a basket for him. She set the basket adrift in a river to float along. Perhaps someone kind would find him and take care of him. It was the Pharaoh's daughter who found the basket and took the boy and raised him as her own." Mommy's voice grew sad. "She had to let him go. She didn't have any choice."

She repeated the story many times to us, always speaking with a deep passion about how sad the boy's mommy must have been to let him go like that. But she knew her son would grow up strong because God would take care of him. Still "it was sad, very sad," she would say.

I had to agree with her. It was a tragedy indeed for a mommy to lose a child, to be forced by calamity and fear to let him float away with a chance he would have a safe and happy life. As much as I believed the Quran, to me, it was only a story. I had no notion that mommies actually did such things.

What if there was a hole in the basket? What if the baby tipped over and fell into the water?

A few weeks later, Mommy left the house and didn't return. She told Noor she was living at her brother's house, my favorite uncle, until Padar stopped drinking. She had packed her suitcase and left in the night. The evening before, she and Padar had spent a long time talking in their room. I never heard any arguing, maybe because their room was far away from mine. From her comments around the house, I knew that she was unhappy because of Padar's drinking, which had escalated since her cousins' deaths.

The next night at dinner, the table was much quieter without Shahnaz, and now Mommy. I wanted to ask Padar when she would come home. My sisters and brothers were so serious and subdued, I was scared to break the silence. But I finally got up the nerve to ask him.

Padar ate his rice and kofta, Afghan meatballs, deep in thought as if he were trying to solve a complex mathematical problem. He mindlessly sipped his Scotch, not caring to address my question. Shapairi decided to change the subject. She brought up the fighting in the streets in the provinces, young men getting arrested for avoiding service in the army, and protest marches at the university.

We had all listened to the TV before dinner, and it varied drastically from the things Shapairi had been hearing at school. The government's version of the news included parades and ceremonies announcing new medical and educational programs. There existed two completely different Afghanistans. The official version was that of a progressive country marching forward into a bright future as a modern nation. My sisters told me of another Afghanistan, of fighting to force the government to stop changing the textbooks in the schools to ones that teach atheism and socialism.

Students, particularly from the university and high schools, were staging protests in the city streets, and police were making arrests. Padar began warning us not to go too far away from the house—"To school and back," he said.

"We're students," Laila said. "Shouldn't we be protesting with everyone else?"

"Stay out of the streets," he'd tell us sharply.

He looked around the dinner table at us all. "You don't know what's going on. If you're not in school, you should just stay close to the house." He insisted we play only behind the gates. No more soccer games in the neighborhood streets. He knew what was going on, but he was strangely quiet on the matter, as though if he didn't talk about it, it might go away. As we ate the rest of our dinner in silence, the country outside our gates was in full-scale revolt against the government.

———

The next afternoon, I climbed the pear tree by the front gate and waited for my sisters and Zia to return from school. I could see all the way down to the end of the street, and soon neighbor kids with their books and in their school uniforms turned the corner and moved toward me in groups, talking and joking.

Since Mommy wasn't around to make sure we had our homework finished, we fell right into playing volleyball or kickball or a soccer game as soon as my sisters and brothers got home from school. Sometimes I chased neighbor kids on the walls or climbed trees in the orchard and picked fruit, and we ate them or threw them at each other. Playing is a child's form of work, a way of dispensing with the harshness of what existed outside the walls of our home, a place where our lawns were mowed every week, trees tended to, and Mommy's rose garden was weeded and trimmed so the bushes were full and beautiful and fragrant.

When we heard the muezzin's call to prayer, we knew it was five o'clock, and dinner would be on the table soon. Padar would be expecting all of us with our hands and faces washed and sitting in our places ready to eat. This dinner was the same somber episode; a dark cloud had come over him that was becoming unbearable to live with. Dinnertime brought fresh reports of what Ahmad Shah and Shapairi had seen at school. Padar said only that he didn't think it would get much better.

After dinner, I asked Laila and Zulaikha about Mommy.

"Why isn't she coming home?" I asked. They just shrugged. There wasn't anything they could do about it.

Why were they so nonchalant about Mommy being away? Zulaikha was always like that, withdrawn and shy, never wanting to disturb anyone. Laila was busy with her own life—school and volleyball. I missed Mommy something terrible. I spent all day with my baby sister, Vida, waiting and watching for Mommy to come home. If no one did anything, I would have to.

The next day, after my sisters were off to school and Padar drove out of the gates to the embassy, I set out by myself. I had put on a new blue dress Mommy had sewn for me. I wore my black shoes and brushed my hair. I left when Noor was busy in the kitchen, and the maids were busy cleaning or watching Vida. I skipped down Shura Street away from my house before anyone noticed I was gone. I began kicking a soda can down the street. I turned onto busy Pul-e-Surkh Road, a traffic-choked four-lane arterial that ran north and south through the heart of the city.

Six scruffy-looking boys, who were going door-to-door begging, surrounded me, teasing me about my blue dress, lifting my skirt. Their behavior shocked me at first, and I thought of running home. But if I ran home, I would never reach Mother. Besides, these boys weren't any bigger than my brothers and their friends. And I wasn't afraid of them. I pushed my skirt down and yelled at them, "I never wear a dress. If I had my jeans on, I'd kick your butt. I have an older sister and older brother I fight with all the time."

I balled up my fists, ready to swing. They backed off, and just then a gate opened and a car backed out into the street. The biggest one said they should go, and they strolled away in the other direction.

By the time they disappeared around a corner, my heart was beating so hard it pounded in my head. I continued on my way, wary about what lay ahead. It was a warm early-fall day, and I had already begun to perspire from the fright of those thugs trying to intimidate me. Trucks and cars whizzed past me, and I strolled along the sidewalk by the busy boulevard.

I missed Mommy. How could our beautiful life be so terrible that she would leave us like this? All along the walk to my uncle's house, I tried to decide what I wanted to say to her. *I need you, Mommy. I miss you.* Or maybe just a question: *Why are you staying away?* The house wasn't the same without her. Trucks rumbled the road, exhaust fumes smelled terrible, and I was scared, but I had to see her and let her know how much I missed her.

It must have taken me an hour or more to walk to the exclusive neighborhood where my uncle lived. By the time I reached the front door, I was shaking. The housekeeper let me in with a surprised look. I stood in the grand entryway while she went off to find Mommy. If our house was elegant and expansive, this home was royal, with marble floors and crystal chandeliers and a sweeping staircase and dark wood walls. A large bouquet of flowers in the hall, a spray of red, orange, white, and purple, gave off the fresh smell of cool garden air. My uncle was in banking and finance, and his wealth was obvious.

My uncle strode down the hall, dressed in a well-tailored suit, his light-brown hair slicked back off his shiny forehead. I thought he was one of the handsomest men in the city, tall, regal, and well mannered. He greeted me with a care that always made me feel like I was his only child. He took my hand and led me into a parlor with elegantly upholstered chairs and a sofa and the most intricately woven carpet. I sat in a comfortable wing chair. Mommy came in and took a seat across from me while my uncle took a seat on the couch. My uncle's wife, my aunt, sat in an upholstered chair next to Mommy, staring at me while she puffed on a cigarette with angry breaths. I wanted to run and leap into Mommy's arms, but ours wasn't that kind of relationship. She gave me a vague smile. I couldn't tell if she was glad to see me, but I knew I was so happy to see her. I sat across from her and folded my hands in my lap.

I asked her why she didn't come home.

My aunt snapped at me before Mommy could say a word. "Tell your father to stop drinking. She won't return unless he stops."

"Don't put that on the child," my uncle said. He sat on the sofa with one leg crossed over the other; one shiny shoe gently bounced as he spoke.

It wasn't until my uncle's words soaked in that I realized my aunt was serious. She wanted me to speak to Padar, tell him to stop drinking. What could I do about his drinking? Mommy didn't say anything, even though I looked to her for some encouragement, something I could hold on to. How could she expect me to go home and straighten things out?

Uncle worked to soothe his wife. He kept telling her to be careful what she said to me, that I had just come to visit my mommy, not to negotiate a settlement between spouses. His voice itself was calming and mellow; he spoke so warmly and thoughtfully. Mommy looked only at her hands, then in the air above us all, as if she were trying to decide what to do. Finally, my aunt said something that stopped me cold.

"Your father is making your mommy's life a living hell. He knows she has a bad heart. He will kill her one of these days."

The air in the room became thick, and I couldn't breathe. *Kill her.* Those words floated in the air, and even my articulate uncle, who I supposed had comforting words for every situation, seemed uncomfortable. To my little-girl mind, the thought of Mommy dying was far from me. Something I had never considered. Despite her heart problems, she always seemed so full of energy, ready to embrace life as it came her way.

I just wanted her to come home. She looked at me with her sad eyes like she had so much to say, and for a beat of a second, I saw a woman at a crossroads.

I leaned forward and stared down at my uncle's highly polished shoes. He was dressed so flawlessly, and the books on the shelves behind him, the lamps and drapes, gave the room a luxurious, secure feeling. The house seemed perfect. Why was it that the war in the streets had somehow seeped inside our Shura Street house and not this one?

"Enjeela!" my aunt said. "Go now." She waved her hand toward me in the air. "Get up, go."

I stood, thinking Mother would protect me from this angry woman, but she had only this sheepish look on her face, as if her sister-in-law was a woman she didn't dare cross. Even Uncle fell silent in her presence.

"Go and tell your father what I said—she's not coming home until he stops drinking," she said with a dismissive wave.

I went into the hall by the door and turned to them in the parlor. I was certain Mommy would come to me, comfort me, but she only sat and stared at her hands, not moving. I wanted to run to her, but I had just been told to leave. The whole house went into an eerie silence, as if I could hear things only from a great distance.

Uncle told a maid something. She strode past me and opened the door. She led me out to the street, and we walked together toward my home. Everything came into sharp focus as we briskly strode along the boulevard. Soldiers were everywhere, on streets leading off Pul-e-Surkh Road. Truckloads of soldiers and equipment rattled past us in traffic, noisy and harsh. Our beautiful city had turned into an armed camp, a military outpost full of men and their bristling weapons. I walked right through them, past their guns and bold faces, with my aunt's message burning inside me.

6

THE BROKEN CIRCLE

At the dinner table that evening, I sat up straight in my chair with my face and hands freshly washed, still shaken from my journey that day. My aunt's meanness rummaged around inside me, stealing my appetite. I played with my fork, waiting for the right instant to deliver her message. If Padar didn't stop drinking, Mommy wouldn't come home. I wanted to reach over and slap the glass of Scotch out of his hand, but he would beat me if I did such a disrespectful thing. As had been the custom since Mommy left, Padar barely spoke, only sipping his drink and then eating. I sat a few chairs down from him with Zia between us, out of his reach. I tried to gauge how angry he was tonight, but he was so absorbed in his thoughts he hardly even looked at us. I had to speak up. A weight rested on my shoulders, unlike my sisters, who ate and chatted, and Zia, who smiled and joked like always.

"I saw Mommy today," I finally blurted out. Ahmad Shah sighed. Shapairi stared at me with an evil eye, as if she wanted to whip me with a cord as she'd done before. The whereabouts of Mommy was not a subject we discussed openly. Everyone knew where she was the same way I knew, from Noor. Padar lifted his head slowly.

"Where?" he asked, gripping his drink.

"I walked to Uncle's."

His face flushed; he began to stammer at Noor, who sat cross-legged on the floor at the far end of the dining room eating dinner. "Did you know this?"

Noor shook his head to say that he knew nothing about it. Laila and Zulaikha stared at me in shock that I had done such a thing on my own. Zia smirked. Padar turned to me.

"What did she say?"

"Auntie said you must stop drinking or Mommy won't come home." I held my breath after all the words came out. I squeezed the seat of my chair with each of my hands to hold down the shaking inside me. No one moved. If he jumped up and reached for me, I planned to duck under the table.

Padar furrowed his dark eyebrows and gave me a puzzled look as if he didn't understand my words. He lifted the glass of Scotch to his mouth and took a long swig, then slammed the empty glass on the table. I could tell by the determination in his eyes that he would give up breathing before he gave up his Scotch. My heart threatened to tear through my chest it was beating so fast. Yet my chest puffed out a bit, feeling strong for the first time in my life—I had told him the truth we all wanted to say to him.

All of us waited in silence. The eruption would come. It always came. A fork scraped a plate, but not a word passed between us, only a silent wish for calm.

He pressed his mouth together, his mustache covering his upper lip, and he eyed me, furrowing his brow, with a malevolent glare that said *You better not ever talk to me like that again.* He kept his dark eyes on me the entire meal. When I left the table, he was still there with his shot glass of liquid. There was no poetry reading that night.

———

Mommy came home a few days later. If something had changed between Padar and Mommy, they didn't tell us. None of us knew of any commitment by Padar to stop drinking, but his drinking did diminish from then on. With Mommy around, life began to take on its former ordered rhythms. She would have Shapairi check everyone's homework when they came home from school. Vida and I were the only ones still not in school, so she checked us to make sure we were clean and ready to sit down for dinner when we came in from playing. Mother had a way of restoring order, of getting things done. The house was cleaner, organized, and my life felt safe. I stored away that conversation with my aunt about Mother's health. She seemed fine, though I knew she and Padar spent a lot of time alone talking. With her around again, he began to drink less.

I didn't see Shahnaz too often, but when her husband, the airline pilot, was on a long flight out of the country, she returned home to eat with us. She always made time for my sisters and me—reading or talking to us. In those times, we were all together, and everyone was happiest. For a while, I had forgotten the trouble that I had seen on my walk to Uncle's and the talk of my older siblings about the goings-on outside our walls.

A couple of weeks later at dinner, we were talking and laughing and asking questions, and I asked if we could go visit Uncle.

Mommy was quiet, pushing her food around her plate.

"They are out of the country, Enjeela," Padar said. His tone was so matter-of-fact that I thought it was merely another business trip.

"When they get back, we could go see them."

"They aren't coming back," Mommy said. She went on, with real reluctance in her voice, to tell us they'd moved all their business to Germany. They had flown out last week while they could still get visas.

An emptiness came over me. Some people were fighting to live the lives they wanted; others were leaving. I knew Padar would never leave

Afghanistan. He had said that many times. How many others would leave too? Would we end up the last family here?

Professionals and businesspeople all over Kabul were disappearing. At Shapairi's school, teachers just didn't show up for class. Rumors flew around that they had been jailed by the new regime for not teaching what the government wanted. Either that was true, or they had fled the country to avoid being imprisoned. Neighbor kids we used to play with didn't come around any longer. When I asked about them, Mommy said their families had moved away. Where was everyone going?

Almost every afternoon, Mommy gathered us together and retold that sad story of Moses, abandoned in a basket on the river by his mother because of the Pharaoh's edict that all firstborn boys must die. His mother had to make a choice: let him die or let him go into the waters of uncertainty. She would always end the story with a question none of us could answer: "What was a mother to do?" Then she would search us up and down with her large brown eyes as if her sadness could explain.

———

One morning, I heard a lot of noise in the hall by the front door. I ran from my bedroom to the hall and saw Shapairi, Vida, and Mommy all dressed up like they were going shopping.

"Where are you going?" I asked. "Can I go?" I didn't understand why I wasn't included in her shopping trip. Mommy knew that I loved shopping—picking out clothes, eating sweets, buying bangles, and watching all the other shoppers.

"Not today, Enjeela." Her voice was firm. "We have some special errands."

"Why can't I come?"

Shapairi walked out the front door without a word. Mommy held on to Vida's hand.

"I can help you with Vida," I said.

She had that cold insistent look of hers. "No, you can't come. You have to stay here." She took Vida out the door and closed it behind her. I ran outside after them.

"Mommy, Mommy, let me go too," I said, nearly crying. "I'll be here all alone."

"Noor is here," she said, not even turning to me.

"Please, please, take me too," I begged her. "Why can't I come with you?" She pushed Vida into the back seat of the car, and before she closed the door, she said to me, "We're going to get our photos taken." Then she slammed the door.

I stood in the driveway awhile, gazing at the open gate to the street. Why wasn't she taking me to get a photo? Another bit of emptiness crept in. I returned to my room and tried to distract myself from feeling rejected and lonely by playing with a doll or bouncing a ball. But it was no use.

All day, I moved around in a daze, trying to sort out why they would get their photos taken and not me? All the things I had ever done to make her mad at me tramped through my brain until I got a headache trying to figure out what was wrong with me. Was I too much of a tomboy? Did I get my good clothes too dirty as she always told me? Why would my two sisters get all dressed up and leave with her and not me? What had I done wrong?

That day, I remember spending a long while up in the pear tree by the gate, watching the road, waiting for my family's return.

Mommy never explained anything to me about the photos, and it was quietly dropped.

Over the next month, Padar stayed very busy with the men who came to our house to talk business. He and Mommy kept up their heated conversations behind closed doors. But we knew they were talking about what they needed to do with their properties. The new socialist government was undertaking a land reform movement that would transform private ownership of property across the entire country. Mommy wanted to sell them. She kept saying that the Parchami would take them anyway. Padar didn't want to at first, but he seemed to change his mind as the reform movement within the new government gained steam. It was at about that time that the army began setting up roadblocks in the streets of Kabul, checking identification papers, and arresting people.

A month or so after the photo incident, after my brothers and sisters left for school, I went looking for Vida. I often sat in her room in the quiet mornings, playing dolls with her, making her laugh. She was such a vibrant little sister, and we were very close. I usually found her on her bed or the floor, playing with her favorite doll, waiting for me to spend time with her. This morning, when I entered, she stood by a small suitcase, dressed in a traveling coat. Underneath, she had on one of her nicest dresses and a new pair of black shoes on her feet. Her hair had been brushed back. The maid helped her button her coat.

"Where are you going?" I asked my three-year-old sister.

"Bye-bye," she said and reached for my hand.

The maid took her hand instead and grabbed her small suitcase. Ignoring me, she strode down the hall toward the front door.

"Where are you going?" I asked, padding after them. The maid put the suitcase on a stack of luggage by the door. Noor and another maid were loading them into the trunk of the car.

My sister Shapairi, also dressed to travel, stood by the car, which had been backed in so the trunk was open near the front door. Noor packed the trunk carefully, working each piece in so all of it would fit. Who was leaving? Shapairi and Vida? How could they be leaving? Where were they going?

I heard Mommy's high heels clicking on the marble floor behind me. She was dressed to travel too. Her luggage was already being stowed in the car.

"Where are you going?" I asked.

"I have to go, Enjeela, to have a heart operation. In India."

"I can come with you. I can help you." I reached out to take her hand, but she brushed me off.

"No, you can't. You have to stay here with your sisters and brothers and father."

"When are you coming back?"

She looked past me through the open front door. I could hear Noor and Shapairi talking about their luggage and the trip.

"I don't know." Her hair was perfectly curled; her coat and shoes were new. She brushed something off the front of her coat.

"I have to go with you," I begged. "You can't leave me here."

"Oh, Enjeela, you're being dramatic. The rest of your family is here. You won't be alone."

She maneuvered her way around me, and I followed her outside. I begged her again to let me come with her; I needed to be with her and Vida. What would I do without them? Mommy didn't turn around to look at me again.

Noor had the car packed, slammed the trunk, and stood by it with a blank stare on his face. I looked at him as if he could help me, but he only shrugged and turned to the house.

It had rained the night before, and the grass and dirt by the driveway were moist and still damp. "Mommy," I pleaded, "you can't leave me here alone."

She slipped into the back seat, and the driver closed the door. The car started and slid slowly out of the drive, and I could see the back of Mommy's head, her hair perfectly coiffed for her flight to India. She didn't turn back once to wave or smile or give me any hope that I would see her again. I watched the car disappear around the corner at the far end of the street. I continued to cry and call to her, thinking she could not be leaving so suddenly without telling me when I would see her again.

I sank to my knees in the grass that had turned muddy in the rain. Noor came up to me and said something. He tried to pull me up by my arm, out of the grass and mud, but numbness had taken over my body, and all the strength had run out of me. I flopped onto the grass, my face in the muddy water. What had I done to deserve this? Tears erupted, racking my body with uncontrollable sobs. I couldn't understand why she would leave me behind. Even after I begged her to take me with her. What would it be like from here on with just Padar?

Padar came home that night from the embassy with two cases of Scotch whisky stacked in the trunk of his large sedan. Noor went out and helped him carry the boxes into the house. Padar didn't say much at dinner that night. Our family was now Padar, Ahmad Shah, Zia, Laila, Zulaikha, and me. Four of us were gone. Six of us were here. We watched in silence as he drank his Scotch all through dinner. He sipped his Scotch after dinner, slumped on a sofa in the family room. He drank his Scotch into the depths of the dark hours of the morning.

Mommy had left us.

7

INVASION OF FRIENDS

The twenty-fifth of December 1979 was a cold day, with chilly winds whipping off the snowcapped mountains to the north and sweeping across the city, a harbinger of a new way of life that marched in with a rumble. I was sitting high in the pear tree that afternoon, bundled up against the cold. The winds left a clear, icy-blue winter sky. I pulled my coat tighter around me and braced myself against a branch, waiting for my sisters to come home from school. From my perch, I could see the fruit trees that filled the acres around our house, and the volleyball court and the maids' quarters and guesthouse, and in front of me, the gate that led to the street.

Mother had been gone for more than a year; my sisters and I kept asking Padar when she would return, but he would only shake his head and mumble something unintelligible under his breath. Several times, I overheard him speaking to Noor about her. Padar had spoken to Mother on the phone. She wanted all of us to join her in India, but he told Noor he would never leave Afghanistan. Even though the fighting grew worse, he loved his country. It was his home. There was a tinge of anger in his voice as he talked. Why should he run away from his own country? I knew Padar as an optimist, a man who believed the best about men. That they wouldn't act like mad dogs forever. But he had little insight into the future. How events would overtake all of us. The army had assumed control of nearly every aspect of daily life, the police, the courts, the schools, the prisons. Still, the unrest continued. There was an exodus of friends and neighbors, doctors and lawyers; anyone whose loyalty to the new government was questioned either fled or was arrested.

I sat for hours that cold day in the limbs of the pear tree, imagining that if Mommy would only see life through Padar's eyes, that Afghanistan was his home, for better or for worse, she would come through the front door with all of her luggage, give me a hug, pat me on the head, and start telling everyone what to do. She would ask why wasn't this clean, and what's that on the floor, and then she would sniff the air and ask what's that smell? She would make everyone clean until the house sparkled. And then she would take me shopping to the bazaar for new fabric to sew us clothes and buy me ice cream. Everywhere in the house, she stood there with her hair neatly curled, dressed in a chic skirt and silk blouse, eyeing me in case I didn't wash my hands or brush my teeth or my hair was out of place. I kept wondering if she would have taken me with her had I been better at staying clean, had I dressed nicer like Shahnaz and Shapairi.

That morning dragged on, and I was thinking about showing up in the kitchen to see what Noor was cooking and to warm myself and find a tasty treat, when the branches of the trees began to shake. I thought it must be an earthquake. We had one once, and many buildings had been destroyed. Just then, warning sirens went off all over the city. These were the emergency warning sirens for disasters, not the police or fire sirens. The rumbling grew louder, and something large and mechanical rolled up my street. I scurried down, hit the dirt hard, ran across the grass, and clutched the gate, squeezing my face through the bars.

A long line of dark-green machines trundled up the road, churning up dust, creaking and grinding. I remember that I didn't have any idea what these machines could be. They were some form of tractor.

But these were much larger than tractors, and they were covered with green metal plates, and each of them had long barrels sticking out of the front. They reminded me of the barrels of rifles, only they were far too long and heavy for a man to carry. I had never seen an army tank, and I didn't know until later what they were used for. They had a blazing red star painted on their sides, and soldiers with grim faces were on top pointing machine guns. They didn't look at all like Afghan soldiers, who were thin and wore baggy uniforms. These men were ruddy, well fed, and had the hard look of warriors ready to do battle.

The line of tanks with their metal wheels paraded by; soldiers pointed their guns at people on the street as they passed. The tanks billowed grimy exhaust, and the clatter of the treads was so loud, I was sure they were tearing up the pavement. I hung on the wrought-iron bars that vibrated in my hands and stared down the street—a tank stopped in front of our house, its motor idling.

I stood petrified, my hands fixed to the bars as I stared up at the soldier on top of the tank, who stared back at me, both his hands wrapped around his weapon. I smiled up at him. And he looked away. At that moment, I was more amazed at the sight than afraid of these soldiers. The war had always been somewhere else, not on our street. And they looked so out of place, staring at us as if we were the intruders, not them. Noor grabbed my arm from behind and pulled me inside the house and slammed the door behind us.

"The Russians are taking over the city!" he yelled at me. "You can't go outside anymore." I followed him around the house, locking doors and windows. He quickly explained to me that the machines were Soviet tanks and those were Soviet soldiers. They had invaded our country. Fighting had erupted across the provinces of Afghanistan, and now the war had arrived at our gates. For so long, Padar had made it sound as if we would always be safe inside our home; it wasn't possible that war could come so close. Noor deeply feared the Soviets, and his fear seeped into me, and we rushed to secure the house. The way he spoke of them as invaders, they seemed unpredictable. I didn't leave Noor's side the rest of the day. When he went into the kitchen to cook, I climbed on the counter and watched him, trying not to shake from the thought of being so close to the war happening just outside our home.

When my sisters and brothers returned from school, they had passed by the tanks in the street and couldn't stop talking about the soldiers everywhere. The Soviets had surrounded the schools and important buildings in town and had flooded the streets with checkpoints and inspections.

At dinner Padar told us that we should stay inside for a few days, which meant the older kids would not be going to school. If the students started protesting again, there would be more shooting. It would take a few days for everything to calm down.

A few nights later, Padar turned on the radio in the living room, and we gathered around. The new president, Babrak Karmal, gave a speech explaining that the Russians had come to the rescue of their Afghan friends. That was the first time I had heard of the mujahideen, the freedom fighters in the mountains. Padar loved Afghanistan. He had taught us songs and poems about our country, that it was our motherland, a sacred land that no one could drive us from. He had read to us stories of how Afghan fighters had defeated the British and a whole parade of invaders. And now the Russians with their tanks and machine guns had invaded to do what he believed could never be accomplished. The Soviets had taken over the government and forced the Afghan army to fight with it against the mujahideen, who were primarily conservative, traditional folk of the countryside.

He doubted that the Parcham government would ever be able to carry out their socialist agenda for the country. They could not confiscate the land from every large landowner for their redistribution plans. He sat rigid and wide-eyed, listening in a sullen silence, moving only to take handsome gulps of his Scotch. By this time, we all knew what this meant for him—his land, his houses, his years of hard work and saving and investing would be stolen from him by this government.

———

The rattle of war, of guns, bombs, and tanks rumbling over pavement, became a nightly occurrence. I was now afraid to sleep alone, so I went to Laila's room. When Zia and Zulaikha couldn't sleep, we'd all end up there. The sounds of chaos outside went on for a few days, and then, as Padar had predicted, it died down.

Padar went back to work. But we stayed home. We played card games, told jokes and stories, and tried not to think about what was happening around us.

"Do you think Mommy's ever coming back?" I asked Laila.

"Not with all this fighting going on."

Zulaikha didn't say anything.

"Why do you think she left without us?" I asked.

Zulaikha shrugged. "Does it matter?"

"Are you guys going to play?" Zia asked, throwing down a card.

Zulaikha was so quiet; she rarely shared her thoughts, but it surprised me that she didn't seem to care that our mother had left with no notes or calls to any of her other children. Since she had left, our once well-ordered life had fallen to pieces—no one except Padar could tell us what to do. We didn't listen to the maids or even Noor when they told us to clean up. We took showers when we wanted to, and no one did their homework. We ate well, but only because of Noor. For the first couple of weeks, we fought over everything: who had won a certain game, who was the best at cards, who would go and fetch food from the kitchen. Even soft-spoken Zulaikha and her closest sister, Laila, got into a fistfight. Zia had to step between them. We stayed up as late as we wanted and rose when we wanted. Our rooms became desperate for a cleaning.

"What if she didn't want us anymore?" I asked.

Zulaikha gave me a curious look that said *Why would you think that?* "What if she didn't have room on the plane?"

Shahnaz worked for the national airline. She could have helped us get tickets.

"Maybe she was tired of all the questions you ask," Zia said, throwing down another card and nodding at Laila to take a turn.

"Maybe you're too sloppy," Laila said, half smiling.

"Your room is a cesspool," Zia said, trying to hide a smirk. "I can smell it from a thousand miles away."

"Your fingernails are always dirty, and you're a tomboy," Laila said. "You know how she wants everything to be perfectly clean."

"Padar will take us to Mommy," Zulaikha said, always one to take a serious bent.

"But he won't leave here, ever," I said.

"Well, if you know everything already," Laila said, tossing all her cards on the floor, "then you tell us why she left us behind."

Laila glared at me, waiting. Zia laughed, trying to lighten the mood.

"All right," he said. "Mommy will return, or we will go to her. Either way you will both be right. Can we play now?"

Laila picked up her cards and bit the inside of her cheek as she pondered her hand. I thought of many reasons why Mommy could have left them behind too. Zia and his messy bedroom and his reluctance to shower. And Laila and her single-minded focus on a game, even if she'd been called a hundred times to dinner. But under the smirks and humor, a well of fear bubbled up—what if they were right about why Mommy left?

———

One night the electricity went off, and it didn't come back on for several days. Noor cooked dinner over a fire in the yard, and we ate in the dark. As the blackouts become more frequent, so did our use of kerosene lanterns that Padar had found. Noor went to the market each day to buy food. He always came back exasperated with the soldiers, who dominated the streets. He feared the shopkeepers would just up and close. Everyone seemed to talk under their breath out of fear of being overheard by the secret police or the Soviet soldiers. Noor said there were far fewer people in the city; many people had fled to rural areas or had left the country.

Padar would never leave, and Mommy would never return to a nation at war. I used to daydream that she would suddenly appear to rescue us. But with every day that passed, she became less clear in my memory; at times I could see only a mere outline, though I could hear her voice. Even when I tried to listen for her in my head, the familiar firm sharpness of her words would be drowned out by the sounds of tanks, gunfire, and trucks full of grim-faced soldiers. I wondered if I would even recognize her if she came to the door.

I spent many days up in the pear tree, watching the tanks and jeeps and soldiers passing by. Planes streaked low across the sky; the rumble of their engines made my legs shake.

The government wanted to turn Afghan society into a socialist state overnight, wiping away centuries of religious thinking and tradition. They had already changed the textbooks in all the schools, taking out any reference to Muslim faith. They even changed the national pledge that each child recited every morning to include loyalty to the socialist state of Afghanistan. They arrested the popular teachers, administrators, and professors who refused to change. These purges and demands only fueled the discontent of the people, which spilled over into protest. Kabul settled into a state of unrest, with its citizens constantly taking to the street in active revolt. Kabuli students passed out flyers about the planned marches, and people from outlying villages poured into the city to show their solidarity. Shopkeepers closed their stores. The marches were meant to be peaceful, Padar told us at dinnertime. But they were shouting slogans denouncing the Parcham and their socialist agenda, so the soldiers fired on the crowds. People were being killed. After the violence escalated, the protests spread to the high schools.

Early in the new year of 1980, students at Ahmad Shah's high school marched to the police barricades, shouting slogans against the new regime. When they wouldn't disperse, the guards fired at them. One of the girls from Shahnaz's high school who was shouting the loudest was shot dead by a soldier. Ahmad Shah talked about her all the time. She was a hero, and her name became a battle cry to the other students. They would shout, "Miss Nahid!"

Shortly after high school students joined the protests, truckloads of Afghan and Soviet soldiers began rolling through the neighborhood. They were searching for teenage boys in order to force them into joining the army. When the truck stopped in front of the gate to our house, soldiers dismounted with rifles in their hands. One of the maids went to warn Padar, who was in the living room. He quickly found Ahmad Shah and told him to cross over the back fence and hide on the neighbor's roof until the soldiers were gone. The soldiers barged through our front door. Padar met them in the entryway; he was very cool and calm. All of us watched from the hall as the soldiers dispersed and went room to room searching for my brother.

"We have no teenagers," he kept telling them nicely. "I don't know why you are coming in here."

The soldiers kept searching, brushing past Laila, Zulaikha, and me in the hall. I watched one of them following the others. He looked no older than Ahmad Shah, who was only sixteen. He moved along, unsure of himself as he pointed his rifle at the ceiling. With a sad droop to his eyes, he poked his rifle into the rooms that had already been searched by other soldiers. They must have forced him into the army just as they wanted to do to my brother. They opened every room and closet, even the maids' quarters outside, anywhere a person could hide. I felt sorry for him and for what was happening to all the boys.

When they left, they piled into the truck and moved around the corner to the next street; Ahmad Shah crossed back through the yards and hid on our roof until the soldiers cleared out of the neighborhood.

That night, we were all mostly quiet as we ate around a kerosene lamp in the center of the dining room table, except for Ahmad Shah, who talked with his chest puffed out about how he had outwitted the army. He was too smart for the new government; they would never catch him.

Padar didn't say much except, "Tomorrow they will come for Zia."

We all grew quiet and finished our dinner.

The next morning when we awoke, Ahmad Shah had disappeared. Padar told us he had gone to join Mommy in India. As much as I missed him, I knew he would be safe there. I wanted to be with him. We didn't need to ask Padar how he had been able to escape the country or whether we could go too. We knew that eventually we'd join our brother and our neighbors, who were disappearing from our street nearly every day. When we were alone with our friends, we often asked them, "When are you leaving?" or "Where is your family going?"

Looking back, I can say it was constantly in the back of my mind that someday in the middle of the night, just like Ahmad Shah, we'd be whisked away to somewhere safe. But we also knew it wasn't a topic Padar wanted to talk about, so this conversation was always among ourselves.

Now there were five huddled around the lantern at family dinners, but it felt like there were only four of us—Zia, Laila, Zulaikha, and me. Every night, Padar drank more until he became incoherent, often raving about what was happening to Kabul and cursing out the Soviet soldiers. When he wasn't drinking, he withdrew into himself, deep in thought, as if he were engaged in some internal debate.

Once Ahmad Shah was gone, the rest of us children decided that we didn't want to be alone at night, so we moved into his room. His was the largest, with a stereo and a king-size bed and a huge closet full of clothes. We took turns sleeping on it or on the floor. I felt safe there with my other siblings, and except to eat or go to the bathroom or to change clothes, we seldom left the room.

———

"Enjeela," Padar called from far down the hall one evening. "Come here now, I need you."

It was late; we were sitting in Ahmad Shah's closet playing cards and telling stories. My sisters looked at me and nodded for me to go. We had been telling ghost stories, trying to outdo each other and not act scared.

"Go see what he wants," Zia said, "before he comes in here and bothers all of us."

He called me again, this time more urgent. I rose and left the closet. When I found him near the entryway, he was leaning against the wall. His suit pants were wrinkled, his white shirt looked like he had been sleeping in it, and his hair hadn't been combed in days. He had a wild look in his eyes.

"Call Uncle for me," he demanded. "I have to talk to him now."

He followed me, shuffling his feet as I walked to the hall phone and dialed his brother. The phone rang, and when my uncle said hello, I returned the greeting and handed Padar the receiver before walking back to Ahmad Shah's room. They talked for hours, Padar sometimes arguing, sometimes listening. I had never heard him fight with his brother before. They talked often about what to do with the farmland. The two of them had spent a lot of their money to make those farms prosperous and hire the workers. Now the war threatened to take it away. Padar ran his fingers through his long black hair, brushing it back while he talked. The government wanted them to surrender the land for redistribution. Uncle wanted to find a way to sell it before that happened. Padar wanted to turn it over to the farmers who had worked it all the years he and his brother had owned it. If they didn't do something, the government would take it anyway. They went back and forth on the phone, trying to figure out what to do with it. I sat in Ahmad Shah's room, my ear to the door, with my sisters and Zia listening to one side of the debate.

Padar argued that he would die first before he let the government have the land. The Parcham would give it to someone who didn't know how to take care of it. This was the first of many arguments between them about the farmland. The conflict outside our gates that Padar tried to guard us from had now seeped in.

Because of the turmoil in the schools, the government closed them down for a few months. When they reopened in late March, Zia, Zulaikha, and Laila began attending again. Other than Padar and the household staff, I was alone at the house for the first time since the Soviets arrived. I had returned to my perch in the pear tree by the gate, waiting for my sisters to come home so we could play. I had become so accustomed to the tanks that lined the street in front of our house that I hardly noticed them anymore.

One day Zulaikha and Noor came flying through the gate, calling for Padar. Zulaikha looked ghostly, all of her skin covered in a fine dust. Her school uniform was filthy, and tears streaked down her face, leaving flesh-colored rivulets. Her eyes were a watery red, like she had been crying for hours. Her tightly braided hair had been pulled loose, and dust-coated strands were everywhere. I jumped down from the tree and ran across the courtyard to them as they reached the front door.

"What happened?" I asked. Zulaikha tried to talk, but she could not stop weeping.

"Let's go inside," Noor said, pushing me roughly toward the door, something he never did. His eyes were terrified. I followed both of them into the kitchen, where Padar sat at the table sipping chai, lost in thought. I often found him like this during the day when he didn't go to work—lost in a trance, blocking out everything around him.

"The Russians are bombing the schools with poison gas," Noor said almost in a whisper, as if he couldn't bring himself to say it aloud.

"Where is Laila?" Padar asked sharply, snapping out of his thoughts. She and Zulaikha went to the same school. Zulaikha began trying to explain that there was gas that smelled, and it was everywhere. Kids had just started fainting, and she could not find Laila in the chaos.

"She's there somewhere," she said, exhausted. "Kids were throwing up and falling down . . ." She trailed off in another eruption of tears.

Padar ran out of the house, down the driveway, and down the street toward the school. We waited for him by the gate. While he was gone, Zulaikha cried and shook so hard she couldn't talk. All of us began to fear for our sister. In a half hour, we saw Padar rushing back up the street carrying Laila, her feet and arms dangling, her head lolling back, and her mouth wide open. He brought her inside and placed her carefully on her bed. For several long minutes, Padar tried CPR, but still she didn't open her eyes or rouse. He picked her up, cradled her in his arms, and rushed outside to his car. Noor opened the back door, and he laid her gingerly across the back seat.

"Stay inside and lock the doors," he said as he jumped behind the wheel. We stood frozen in the doorway, the sounds of screaming and crying echoing in the distance as he sped off to the hospital.

Zia and Zulaikha kept talking about what had happened to Laila at the school, but I could only picture her unconscious body, limp and lifeless. The poisonous gas had done something to Zulaikha too, because she wasn't herself. She was lethargic and drowsy, and it was difficult for her to complete her sentences. I had never felt any fear running through these streets before, but now this invasion had penetrated our walls, emotionally and physically. I could be killed. We all could be killed. *What if Padar gets killed? What if he doesn't return? How are we going to live?* Something slipped away from me, from all of us. I wasn't old enough to understand exactly what it was. Death and dying were as close to me now as my own beloved sisters.

I must have been up in the tree for an hour or more when Padar pulled into the drive. Laila was sitting up in the front seat. Noor came out to help her into the house. I jumped down from the tree and met everyone else running out as we all gathered around her. She was weak, and her skin was pale as a full moon. Padar shooed us away as he and Noor brought her inside and settled her in the living room. She wanted to sleep, but the doctor had told Padar to keep her awake. If she fell asleep, she could fall into a coma, maybe even not wake up. She didn't want to talk, though, so while Noor fed her, we tried to get her to smile with cheers like the ones she always did for us on the volleyball court.

When it was my turn to talk, I knelt and looked up at her. Propped up on the sofa, she stared down at me. Her face had been washed, and someone had combed the fine dust out of her hair. She gave me a vacant look as I recounted the fun times we'd had together, the games we'd played together, and how when she got better, we'd go outside and run in the yard and play volleyball, and everything would be like it was before the tanks arrived. Her eyes were expressionless as she listened to me. I don't think she believed a word of what I was saying. I wasn't sure I did either.

8

UNEXPECTED VISITOR

One summer evening before Padar had barely drained his first Scotch, there was a loud banging at the front door. Mommy had been gone for nearly two years, and this banging on the door brought me running. Had she come home? Not a day passed that I didn't wonder if she were alive.

The beating against the door kept on until Padar swung it wide open. Several grim-faced men in business suits filled the doorway; Russian soldiers with rifles slung over their shoulders stood tall behind them in the driveway. They began talking to Padar in Russian, so I couldn't understand what they were saying, but Padar responded in an argumentative tone, which grew angrier as the discussion went on. They talked while standing there in the doorway well past dinnertime.

When it was over, Padar slammed the door and stomped into the living room, cursing and fuming. "They want me to spy for them," he said, slouching into his chair in the family room. He slugged down a fresh drink and stared red-faced at the wall.

"How?" I asked.

He only shook his head and gazed off into space.

That summer, the same men came to our door often, talking with Padar outside our front door hour after hour. Afterward he would come inside, angry and flustered and swearing profusely. They wanted information from inside the American embassy, and they obviously believed they could wear him down to get him to cooperate.

The Russians told him about American conspiracies and plots against the Afghan people. That the Americans wanted to possess Afghanistan as a base in order to spy on Russia. That Americans didn't care about the Afghan people, but only what they could steal from them. The Americans would rape the land of its minerals and wealth and leave the people with nothing. They insisted that the Russians were friends of the Afghan people. They wanted only what was best for the future of the nation.

Padar hated the Russians, and his resolve to not betray his American employer never wavered. Yet they didn't give up trying to convince him. They followed him when he drove to work, and at the end of the day, they were waiting by his car to follow him home. They became a presence in Padar's life almost as constant and reliable as Scotch.

That fall I began school. On my first day, Padar walked with me. A big black car followed not too far behind us, and he told me to keep looking straight ahead. "Those bastard Russians are following us again." He never appeared to be afraid or intimidated, just angry that they were so persistent and so obnoxious. He never broke down and worked for them, and I admired that he was so strong and fearless. But as brave and strong as he acted in front of the Russians and soldiers, at home he buried himself deeper in his Scotch glass.

By this time we were all sleeping on the floor or the bed or in the spacious walk-in closet of Ahmad Shah's room. Padar often stayed up late drinking, and it was in those fall months after I started school that Padar and Uncle finally came to an agreement about the farmland, which plunged our home into an even darker place. They made the decision to walk away and deeded the land to the farmers who lived there. Though it was what Padar wanted, he knew that it would be more difficult to support us without the revenue the farm had brought in. I rarely saw him sober after that, and soon he began channeling his extra energy and drunkenness into midnight poetry sessions, which we were all required to attend.

In the darkest part of a winter morning, he held a bottle of Scotch by its neck as he badgered us awake.

"Come quickly!" he demanded with a tone that wasn't meant to be argued with.

Sleepy, tired, half awake, we gathered in the living room. He slumped into one of the upholstered wing chairs and motioned for us to sit at his feet. Candles and a kerosene lantern lit the room in an eerie glow. I tried to hide in the half shadows, but he waved me closer into the light. Poetry was his great comfort, and somehow he must have thought it would protect us too, keep us from falling into the dark hole he had found himself in and was trying to climb out of with the help of Hafiz.

"Laila, recite," he demanded.

Laila, who had recovered quickly from the gassing, rose slowly and tried to stumble through a poem. Her lackadaisical memorization of poetry infuriated him.

"Okay, that's enough of that, sit down."

He would go around to each of us, still rubbing our eyes and yawning but aware of Padar's irritability. When he came to Zia, who was never exact, precise, the way Padar liked it, Zia faltered and would try to make a joke about it, but Padar signaled his displeasure with a hefty grunt. This lack of attention to the music of the sentences flustered him. As if his whole world would be at rest if he could hear a beautiful poem. He had taught us all about poetry, how to listen to the words and enjoy the beauty of the language, but he was too drunk now to notice how afraid we had become and that even if we knew a hundred poems perfectly, we feared it would not be enough to keep him off his path to insanity.

This early-morning session grew tenser as he demanded more, his voice sharpened into a weapon.

When he came to me, I had one poem I could recite with conviction and depth, the way he thought poetry should be felt. If I could please him with my words and make this stop, then I wanted to do it.

"Enjeela, recite." He pointed at me.

I slowly rose, the ethereal darkness all around me, and edged closer into the dim smudge of light radiating from a kerosene lamp. I spoke:

Within the Circle
The moon is most delighted when it is round
And the sun is the vision of a pure circle of gold
That had been refined and surfaced in flight by
    the creator's lighthearted kiss

And the different kinds of fruits rounded to
    swing freely within the circle
From the branches, it appears the origin of a
    sculptor's hands

And the pregnant belly curved and shaped by ex-
    cellent of its kind by the soul within . . .

As I recited, Padar rocked back and forth, his index finger to his lips, and his eyes drooped closed. He was either meditating, or he was asleep. Somehow the words had given him peace. I stood in the half-light, and after a few moments, we could hear the regular breathing of sleep. Finished, I waited in the flickering light of kerosene flames. We sat around him in a half circle; the other half lay in the empty darkness behind his chair. The other half of our family—Mommy and Vida, Shahnaz and Shapairi and Ahmad Shah—was absent.

These sessions went on almost every week, deep into the winter, as the conflict became a war. At night, when the clamor of the city had died down, and Padar had released us from the broken circle, we could hear the battles being waged in the far-off mountains. The distance tempered the constant explosions—they sounded like fireworks. As if the countryside were in a constant celebration.

That winter was one of the coldest to ever hit Afghanistan. The snow on the mountains around the city was a thick white blanket. We had little electricity, and Noor gathered wood to burn in the fireplace in the living room. Padar brought home a coal-burning stove for the family room that he vented through a window, and in the freezing hours of the afternoon, we gathered around it, dressed in everything warm we could find, and told stories and ate dinner and waited out the weather. When it didn't snow, we played outside, jumped off the roof into the pillows of snowdrifts piled up around the house. When it was too cold to go outside, we huddled in Ahmad Shah's room, played a card game called *fis kut* (the game is much like gin rummy only with more players), and told scary ghost stories until we were so tired we fell asleep on the floor, close together to fight off the chill, all hoping as our eyes closed that Padar would sleep through the night.

I thought about Mommy the most when we played fis kut.

"I don't think we'll ever see Mommy again," I said.

"You are mistaken as usual," Zia said, picking up a card.

"Look at us. We live like animals," I said.

"We are animals," Zia said.

"Speak for yourself," Laila said, her voice lifted up like she had it all planned out. "I can't wait for the mujahideen to destroy the Russians so I can play volleyball again."

"Do you think we'll be able to go back to school soon?" Zulaikha said.

"They are making the kids speak Russian now and join the communist clubs," Zia said. "Soon we'll all be eating borscht."

Padar had forbidden us to join the youth clubs the Russians had set up.

"Padar won't let us learn anything Russian," I said.

"That's why we're staying home, so we can eat our kabobs in peace," Zia said. "Now it's your turn to play, so stop talking." Zia laughed and I laughed.

"See, already you have forgotten Mommy," Zia said. "All you need to do is play more fis kut, and you'll forget her completely."

We all looked at him. Zulaikha's lips curled up in fear. Laila looked angry.

"Padar won't leave us," I said.

"He's already left us," Laila said.

"Don't talk like that," Zulaikha said.

"Why not?" Zia said.

"He's taking care of us, the best he can," I said. "He won't leave us."

No one said any more as we continued playing our game. We played by the hour, day after day, week after week. We were becoming expert at it until we knew every rule and every trick. The more I thought about it, the more I had to agree with Zia. Playing games did allow me to forget about Mommy. I couldn't remember what her voice sounded like or what it was like to be really clean.

It was one of these freezing winter nights that I saw the man with the white horse.

He walked right out of Ahmad Shah's closet toward me. He was an old man, a very old man, with a long white beard, and his clothes matched the brilliant white of his horse, who had a princely saddle, full mane, and a bushy tail. He stood tall and strong next to the man. At first I was certain they were ghosts. But we had been telling ghost stories all night long, so then I thought I must be asleep and it was a dream.

"I can see you," I said to him.

The man stopped and stared down at me. He held the horse's reins as if he were taking it out for a midnight ride to see what was left of the city.

"Are you awake?" he said, a lilt of surprise in his voice.

I told him I was. "Who are you?" I asked, suspecting already that I might know who he was.

"You can see me, little one?"

I sat up and nodded. He was as real to me as my sisters and brother sleeping beside me.

"You must be very special to see me. No one sees me." He smiled at me and tugged on the reins of the horse. "I must go," he said. "Go back to sleep before the others wake up." His voice was warm and caring. None of the others even stirred.

Before he left the room, he turned to me. "Don't tell anyone you've seen me."

"I won't." I watched him disappear back into the darkness of the closet.

The next morning, I woke up slowly as I tried to make sense of my dream. It had to have been a dream, but it was so real, so alive. The bearded man in white had been so close to me, and I thought I could smell the musty odor of a sweaty horse.

I saw him several more times before we moved. He told me many times how special I was that I could see him, and for the first time I understood that specialness as something I could do that my sisters and Zia couldn't—I could see the bearded man with his white horse and warm smile and gentle voice.

In January, we moved. It was getting harder and harder to live in that big house since giving away the farmland. Keeping it warm and clean was impossible. Padar still worked at the embassy, but his workdays were becoming more sporadic. Some days he was too drunk to leave the house.

The small house, a couple of blocks away from the one on Shura Street, was easier to keep warm, though it didn't seem much warmer. In the spring we moved again, this time to a tiny house in a very different neighborhood. It was here that Noor, who had been the only staff that had moved with us from Shura Street, left us. Our family continued to get smaller, just like our home, and it was difficult for me to believe that Padar could take care of us on his own.

Every time I lay down to sleep, I let my thoughts drift to the man with the white horse and his words of comfort to me. He had followed me from house to house, and I would float away with him into a land of peace and beauty. I began to think that maybe there was a reason to hope. He said I was special, so it must be true. I must have some peculiar gift since I was the only one who could see him. Through the cold days and shivering nights, I knew I hadn't imagined him. He was as real as the war to me.

Spring arrived, and my aunt and my cousin Izmarai, son of my Aunt Gul, came to stay with us. He was a slender, handsome boy, with blond hair, green eyes, and an infectious smile. Izmarai felt like one of us, fitting into the family as a brother. We were close to the same age, so we played together. Our house was small, and now, not by choice but out of necessity, the kids all slept in the same room. Playing cards and games continued to be the way we would spend our days and nights. We were not allowed to go outside, but I knew the spring flowers and *ashoka* trees were blossoming, and soon it would be summer. Whenever the door opened, the fresh smell of spring filled our small house. The air was changing.

———

One morning, way before dawn, Padar woke us.

"Everyone up. Get dressed," he commanded.

Zia groaned, "Not another poetry session," but this morning's arousal was different. Padar was dressed neatly. His hair was combed, and he didn't sound like he had been drinking. His voice was serious and sober. This was not a midnight poetry session. He held the lantern close to each of our faces and told us to wake up. In his other hand, he held four backpacks.

"Pack a change of clothes in these," he said, dropping a backpack by each of us. "Get up and hurry."

My aunt came into the room and helped us.

"Hurry, children," she said in a calm voice. "Pack quickly."

She sorted through our things and picked out clothes we should take. She worked methodically. She knew exactly what we would need. All of our pretty dresses and city clothes we were to leave behind. She said we were to travel, so we shouldn't pack too much. We had to hurry because we must leave soon.

"Remember, always dress properly, not like you're going out to eat or shop in Kabul, but comfortably."

None of us asked any questions. Maybe we were too tired and shocked in that moment. There had been so much change in our lives the last two years. And almost everyone we knew had already escaped the country. Another move didn't seem odd. Once we were packed, Padar called us to come into the small hall by the door. We gathered around the lantern. By the door stood a big man. He was dressed in traditional clothes, *peran tumban,* and a flowing cape that covered him like a country peasant. He did not carry himself like a peasant, though. He stood erect and had an ease about him. Even under those baggy clothes, his muscles and wide shoulders were obvious. He had long, black, curly hair that rushed down over his shoulders. He possessed a disarming smile and a very handsome and brave-looking face.

"This is Masood," Padar said. "He's going to take you out of Kabul."

Izmarai stood off in the dark next to his mother.

"Is Izmarai going with us?" I asked.

"No, Enjeela," he said. "He can't."

I begged Padar to let our cousin come with us, until he grew exasperated with me.

"Enough, Enjeela," he said. "You have to leave now." He gave each of us money. None of us counted it, but it seemed like a lot. We stuffed it in our backpacks or our shoes. I saw him give Laila a piece of paper with the name of a hotel on it.

"I won't be going with you right now."

"What?" Laila said. "We're going alone?"

"I can't leave yet. The Russians follow me everywhere. If I'm with you, we'll all be arrested."

Laila started to argue, but he raised his hand to signal silence. He had made up his mind.

"This man will take care of you. Don't worry." He motioned toward Masood.

Laila had a sullen glare. Zulaikha shrank back. Zia gaped. I cried. Now, like Ahmad Shah, it was our turn to slip away in the night.

Masood moved out of the shadows. He knelt by me and took my hand so gently, the way a man of great strength would do.

"Little one, are you afraid?" His eyes were clear and steely black. His smile was pure confidence.

I nodded.

"Don't be." His reassuring eyes blazed at me. "I am Masood. I will take care of you better than I will take care of myself. Nothing will happen to you unless it happens to me."

In that instant, I trusted him. I wiped my tears on my *chador*.

He then went to each of my sisters and Zia, knelt by them, and told them the same thing. It was settled that we were to go with him. There was nothing more to argue about with Padar. Masood had a real strength to him that was unmistakable.

"This is a man you can trust. He will take you to Peshawar," Padar said. "Do everything he says. You must go now."

I took a breath.

Padar pushed us along. "I will see you all in Peshawar soon. Now go!"

We filed out the door. I hid my hair under a chador and dried my tears on the edges of the cloth. My sisters wore chadors that covered their entire bodies, and Zia was dressed like Masood. We all wore our newest sneakers. Masood took my hand, Padar closed the door to the house behind us, and we walked into the darkness of the sleeping city.

9

MASOOD

We had piled into a cab, which rode quietly through the dark, early-morning streets of Kabul and turned onto the highway taking us to Jalalabad. The four of us were crammed into the back seat.

The steely-eyed man, whom Padar said we could trust, sat in the front seat telling the driver which way to go. Peshawar, which is right across the border in Pakistan, was only a six-hour drive from Kabul. I knew that because so many of the kids in my neighborhood and at school had fled to Peshawar. Stories floated around that they had escaped the country, driving all night to the border. It was the first stop before going on to other places. We would stop in Jalalabad, and in my child mind, I expected to make it to the hotel Padar had told Laila about by that night or at least by early morning. I knew this from my friends who said it wasn't far to Peshawar by car, maybe a day's drive at most. And Padar hadn't said when he would come to us, but I felt certain he would come after us.

As dawn broke, we were well outside Kabul. The car stopped on a lonely stretch of road beside a bus. We had buses in the city, but this one was different. It looked like an old school bus, with bright-colored stripes painted along the sides. Prayer beads hung from the rearview mirror, and tassels decorated the windows. A stereo on the dashboard blared Indian music.

Masood urged us up and into the bus. The bus was crowded, but we found places to sit on the worn leather seats that were deeply cracked and torn. This wasn't a bus full of city people. I'd never seen so many women in one place wearing the full-face-covering burkas. The men wore peran tumbans and turbans. Only a few of the younger men wore T-shirts and jeans. People stared at us. We were the only children among the passengers. I'd never felt so out of place, like a foreigner.

The bus motor rumbled, and we began rolling, the driver pushing it methodically through the gears as it lumbered up to speed. Outside my window, I watched as we moved farther away from the flat, arid land surrounding Kabul and deeper into rugged mountains toward the Kabul River Gorge. The two-lane road appeared to have been carved out of the side of the sheer rock. On one side of us, the mountain, craggy with sharply angled boulders that protruded from the earth, veered off toward the sky, so we were constantly in the shade. On the other side, the edge dropped off into a tumbling river. We careened one way, then another, as the bus weaved through winding curves, straining the motor as the road rose and then descended so often I couldn't tell if we were going up or down.

The traffic slowed and piled up as we neared a roadblock manned by Afghan and Russian soldiers. Grim-faced Afghan soldiers stepped up into the bus and examined each of us as they made their way down the aisle. They clutched their shiny black rifles as they hesitated, scrutinizing every face. It appeared they were looking for someone from the way they peered down at the passengers in front of me. I thought they'd see my new sneakers. People from the villages didn't wear brand-new sneakers. Then I thought of the money in my shoe. It had been stupid to put it there. As if on cue, they started yelling at people, calling them names, saying they were looking for cowards who were afraid to fight for their country.

I lowered my head. Next to me, Masood sat tall and fearless, never taking his eyes off the soldiers. I saw his hand move to his waist. They stared at Masood but passed him by. A soldier grabbed a middle-aged man across from me. He yanked the man roughly to his feet by his collar.

"Where are you going?" the soldier yelled in his face.

"Home," he said, fear in his voice. "I'm going home."

"You look like one of the escaped prisoners," the soldier said. "We've been searching for you."

"Bring him outside," another soldier said. They dragged the man out and threw him on the road right outside our window.

Four or five soldiers surrounded him and began shouting, "Where are you going? What were you doing in Kabul?" They pointed the gun right at him; one soldier shoved the muzzle of his rifle right in the side of his head. The man tried to answer, but they kept on shouting at him. They called him a dog for running away.

"I would never leave my country," the man said, raising his head from the dirt. "This is my motherland."

The man sounded just like Padar. He always spoke of the motherland; this was where we were born, our homeland; it made us who we were. Everything I was leaving flashed through my mind—my house, my school, my beloved friends, Shahnaz and Saleem, and Izmarai and Auntie. Sadness came over me, as if I was walking away from a great treasure, one I could never replace no matter how hard I searched for something like it. The smell of the ashoka tree came to me, a sweetness on the air, the sign of spring in Kabul, when the city came to life. I would never forget Kabul.

They continued yelling at him, wanting him to admit to something. Now he was on his knees begging.

"I was shopping in Kabul for my wife and daughter." He kept repeating that, but they wouldn't listen.

Masood leaned down close to me. "Go outside right now and tell the soldiers he's your father." He urged me on with his eyes.

Padar said he was a man we could trust, so I didn't even take a breath to think about it before I rose to my feet and made my way down the aisle. I stepped through the open door onto the road. The man held up his hands, pleading with the soldiers, a deathly fear on his face. I'd never seen a man so afraid, so beaten down, as if he could die right at that moment from shame. I'd never seen an Afghan man treated like that before. I pulled my chador tight against my face. I had to think of something to say that would convince these men to let him live.

"He's my father," I said, holding out my hand toward him. "We were in Kabul shopping. We were just going home." I lifted a foot to show off my new sneakers, shiny and white. The same shoe that was lined with new afghani bills to pay for my escape. I wiggled my new shoe at the soldiers.

The man reached for my hand, hesitantly at first, then he took it with a sigh of relief. "Yes, this is my daughter."

I walked slowly up to the soldiers. "Please let him go, please, please, please." I used my most whining voice, the one that always irritated everyone.

An Afghan soldier kicked the man one more time. "You dirt. Get up and go to the bus."

I held his hand, and we boarded the bus. I led him to his seat and sat next to him. He held my arm tight and whispered to me, "You have a lot of courage." He thanked me several times. After the bus had rumbled miles down the road, I took my place next to Masood. I knew he was proud of me from the glow on his face.

"You did the right thing," he said to me.

I could tell by the way Laila and Zulaikha were frowning at me from their seats in front of us that they weren't so happy with my bravery. As soon as I sat down next to him, they let Masood have it.

"Why did you tell her to go out there?" Laila said. "She could have gotten killed."

"Don't ever do that again," Zulaikha said to me. "Those soldiers will shoot you if they think you're lying."

"Afghan soldiers wouldn't hurt a little girl," Masood said, "if they don't think she's trying to escape. Besides, she saved a life."

"You're supposed to protect us," Laila hissed, the anger simmering in her eyes. "She could have gotten killed, and it would be all because of you."

Masood turned away, apparently not interested in having his decisions examined by anyone, especially two teenage girls. As angry as my sisters were, I knew I'd done the right thing in helping that man. And what surprised me most was that I hadn't felt afraid of getting hurt at all. That possibility came to mind only when Laila mentioned it with fire in her eyes. It finally occurred to me that she could be right and that she knew, since she was older and wiser. If Padar were there, I wouldn't have had to go out, he would have stood up for that man. I'd never seen him afraid of anyone, and when those soldiers showed up at our front door looking for Ahmad Shah, he had been so cool in the way he spoke to them, like they were mistaken to think they could be right. As much as I disliked his drinking, I knew him as a brave man who always stood up for the weak and helpless. He would have had something to say to those confused soldiers.

Masood had said if we weren't escaping, they wouldn't hurt us. But we *were* escaping, and we had new sneakers and backpacks full of clothes and money. If they had searched us, they would have figured out our intentions.

I rested my head against the glass and watched the mountains slip by as the bus rumbled on. Padar wasn't here to do the right thing. And maybe what Masood had been showing me was that I was alone here, and I'd have to stand up for myself, and I'd have to make brave choices.

He would help us to know what to do, but it was going to be up to each of us to be afraid or not to be afraid.

———

Masood told us that we couldn't go straight into Jalalabad and then on to Pakistan; we'd be getting off the bus at the first village on the road to Jalalabad. There were too many Russian soldiers on the main road to the city.

The army had set up roadblocks all the way into the Khyber Pass to stop people from escaping. They were forcing men from their cars at gunpoint and sending them off to fight for the government. I thought of my brother Ahmad Shah, who had escaped rather than join the army, and my brother Zia, who in the next year or two would be conscripted to fight too, if we had stayed. Then I thought of Mommy, and I remembered all the arguments she used to have with Padar over leaving Kabul. Everyone in her family was fleeing the city, and she thought that we should follow. I wished we had all flown away with her and my other sisters. It would have been easier to get out back then, before the Soviets came. She should have taken us all. But she didn't, and so I sat with my other siblings, who were now sleeping or staring out the window on a bus to Jalalabad.

The bus wound through the rocky mountain passes, the narrow road hugging the mountainside as we edged along, just feet from a steep cliff. Traffic became heavy on the road, with big trucks of every kind, other buses of villagers and refugees from Kabul, and cars jammed with families with all their belongings tied to the roofs. We slowed to a crawl, then stopped. We sat there for a while, beginning to sweat in the afternoon heat, before the bus driver announced that we would have to get off. A landslide had blocked the road up ahead, and we would have to walk the rest of the way. We gathered our backpacks and filed out the door with the rest of the travelers.

We trudged in a group through the mountain pass that was strewn with huge boulders and dirt. We had to weave our way through the debris, straddling rocks and loose dirt, slipping between larger boulders, until it was too dark to continue safely. Masood found a safe spot up on a mountain slope, and we sat close to each other in the dirt. Some of the other bus passengers stopped with us; others disappeared into the darkness, continuing their journey up the road. I sat close to Masood, and he made himself comfortable in the dirt as best he could. He rummaged in his knapsack and pulled out an apple. Then, from under his cloak, he unsheathed a large, shiny hunting knife. I'd never seen such a large knife before. He carefully peeled the apple with the sharp blade, then cut it into pieces, handing out some to each of us. My sisters and Zia sat close by, and we ate in silence. Masood cut more fruit for us and passed around a bottle of water and told us not to drink too much; we would have to save some for the long walk tomorrow.

It had been a long day—woken suddenly from my comfortable bed and now bedding down right in the hard dirt on a hillside. I was exhausted and tried to make the best of it. My sisters and Zia settled down, and in minutes it seemed I could hear them sleeping soundly. I lay awake, staring up at the Afghan sky. The stars above sparkled—brilliant in the night sky, beautiful and large. In one day I'd been thrust out from my home into a wilderness, and all the light I had were these stars, surrounded by quiet. The sound of bombing that we heard every night didn't reach this isolated patch of earth. My thoughts ran everywhere, wondering where we were going and if we'd even get there. I was too fatigued to think about how hungry I was.

"Are you having trouble sleeping?" Masood said quietly.

He sat nearby in the same position, sitting up with his arms around his legs, since we had finished eating. He hadn't moved.

"Yes," I said. The air had cooled off, and I felt a chill.

He took off his long cape and laid it over me. When he leaned over, I could see guns strapped across his chest, a pistol in his belt, and his hunting knife strapped to his leg. "You were a little lion today," he said. "I'm so proud of you. Now sleep. Tomorrow we will walk far."

He settled into his sitting position, legs against his chest, arms around them, holding them close. I couldn't even tell that he was breathing. He never closed his eyes. His words warmed me—*a little lion*. I drifted off under the starry night.

Deep into the morning, I remember tossing and turning. It seemed like minutes later Masood was shaking me awake. "Get up. We have a long way to go today."

We all rose, and Masood handed out more apple slices. He took his cape back and wrapped it around himself, concealing the weapons strapped against his large torso. The other bus passengers had already left; it was just four kids and Masood. Once everyone was standing, we set off, following Masood's path as the sun rose.

The farther we walked, the thirstier we became. Hunger and thirst weren't feelings I was used to. He pushed us all day. When I told him how tired I was, he would tell me just a little farther. "We can rest up there." He would point to something up ahead, but we never stopped there.

Late in the day, the road dipped down alongside a river, but still there was a twenty-foot drop-off to the river's edge. We were all thirsty, but it was too far to jump down, and even if we had, the wall was too steep to climb back up to the road.

"Look there," I said, pointing to a tire floating in the river. Someone had anchored the tire in the river and attached a rope to it, which was tied to a nearby tree. I climbed down the rope. One by one, everyone followed until we were all by the shallow river bank. We cleaned up; washed our faces, hands, and arms in the cold water; and drank as much as we could. It was a relief from the brutal trek, and we all relaxed in the moment of rest.

We were having a great time until Masood shouted, "Tanks are coming! Get in the water!"

Masood hated and feared the Russians and didn't want to be seen on the road when they passed. We jumped into the water and held on to the tire that kept us from being swept away with the current. None of us knew how to swim except for Zia. The river rushed swiftly around us, swirling and pushing against us. Masood submerged his head, and we all did likewise. We could feel the vibrations of the tanks rolling by in a long line. I had to come up for air a few times, as did everyone else. When we didn't hear them any longer, we waded into shore. Dust clouds from the passing tanks lingered in the air, leaving a fine patina of dust over us. We stood on the shore for a few moments catching our breath. This was not going to be an easy walk through the countryside. Every day we were going to confront life-and-death situations. This wasn't a game we would be able to talk our way out of as I had on the bus. There was going to be hiding and running and being afraid and not being afraid. When Masood said it was time, we silently climbed up to the road to continue on.

Our walk lasted several days. Masood would let us stop only every couple of hours. We ate sparingly along the way: slices of apples, dried fruit, a tough brown bread, and water. The travel was exhausting, and we'd slump to the ground at each break to rest our legs. We slept in the open on the side of the road. I had never done that before and neither had my sisters or brother. I never thought I'd enjoy seeing the stars, so vivid and bright in the sky, millions of speckled worlds spinning around me in the night. I had spent my whole life, as much as I remembered, being taken care of by Noor. If we needed to eat, he fed us; if we ran out of food in the house, he went to the market. If we made a mess, one of the maids would clean it up. If our clothes were dirty, we changed into clean ones—washed, ironed, and hung up for us, ready to wear. Now for three straight nights, we had slept on the cold earth, worn the same clothes, and ate apples and pears and rough bread that Masood pulled from his bag. My new tennis shoes, white and shiny just three days ago, now looked like I'd worn them for years. The cracks were filled with dirt, the porous soles were caked with dirt, and the laces had turned a dirty brown. I missed Noor and the house on Shura Street and Padar.

When we arrived in the first village, our resting spot was nothing more than a cluster of mud-brick compounds, behind which we could see the thatched roofs of tiny houses. These small compounds were clustered along a dusty street that ran down the middle of the community, emptying into a small square. There was a uniform brown dullness to the buildings. As nondescript and rustic as the place appeared to us, Masood assured us we would find what we wanted most here: a place to sleep, something nice to eat, and water to wash. Cows, chickens, and sheep were everywhere along the lane. I was so hungry; if I had had the energy to catch one of them, I would have wrung its neck like I'd seen done and begun feasting on it there in the middle of the street. We slumped to the dusty ground in exhaustion while Masood talked to one of the villagers, who agreed to feed us and give us a place to sleep. He motioned us toward an outdoor cooking stove, and we watched a few village women cook rice and vegetables. The women looked like they wore the same clothes they slept in, faded gray chadors and baggy *kameez*. When the food was ready, they placed the meal on a large platter and gave us each a little plate with a small serving while they began sharing what was left on the platter. They didn't give us forks or spoons. We all watched the villagers for a while as they ate with their hands. We had never eaten with our hands before, but when hunger claws at you till you think it is going to burst you open, it is not too hard to pick up the rice with your fingers and stuff it in your mouth. I ate with my fingers, as the villagers did and as I'd seen my countrymen do before, and it was the best rice and vegetables I'd ever had.

After dinner we went down to the river to wash. After washing, we watched the villagers prepare for the evening. Once inside one of their huts, we sat on the hard-packed floor. There were no beds, no electric lights, and no running water for showers. When it was time to sleep, most of them curled up on the dirt floor, so we did the same. There were few blankets to go around, so we used our own clothes to cover us.

That night, as my tired body dragged me off into sleepiness, images of Noor setting plates of food on Mommy's long dining room table flashed through my thoughts. The rhythms and routines of village life were so different from what I grew up with in the city. I had lived in a different world than the people in this village had.

We stayed in this place for a while, waiting for Masood to decide when it was safe for us to continue on our journey. We soon settled in to their rhythms. We rose each morning and washed in the river to start the day. Since we also drank directly from the river, which was the only source of water, I learned to look around and make sure I wasn't downriver from village cows and sheep and other animals that would stand in the river and foul it with their waste while they lapped up the water with their tongues.

Village life was far removed from life in Kabul. The kids were dirty and wore tattered clothes, and the women, who worked hard in the sun, slept in the same clothes they had worn during the day. My sisters and brothers and I had whole closets full of clothes, and we had toys and bicycles and watched TV at night in a plush living room. In this village as dusk closed in, I watched a few of the kids play a game with sticks and rocks while they ran around in their tattered clothes. At night, as I slipped off into sleep on the hard dirt floor after a meager dinner of vegetables and rice, I wondered if my memories of Kabul were the reality in Afghanistan.

One night after everyone went to sleep, and a quiet had descended over the village, Masood woke us. In a hushed tone he told us to get our things; our way was clear to continue on. We were leaving.

"This is a very difficult part of the journey, so we must stay together," he told us as we moved quickly down the dirt road. We were heading deeper into the countryside. He explained that we would have to go around Jalalabad, and the shortest way was through a large marijuana field. It was well guarded on all sides by the farmers, and he had received special permission for us to walk through it. "I paid them to let us pass," he said. But he said we must be quiet and stay together and concentrate, or the unpleasant smell of the tall plants would overcome us.

I'd never smelled anything so rotten. The field was so vast and dense with plants that the concentrated aroma of the marijuana plants had turned into a putrid stench that burrowed into our noses and seeped down into our stomachs. It was like walking through a garbage dump where animal carcasses and waste food had been left to rot, producing one large overwhelming odor of death. We gagged every step. I wanted to throw up, but Masood prodded us to keep moving. We didn't dare stop, worried that the stench would overwhelm us to the point we would be unable to continue. He carried a lantern and held it out in front of us and warned us to watch where we stepped. The field went on for miles. I figured this because we had to walk all night to get through it.

"There are scorpions and spiders, but don't worry, if you get bit, it won't kill you. I know exactly what to do."

I knew scorpions well. I'd seen them when I walked to school or down by the Kabul River, where we went at times to picnic or to throw rocks in the river. They were a greenish brown, with spindly legs and a curling tail with a poisonous sting on the end. Masood tried to reassure us we'd be fine because they had poor eyesight. They were all over, and we often saw them scurrying out of the light of the lantern.

The odor was so intense it overpowered us no matter how hard we tried not to think about it. The sour smell settled in our stomachs, and every so often one of us would stop and start retching. Masood turned and waited when one of us was throwing up, then he marched on and we followed.

To keep our minds off our sickness, we talked about our days in Kabul. About how Shahnaz and Shapairi were the most beautiful girls in town and how boys used to follow them around when they walked to the store. And how boys would drive by in their cars and whistle at them. And how suitors would come by the house wanting to speak to Padar to ask for their hands, and he would kick them out for being rude, or too young, or too old. And the fun we had at our parents' parties, with our friends, and during the holidays, when the family would gather to eat and talk.

"Will we ever see those days again?" Laila asked. "Go to the parties that we used to have in Kabul?"

A party? With every step we moved farther away from our home, my fears grew that we'd never see either of our parents again, that we would be stranded in one of these villages, eating rice and vegetables with our hands and sleeping on dirt floors for the rest of our lives. In the darkness that night, I began thinking maybe our parents were just trying to get rid of us by sending us on this journey. *A party?* I pictured myself eating with a fork again and smiled through another spell of gagging.

10

THIS IS YOUR LOT

Just after sunrise, with the sun at our backs as it peeked through the ragged edges of distant mountaintops, we tramped into another village of squat mud-brick houses that rested along the banks of a stream. By this time, all of the villages looked the same, born out of the Afghan dirt that had left a muddy hue to every building and every wall. The dirt path down the center of the village looked much like the others we had walked through, but here, we were greeted. A line of raggedly dressed children with dirty faces and hungry eyes watched us as we passed. The chilly air made me shiver, and I had a fatigue I had never felt before. I wanted to lie down in the dirt of this dingy settlement and sleep. I couldn't put any more weight on my feet; my tennis shoes had rubbed against the back of my heels for too many hours. Laila, who had been throwing up all night, limped behind me, barely able to take another step. Zulaikha and Zia were both slump-shouldered and weary. Spent beyond our experience, we collapsed in a silent circle in the dust in front of one of the mud-walled compounds. None of us spoke when Masood left us to meet with one of the villagers.

It felt as if we had all changed in the week since we'd left Kabul. Laila, a natural leader with energy and confidence from her years of volleyball competition, who pushed all of us to perform better or play harder, was now collapsed over her knees as if she was never going to stop throwing up. Across from me was quiet Zulaikha. Her thoughts were a mystery to me. My adventurous brother Zia's fun-loving demeanor had now turned so serious. Once I had my sneakers off, the sharp pulsing in my feet began to ebb, so I moved close to Laila and put my hand on her shoulder to let her know I was there. Her body convulsed as she retched. She was the one who had always taken care of us, but what if she couldn't continue? I watched Masood across the courtyard as he spoke to a man.

I tried to remember why Padar had sent us away without him. Was he truly going to meet us in Peshawar? What if he got so drunk he fell asleep and never woke up? And while he slept, his cigarette fell out of his mouth and lit the house on fire? That nearly happened once. The flesh of his arm had blistered such an ugly, painful red that we had to take him to the hospital. A fear rose within me that he would never come for us. That we were now alone.

I covered my face with my hands. I wanted to cry. I knew I shouldn't. Even though I was the youngest, I didn't want my sisters and brother to treat me like a child for the rest of the way. I especially didn't want to let Masood think I was too weak to make it through the journey. I took in a deep breath and opened my eyes. I would not let myself act like a baby.

Masood stood on the other side of the dirt yard, by two wooden doors in the mud wall, as he talked with an old man. I could see the man's face clearly—a scruffy gray beard that hadn't been combed in a lifetime; a weathered, parched face like a discarded piece of leather; and a mouth of missing or cracked teeth. He wore a dirty sand-colored peran tumban, the traditional dress we saw often in the countryside. I could hear Padar's voice run through my head—*Don't trust him, don't trust him.*

The wooden doors separated the part of the village we stayed in from where the rest of the people lived. It was the private compound of the local villagers. The part we stayed in was for travelers. In a couple of days, we all recovered from our walk through the marijuana fields. My curiosity returned, and I began to wonder what life was like behind those closed doors.

Laila wouldn't have anything to do with my snoopiness. She kept telling me to stay close to her, that this was a dangerous place, and I shouldn't just walk around and look into people's houses or ask what they were doing. She warned me to not go too far from her. But it was difficult being around her. What did she know? Every day, she constantly pestered Masood about how long we were staying in the village. She wanted to know why we couldn't just keep walking and get out of there. Why was it taking so long to get to Peshawar? Then Zulaikha would pipe up and start complaining about the food and the hut we slept in. Pretty soon we were all snapping at one another. Masood only smiled at all the questions and demands. "You should be happy," he told us one day, "that you don't have to live here. We are just waiting till it's safe to pass. Then we will leave."

Each day, the bombing in the mountains became more intense. Explosions in the distance sent small tremors through the earth as we sat on the ground eating our rice and vegetables. At night when sound traveled, we could hear the rat-a-tat-tat of machine-gun fire and jets streaking overhead. During the day, helicopters passed overhead, and we could see the guns and bombs. The war was close enough that Masood insisted it was too dangerous to go farther right now. As soon as he had news that it was safe, we'd move on. Meanwhile we were stuck in this dreary place, eating just enough rice and vegetables to keep the hunger pangs away.

Day after day the old man with the cracked teeth came through the wooden doors, delivered our food, then disappeared behind the doors, leaving us to ourselves. He would often stare at me and my sisters as we played. I watched him look us over one day, like he was trying to value livestock in the market. I turned away from him, renewed in my determination not to go near him. But I couldn't sit still at times not knowing what he was doing on the other side of the gates.

One day when he finished bringing lunch, I waited until he returned to the other side, then snuck over and opened one of the doors and peeked inside. The other part of the village looked similar to our side, but this one was full of kids—hungry, gaunt, toyless children. One girl who appeared close to my age stood out: she moved around to her chores with vigor others didn't have. She still had passion for life, despite her dismal environment. Here was one girl who appeared to have stayed above it all.

She must have been babysitting, because she ran around chasing after the little kids. I didn't speak to her, because she was so busy. Every day, she wore the same black baby-doll dress and green pants—a peran tumban—and she kept her black hair stuffed under her black chador. She was skinny and dark skinned like so many of the other children. Finally, one day after the gray-bearded man dropped off our food, I snuck into the other side and furtively approached her.

"Salaam, I'm Enjeela," I said, raising my hand to shake hers.

"I'm Mina," she said with a smile, the first one I'd seen from anyone in this village. She had the sweetest nature to her. I wanted to be friends.

"Would you like to play?" I asked.

"I can't right now." She looked around at the yard full of kids. "I have things to do, but if you meet me back here in a couple of hours, I can."

When I returned later, she was seated on a rock waiting for me. I sat beside her, and we talked like we had always been sisters. I couldn't contain my joy at finding a friend to play and talk with. I could see by the light in her eyes that she enjoyed it as much as I did.

"Do you know how to play *juz bazi*?" I asked.

She shook her head.

I explained the simple game to her. It's a jumping game where each player takes turns, similar to hopscotch. We played for a long time. For the first time since leaving Kabul, I forgot completely where I was; we were just two little girls enjoying a moment of friendliness. We were both caught in a reverie of fun until a shrill voice tore through the air. I cringed and looked around. It was an old woman, shriveled in her face by sun and work, who stood in the door of her hut screaming at my friend.

"Come here, you little bastard. You have a lot of work to do."

Mina ran off and disappeared into the darkness of the hut. I stared at the door of that ragged hut she lived and worked in. I felt an instant sadness for her to have such a terrible mother.

We played every day after her chores were done. I never asked Mina about her mother. And Mina never complained.

One day Mina taught me a game called *panjoque*. It's a popular game played with rocks that requires fast reflexes and good balance. We each collected ten small stones we could hold in the palm of our hand. We would throw them up in the air, flip our hands over, and try to catch as many as possible on the backs of our hands. The ones that fell on the ground we'd group into a pile close by. If we caught at least one, we'd throw that one up in the air, and before it landed, reach down and grab the ones in the pile below us, then reach out and catch the one we had just thrown up. We'd keep playing until one of us was successful and won the game. Sometimes I won. Most of the time Mina won. We played it a lot.

After we finished, we sat in the sun, and she asked me to tell her what it was like living in Kabul. I told her about how I used to sit on the highest branches of a pear tree in my yard and watch the neighborhood. I told her about a suitor who came for my sister Shahnaz. His name was Saleem, and Shahnaz was in love with him. He used to follow Shahnaz home from work every day, but they couldn't exchange words because that wasn't the custom.

I told her about when Saleem's family came asking for Shahnaz's hand in marriage and how they came to our home with beautiful gifts for my parents and Shahnaz. Then the engagement party Padar threw—it was the biggest celebration we'd ever had in our home. And there was so much food and drink. More than five hundred people were invited to the wedding, and ambassadors and dignitaries attended. And they brought the most expensive jewelry as wedding gifts because the higher your social status, the nicer the gift you gave.

Mina sat wide-eyed, listening. As I told her about all my brothers and sisters and going to school and learning how to read and write, her eyes brightened. The world was opening up for her the way the petals of a flower unfold in the sunshine.

Every time Mina and I were together, she asked me to tell her more stories of Kabul. I told her about how we'd get all dressed up in new clothes and drive to the theater with my parents and watch live plays. My favorite of all time was the very first play I saw, *Snow White*. After I explained to her the story of the wicked witch and beautiful princess and handsome prince who saved her life with a kiss on her lips, she gave me a blank stare—she'd never heard that story.

I told her my dream was to return to Kabul and wait for a handsome prince, all decked out in the most gorgeous clothes, to come and ask for my hand in marriage. We'd have the greatest engagement party ever. I would be married at the Kabul Hotel, just like Shahnaz and Saleem. My wedding would be just as grand. I'd wear a green dress for the *nikkah*—the first part of the ceremony, where the bride and groom exchanged vows and signed the marriage contract. And I'd wear the most stunning white dress for the ceremony afterward. And there would be thousands of guests to celebrate with us. My prince would ride a horse or drive a car or fly a plane—I didn't care, but I believed he would come for me one day.

After I finished, Mina was silent for a long while. Her eyes had grown large. She spoke very softly when she told me that weddings in her village were not like that at all. People didn't have much money or many clothes. They did wear the traditional green dress but wore it for both parts. She'd seen lots of weddings, I sensed, because she seemed to know exactly how they were done in the village.

I could see in Mina's eyes that she had a yearning to see the world beyond her village of dirt hovels and the tedium of grueling chores.

"Would you like to come to Kabul with us when we return? You could be my sister," I said. "You can go to school with me and learn to read and write."

Her smile came alive, but she said nothing.

The next day I went to meet Mina in our usual spot. She wasn't there. I looked everywhere, but I couldn't find her. The same happened the following day. I told Laila I was worried something had happened to her, and she said I should just keep to myself. No one knew what went on around the villages. I couldn't believe that she didn't seem to care. On the third day, I found Mina waiting for me. Deep-purple and red bruises mottled her neck and face. She looked like she'd been in a desperate fight. She tried to play, but she was still in a lot of pain. She never said what happened, so I pestered her.

She finally told me that she had been beaten. I asked why her parents would beat her.

"Why are your parents so mean to you?" I asked.

"They're not my parents," she said. "That man's my husband. That woman is his other wife. They don't like me to play with you so much since I have a lot of work to do taking care of the little kids."

All the village sounds disappeared for a moment as I tried to understand what she had just told me. She studied her hands and pulled at the cloth of her peran tumban. I thought of the old man's ugly face and angry grin. All the light in her eyes left. They filled with tears. "He bought me from my parents when I was seven."

I didn't know how married couples did it, but I knew they had children, the details of which seemed to be made of mysterious things—things older girls would whisper about. I knew that a man had to court a woman and be desperate for her to get her to marry him, and a girl should be much older than seven to be courted. My parents certainly didn't *sell* Shahnaz to Saleem.

The only thing I knew about marriage was what I learned from my sister. Husbands were supposed to be in love with their wives—like Saleem and Shahnaz, and Snow White and her prince. I tried to think of some encouraging words to lift her spirits; she looked so defeated— not like the joyful Mina I had met just a few weeks ago.

I asked her about her family, but she couldn't remember what her parents were like or where her home even was; she had been so young when she left. She'd been in the village with this man and his other wife for more than two years. This gray existence had wiped away any memories of a happier time with her family. She had no hope or expectation of ever seeing them again. Shock ran deep inside me that parents could abandon a child for money. I knew wives didn't walk away from their marriages. I was separated from my parents, but it was a different situation. We were on a journey to reunite as a family. But Mina would never see her parents again. She couldn't even remember what they looked like. The whole world was closed off to her. She didn't know anything about the world outside the sharp boundaries of her tiny life until I had shared my memories of Kabul. I wanted to cry for her.

Mina was going to spend the rest of her life as a slave. It made me angry. It made me so glad for my family and all that they had shown and taught me. I had such a treasury of memories inside me: My sister Shahnaz reading her romance novels to us kids. Mommy's stories from the history of Islam and of Afghanistan, and the books and poems Padar would read to us of heroes and fairy tales on those dark nights when the electricity was out. I knew there was much more to know and explore than what had been forced on her. I could not let her continue to live like this.

I went to Laila and told her about what had happened to Mina, how her parents had sold her and she was the wife of that terrible old man who brought us food. Laila was already upset about staying in the village—this brought her to a level of rage. She agreed with me that we needed to leave and that we should buy Mina from the man and take her with us as a sister. She had the money to help.

Later that day, we spoke with Masood. We squatted in the dirt with him, speaking in low tones. Laila was beside me.

"We have to take Mina with us when we go," I demanded.

"We can't take her with us," he said.

"Why not?" I said. "She's just a slave here."

"It would cause too much trouble."

"We can buy her. I have money. Laila has more."

He shook his head of long hair. I could see the resolve on his face.

"You have to know something," he said. He glanced around as if he wanted to make sure no one would hear us.

"What?" I said with insolence. "What do I have to know?"

"This happens every day in Afghanistan."

"What happens?"

"Little girls are sold to men like this every day. This is her lot in life. It can't be changed." Masood was deliberate and firm in his explanation.

Laila and I gawked at him.

He shook his head and looked off.

"We have to help her," I said, not accepting that there was nothing he could do. Masood was a good man; he had helped us through so much already. Surely he knew this was the right thing to do.

"Enjeela, listen to me." He settled his dark eyes on me, and now he wasn't smiling. "If we try to help her in any way, it will put us all in great danger—you and you," he said nodding to each of us. "And Zia and Zulaikha." He rose and glanced down at us, unsmiling. "It is your lot to go on from here, and it is Mina's to stay. No one can change that." He turned from us as if he had more pressing things to do. I knew he wouldn't change his mind. He was like Padar. He had made up his mind, and he expected us to accept his decision.

That day and all that week, I moved around in an anger-fueled daze. Every time I saw Mina and spoke to her, her desperation grew greater. She had lost that joyful sense of acceptance she had possessed when I first met her. It reminded me of my own desperation. I couldn't help but think what happened to her could happen to me. Every bit of anger I felt about Mina's situation, I felt for my own. I thought about Mommy leaving and Padar sending us away. Parents weren't supposed to abandon their children. Our two plights mingled into an inferno of rage inside me. I wanted to forget I even had parents, that I even had a home.

Mina never mentioned the beatings again, but her fresh purplish welts said they hadn't stopped. She seemed weaker, with less determination. I told her we'd perform *namaz* for her. I remembered how the mullah had sung the *azan*, the call to prayer, five times a day. And how we'd pray, say *namaz* together, or attend the mosque, the boys and men on one side, and the girls and women on the other. Here there was no *azan*, and no one said *namaz* either.

All the light in her eyes had been beaten out of her. She walked around a mere shell of herself. I hated every minute we were in this ugly village. The sight of that man—her husband—made me want to yell and scream at him. But Masood had warned me not to interfere, not to say anything a little girl shouldn't, or my life would be in danger; all of our lives would be in jeopardy.

Mina and I prayed together. We prayed that no one would ever beat her again. And for me to see Mommy and Padar again. We did this every day for several weeks, and I began to think things were changing for her, to believe that Allah heard our prayers.

Then one morning, Masood came to me.

"Sit here, Enjeela," he said, pointing to a place beside him. He had a serious expression. "I want you to stay in our camp. The neighbors are going to have a funeral today."

"Who died?" I asked, surprised.

"I don't know." He averted his eyes. My heart began to tumble like it would fly right out of my chest. I didn't believe him.

"Is it Mina?"

"No, no," he said. "Just stay here for today. Pack your things; we're leaving early in the morning."

I shot up from my seat and ran to the other side of the village, expecting to see her smiling and waiting for me. We would play *juz bazi*, then tell stories, then have a tea party. When I got to the other side, I looked around and she wasn't there. A body wrapped in white sheets was laid out on the ground, and seated beside it were Mina's husband and his other wife. I searched every other face in the crowd of people who were surrounding the corpse, but Mina wasn't among them. But I didn't see any children in the crowd. Maybe they didn't allow children to attend. Not even child brides.

Other villagers stood around the shrouded body. The old man sat, and when I made eye contact with him, he gave me a hateful stare from across the courtyard.

I had never known hate for another person before I met him. Even the soldier in Kabul who came to our house searching for Ahmad Shah or the Russian men who harassed Padar hadn't made me feel this burning distaste. As if I'd swallowed some fruit of awakening, my eyes were opened to the evil in men's hearts. As I stood there staring back at the man, my knees became weak. I broke his gaze and collapsed in the dirt. I cried as I continued to search for Mina in the crowd. If it wasn't Mina in the shroud, then where was she?

Zia walked up, put his hand on my shoulder, and told me that I needed to come with him; we would need to eat before it was time for us to go. As I rose to go with him, I could feel an emptiness in the village behind me, that the light Mina had brought to it was gone—all that remained were tattered clothes hanging on skinny bodies in the dust, and in the center, the wicked man and his brutal wife. If Masood was right, and all of Afghanistan allowed such despicable traditions, I hoped the entire country would collapse into dust too.

As we ate, Laila kept saying that Masood was right, if we tried to help her, the villagers would probably beat us, or maybe kill us, too. Our money wouldn't have solved anything. Masood just shrugged when I glared at him.

"What if it's not her?" I cried. "We're just going to leave her behind?"

"It's too bad," he said. "But her lot is here with her people."

Their willingness to just slough off Mina's life as if she were some worthless possession turned me rancid inside. I went to my makeshift bed and lay there tossing and turning all night, unable to sleep. Every time I closed my eyes, I saw her smile. How could we leave her with this animal for a husband? I couldn't stop crying.

We rose early, shouldered our packs, and stepped into the darkness. We passed the last mud hut shrouded in quiet shadow. The dusty path wound through the rugged countryside as we followed close behind Masood's brisk steps. I prayed for Mina as we walked, that she was alive and would sleep safely in peace, and that one day soon, she'd know the love and joy of a real family.

11

The Wolf and the Lion

A few days after we left Mina's village, we hiked single file through the early morning, down a dusty track leading to another nameless village. My body moved forward, step upon step, but so much of my heart had stayed behind with Mina. The thought of her living for the rest of her life with that intolerable old man as a husband shook any ideas of fairy-tale romances out of my mind. I was a different person than when I had entered that mud-hut hovel. I understood a wariness about life that I hadn't known before. I had been soft and malleable, so trusting of adults and enamored with my life in Afghanistan—now I had been gelled into something firmer, more complex, and guarded. I had always believed that my life was in the hands of God—and he would take care of me. But now I wasn't so sure about that; my fate had the feeling of chance to it. I became more watchful about what was going on around me, about the men of this land and their ways. And possessed of a new determination, I would not lie down and let evil happen to me. I had to be as courageous as possible—and if I died, then so be it. If it was my time, I would die; if not, then I would live. But I would not let these men make a victim of me.

I'd never felt so alone, so stripped of everything that could protect me and my sisters and Zia. Only Masood stood between us and the dangerous wolves of the Afghanistan countryside. As protective and loyal as Masood had seemed so far, I still feared deep down that he might disappear into the night and leave us at the mercy of these wicked men who lived in their dirt houses. I'd made a trade in that little place: my simple way of seeing the world, for Mina's face, her vibrancy, her deep desire to see beyond her narrow life she'd been fated to, sold into slavery by her parents, into an anonymous existence. If she couldn't leave with me, I wanted to live for her, for what she could have discovered.

The dust coming off the road settled into every pore of our bodies, on our clothes, in our hair, and covered the bits of food we ate out of Masood's pack. I lost track of how many days we walked. Sleeping under the stars on the side of the road in the hard dirt. We must have traveled a good distance, because the land began to change. It became slightly undulating, and then we passed through an area that at one time must have been heavily wooded, but now the forest had been thinned down to scraggily looking pine trees. The green pine needles broke up the pervasive brown scenery of the rocks, boulders, and dirt that all melted into one tone of dried-out earth. We finally came to another village; it looked like a fortress with a mud wall surrounding it—threatening to keep us out.

Inside the gates, we found an open area that had been turned into a makeshift campground filled with tents. Others escaping Kabul had ended up in this same remote place on their way to Pakistan, just like us: families, groups of men, and some who were alone.

Masood surveyed the place and turned to us. He squatted down to eye level, and with an ominous tone, he said to us, "Don't talk to anyone here. Don't trust anyone. Stay with each other, and don't wander off." He stared especially hard at me and repeated, "Don't talk to strangers."

I had no intentions of trying to make any more friends. Walking through the tents, I quickly noticed that most of the travelers carried Kalashnikov or hunting rifles and looked at us warily as we passed, as if they were sizing us up. From the way they dressed, some of them must have come from Kabul; others were in the traditional dress of the countryside, but they all were tense and suspicious. The cities and towns were emptying out in the face of the growing arrests and torture by the army. People didn't trust each other. Some could be spies sent by the government to see who was escaping.

Everyone was suspicious of anyone who was curious or overly helpful. So it was best to keep to ourselves. Laila took to holding my hand to make sure I stayed with them when we walked through the camp. But when she wasn't looking, I often snuck away to see the camp for myself. I didn't have the same fears as my siblings of getting hurt. I was a little girl; I wasn't a threat to anyone. Who would bother with me? But still, every time I returned from exploring on my own, Laila chastised me for being so careless.

The days of our stay blended into weeks. Around the cooking fire at night, some of the men talked openly of one of the travelers: a woman named Fatima. They were concerned that she wouldn't make it through the mountains. One of them asked what would become of her daughter. Someone said they thought she would die if she was alone. She didn't seem able to take care of herself. My curiosity got the best of me. Why couldn't this girl take care of herself? I wanted to meet this girl and her mother, but Masood had told me to stay close to my sisters. Laila warned me every day not to wander off. And for some time I didn't, but then I couldn't restrain myself any longer, so one day when Masood and my sisters and brothers were preoccupied, I wandered off to find that girl and her mother.

Fatima and her daughter weren't difficult to spot. I'd seen her wandering the camp at times, weak and frail-looking. She had pale skin and walked with a listless gait, as if she didn't have the energy to spare even to take a few big steps in a row. She wore a white chador on her head and a peran tumban under a gray dress. Her hard life must have worn her down. She walked around with her eyes to the ground as if she was too weary to even lift her head. She wore a perpetual frown, as if she didn't expect to complete her journey. Maybe she had heard what people were saying about her and had resigned herself to letting it come true, and one day she'd simply drop dead. Her daughter, Shakila, who was eighteen, was also very quiet and reserved. She appeared delicate and lovely, with long black hair, brown eyes, and deep olive skin. And she was very devoted, tending to her mother's every need because the slight woman could do little for herself.

The camp was a ramshackle affair, with rows of shelters that were nothing more than plywood and canvas tarps thrown over branches and boards scavenged from the area. The camp was laid out in a haphazard maze of narrow alleys that twisted and turned through the entire camp. Making my way through this warren, I spotted Fatima curled up in a corner of her tent, weeping. I gathered she was grieving over her own fate, which to me seemed like a waste of time. Her daughter was very busy taking care of her. The mother hardly left her tent, but when she did, she wore her pain like her own death mask.

Once I knew where her tent was, I strolled by it each day. Most of the time, she lay in the same position as the first time I saw her. The rumor around the camp was that she feared her looming death would place her daughter in danger. A girl alone of marriageable age and who is beautiful but with no family to protect her is the most vulnerable of all people. If something happened to Fatima, Shakila would be at the mercy of any man in the camp who could claim her.

When I looked at Shakila, I saw Mina, her bruised and welted body, and those two devils who had beaten a little girl for playing games with a stranger. This land was harsher on its children than the relentless sun, scorching and unforgiving.

Every time I went by Fatima's tent, I became more provoked to say something. I had watched Padar, with all of his weaknesses, never falter in his determination to help us. I couldn't comprehend why she couldn't be strong for her daughter, the way Padar had been for us. It didn't seem right to me that she would give up in front of her daughter.

One day I stopped at the open flap of her tent and stepped inside. She must have sensed a stranger, and she looked up at me. I was intending only to get her to think about her daughter, to get her to bear up under the hardship that we were all going through, or everyone's greatest fears about her would certainly come true.

"If you're going to die, then it's your time. If it's not, then you won't," I said, trying to inject her with some courage to continue on. Whether we died or not was out of our control—couldn't she see that and know it was best to try to live? "Stop crying. You have to be strong, or your daughter will suffer her whole life."

She stared at me, surprised that I would speak to an adult this way. My every intention was to comfort her with the thoughts that had brought peace to me after leaving Mina. But I could see from her offended look that she hadn't found any comfort in what I'd said. Shakila, who had been busy preparing something for her mother, had a look of horror. I couldn't figure out if it was the very mention of death that had shocked her or that I had dared to speak to her mother the way I had.

My cheeks flushed with embarrassment.

Shakila and Fatima asked me with their eyes to leave and to stay away from them. I wanted to hide myself; I felt so ashamed at what I had said to her. I didn't say it to mean that she should die, but if that was her fate, what could a person do about it but to suffer it courageously?

I ran from the tent door, out through the village gates, and into the thin woods. My head clamored with a sense that I'd injured them both, made them weaker by condemning her to die, and all I was trying to do was encourage her to persevere. I took a beaten path through woods that grew steadily thicker on either side of the narrow dirt track as it rose and dipped over the hills. Driven by my shame, I ran along a path that led deeper into the mountains. I hoped to reach a place to rest, somewhere away from everyone and the voice that ran through my head. I ran and ran until I was so winded I had to lean against a tree to rest. The trunk of the tree was so thick I could hide behind it, and the branches were filled with leaves. I panted in the shade of the great tree until I caught my breath. The air smelled clean and felt cool in the breeze off the nearby river. Down a slope, I could see the mud huts of the village sequestered in a clutch of brown hills.

A small glade with tufts of scruffy green grass lay off to my right. After I caught my breath, I noticed something moving along the opposite edge of the tree line. It circled around one spot.

Hoping to see a deer, I furtively skulked through the trees around the edge of the glade, staying hidden, not wanting to scare it away. As close to it as I dared go, I could tell it wasn't a deer. Rather, it had a shiny gray-and-white coat and dark, piercing eyes. It was a wolf. In a frenzy of movement, it tore and clawed at a carcass, growling as it worked, eating ravenously. Moving closer still, I could make out the horns of a goat, its body splayed in the grass, its feet spiked toward the sky; flies hovered around it. The rank odor of death, pungent and brutal, the smell of blood and flesh, filled the air. I hid behind a tree. Except for the hum of the wolf's growls as it ate, the forest was silent.

The wolf hadn't seen me; it was preoccupied tearing at its meal. Its muzzle was drenched crimson in goat's blood. I froze, mesmerized by the cruelty and majestic beauty of nature right in front of me. I remembered when Padar would have the mullah come to the house before Eids to butcher the calf we'd spent all year raising and fattening. How horrible it was to watch the blood of the calf—whom I'd petted and fed from my own hands—pour out from a slit across its throat. I hated watching it, but it was part of the ritual of our religion. Here in this forest of trees so far from any human eyes, animals were feeding as a way to survive.

After a while, the wolf must have sensed my presence, because it stopped eating and turned its crimson muzzle to me, fixing me with its dazzling black eyes. It lifted a paw and stepped toward me, and I retreated only one pace, daring it to let me into its space. We stared at each other for the longest moment, and I felt no revulsion at the blood that dripped from its teeth so conspicuously bared at me. More than that, I felt no fear of its teeth or its strength or its ferocious nature.

In that moment, I believed I could see right through its dark eyes into it, and it could see into me; we touched each other's souls. I knew its intent, and I thought it knew mine. It was doing only what it had to do to survive, to live among other animals in the woods and the mountains who would do the same to it in a flash if it ever let its guard down. It was free to live, and it lived by eating what it could find. It had no remorse or fear or anger at its life—what it took and what it gave. It roamed in freedom, and it was that freedom from fear that kept it alive. We were kin.

It must have sensed I wasn't a danger to it. It turned back to its lunch, and I backed away slowly until I lost sight of it. Once I found the path through the woods, I tried to retrace my steps back to the village. My heart and mind raced with thoughts: The goat being torn apart. The bloody muzzle of the wolf. Its piercing dark eyes. Its aggressive will to survive.

Fatigue came over me, and I wanted to find a place in the shade, away from the open land sparsely dotted with half-bare trees and low shrubs. I spotted the rocky gray face of the mountain, an outcropping with shady spots recessed into its mottled surface. I made it to the rocks and moved along the crevices and shadows until I found one that opened into a cave. At first I thought maybe it was a lair for animals, but then I noticed the well-worn entrance. Many travelers, like myself, must have found this place before.

I entered into its coolness, touching the wall with my hand to let it lead me farther into the darkness. The surface of the rock felt moist, and that made me think there might be a *shama* here: a pure, clean underground spring. It took me a while to wind my way through the narrow dark cavern before I came upon a circular pool of crystal-clear water, placid and completely silent. The walls were dark purple, and where they ran into the water, the rock turned shades of amethyst and plum. The deep colors of the rocks had a sheen to them, like they were embedded with fragments of diamonds that glistened in low light, making the calm surface of the water sparkle in the sunlight that was peeking through the rock walls of the cave. It took me a few moments to catch my breath; the sight was so overwhelming in its beauty. The solitude and peacefulness of this water and the sparkly grotto had been untouched by war. I felt suddenly able to rest. I knelt down by the water and stared into its clear coolness. My exhaustion began to lift; I felt at peace.

I washed my face in the refreshing water, and it revived me. I sat on the rim of the pool, in the pebbles and sand, and gazed into the *shama*. I thought about life as I stared down at my reflection in the sparkling water—Kabul, and the house on Shura Street, and my bicycle, and playing soccer in the streets with neighbors, and the whole family around the dining table. I heard Mommy telling us stories, and Padar reciting poetry. For the first time in a long while, I thought of Mommy and could hear her voice in my mind. I missed her terribly. I wondered what her life in India must be like. And in that moment, I thought I could see her face in the water—it floated just below the surface. Her smooth skin, the cut of her hair, her large brown eyes that took me all in. Every detail as real as my own flesh. It was a sign that I would see her again someday. I even looked different. The Enjeela in the *shama*'s reflection was thinner, with fatigue underlying her eyes. I hoped that Mommy would recognize me. That she wouldn't mistake me for the wolf I was becoming. Like my kin that I had seen in the woods, gray and sleek, staring at me with bold black eyes and a bloody muzzle. We were the same in so many ways—tenacious and fearless. Everything I loved was gone, and I had no way of knowing what the next village would be like, or even the next day, but I wasn't afraid. I was meant to survive.

Masood and the other refugees from Kabul that I'd met on the road came to mind. All of them struggled to survive the war and the sadness that surrounded us for leaving our homes and families. I thought about Mina, and grief over her situation threatened to evaporate the peacefulness I'd found here. She hadn't escaped. She would never leave her slave existence.

I rose, undressed, and waded into the refreshing cold water. I submerged myself, and then pushed up into the air and breathed in the freshness of the cave. I wiped the wet from my face and pushed back my hair. The water's chill sent tingles through my body. The chamber's walls sparkled, and I felt so secure here that I didn't want to leave.

I floated for a while, staring up at the top of the cave, my arms and legs extended and weightless.

I thought of Masood, of his sturdy determination to get us to Peshawar, and of his belief in me. He would be worried about where I was—he would think something horrible had happened to me.

I suddenly felt panicked and guilty. I quickly swam to the edge of the pool and raced to dry off and dress, and then made my way back to the mouth of the cave. I glanced behind me into the darkness. I knew I had to go back to camp, but I was reluctant to leave. Taking in one last breath of the cave air, I walked out onto the mountain.

When I entered the gates of the village, Laila ran to me, anger in her glare. She grabbed my arm and began pulling me toward our tent. "Don't ever leave like that again," she said, scolding me. "We looked everywhere for you." At our tent, Masood had a relieved look when he saw me. "We were scared something happened," Laila admonished me.

When she settled down, I told her about the *shama* and how beautiful it was, and the water, so perfect and clear. They all wanted to go, except Zulaikha, who was concerned about wandering outside the village alone. When Masood agreed to accompany us, we all went the next day.

My sisters and Zia couldn't believe the calmness and peacefulness of the *shama*. Masood told me the entrance was well hidden, so it was very lucky I had found it. We went there almost every day until it was time to leave that village. When we were in the cave, we all pretended we were in another place, a fairy kingdom or a magical realm, anyplace but a country being torn apart by bullets and bombs.

In the nearby mountains and valleys, the Soviets and the Afghan army bombed the mujahideen mercilessly. When the pounding of the bombs grew louder and too close, Masood said it was time to leave. When we were all packed, he told us that Fatima and Shakila were coming with us. We knew from what we'd seen that Fatima would slow us down, make our journey longer. At first, Laila complained, but Masood said that was the way it would be. Fatima's guide had left her, and she was alone, and they were on their way to Pakistan like we were, with no other way of getting there.

After days of walking and sleeping just off the roads so we wouldn't be seen by other travelers or soldiers using them, we entered another village, famished and tired. The smell of kabobs greeted us. Masood gave one of the elders money to take care of us, asking him to feed us very well. Masood said we needed strength for the rest of our journey because soon we would be turning into the mountains, and our way would get more difficult.

We rested there for a few days, regaining our strength from the days of sleeping beside the road. Soon it was time to move again. By now Laila had stopped complaining about how long it was taking to get to Pakistan. The other refugees fleeing the country were in the same situation. We all had to walk around the war since taking the direct route would get us either arrested or shot.

Masood purchased a donkey for Fatima before leaving the village, and that helped us move faster. Still it took her time to adjust to riding on the back of an animal since she'd never done it before. After a day of riding, she learned to sit sidesaddle on the donkey with her daughter seated right behind her. Masood led the donkey, and we wound single file behind it into the mountains, where the mujahideen were fighting to free the country from invaders.

Bombs and machine-gun fire came from the canyons on both sides of the trail. Still Masood said traveling deeper into the mountains was the safest way to go. The road, now nothing more than hard-packed dirt, wound beside a river. Sometimes it narrowed so that we could pass through only one at a time. We gradually trekked higher, between mountains that rose steep and treacherous on both sides of us.

Our way led through a string of villages, some with walls surrounding them, but many were nothing more than clusters of mud huts by the side of the trail. As we moved farther up the mountain pass, it seemed almost every village we passed was in mourning. Through their openings came the wails of women heavy with grief. I stopped to look into one and saw women seated on the ground in front of a shrouded body laid out on the dirt floor—either a father, brother, or son. The grief of the women weeping was overwhelming. I felt ashamed intruding on their sorrows. Masood stopped beside me. "Funerals," he said. "The sons and fathers of our country are dying in this war." We were all quiet that night as we sat around in the dark, camping between villages. Masood wouldn't let us have a fire lest we attract attention to ourselves, so we lay out under the glittering stars to sleep. The ground seemed extra hard. We ate fruit, some nuts, and whatever else Masood had in his bag. I felt sorry for the mothers and sisters of these villages we had passed through. I was thankful we were alive, and we were not starving. And we were on our way out of this country that was now bleeding to death from so many wounds.

That night, Masood warned all of us that the most grueling part of our journey was yet to come. So we must sleep and gather our strength. I tried to sleep that night, but the images of white-shrouded bodies plagued my closed-eyes vision. I thought of Ahmad Shah and Zia and Padar. Was it better to stay and fight with the mujahideen or to escape with my family? I was glad the men of my family were not fighting, but I was sad that so many other fathers and brothers of my country were dying.

12

KUCHI

The next day, we started early and moved down the path to the mountain trails single file until we came to an open area where travelers had gathered in a makeshift camp. A section of it lay in the shadow of a stand of trees; a stream flowed along the outer edge, up against the rocky side of the gray mountains. Off by themselves by the trees was a family of Kuchi. They were nomads and were brightly dressed, unlike everyone else in peran tumbans and chadors. I couldn't take my eyes off them as we made our way into camp.

"They can put a curse on you. It would be better for us to stay away from them," Fatima whispered in my ear as we passed. "They'll use black magic," she said, warning me not to have anything to do with them.

A wide space lay between us and the nomads. No one else in the camp was speaking with them, affirming Fatima's claims. But I'd heard stories about the Kuchi, that they had no fixed home, lived in tents, and were constantly on the move. They must have many interesting stories to tell. I had never seen such colorful people, even in Kabul. "Look at us, we're already cursed," I said to her. "What more could they do to us?"

As we set up camp, I watched a young Kuchi mother play with her children. She had dark flowing hair and eyes rimmed with black kohl, which made her look exotic and beautiful. She wore a silver stud in her nose and a gold-and-red *bindi* between her eyes. Strings of colorful beads adorned her neck. She draped a green scarf over her head, and her billowy clothes were deep shades of purple and shocking pink and white. The way she played with her children and how her husband took care of their camp, compared to so many of the rough characters we'd met on the road, seemed quite normal. I wondered why Fatima and the other people in the camp feared them.

Even though their clothes were bright, they were very worn. I thought I could use that as an excuse just to speak with them. I approached Laila and Zulaikha and Zia. "They're very poor," I said, pointing to the nomads. "We should give them some money."

"We're poor too," Laila said, shrugging me off. "We hardly have enough for ourselves."

That was Laila, always being dramatic about our situation, as if we could starve to death at any second. I frowned at her, letting her know I was very unhappy with her stinginess. "We have plenty," I said. "Give me a few afghanis so I can help them."

To my surprise, normally quiet Zulaikha also chirped at Laila to be more generous. They argued until exhausted by the debate. Laila dug in her pocket and tossed me five afghanis. As I walked over, I tried to think of a way to approach them with the money without offending them. I decided to ask if they sold jewelry, but first I wanted to let them know that I was interested in getting to know them.

"Do you have any *surma*?" I asked the woman. *Surma* is also called kohl; it's a black powder from the mountains that is used as eyeliner. Mothers in Afghanistan applied it to the eyes of newborns in the belief that it made their eyes bigger and stronger.

She smiled warmly at me and said she did. She searched in a large cloth bag beside her. "Would you like me to put it on you?"

Her voice was pleasant and inviting. "Yes, please." I sat cross-legged on the ground in front of her.

She pulled out a black box and a small wooden stick. She sharpened the tip of the stick with her pocketknife until it was smooth and clean. She then dipped it in the black powder and delicately applied it around my eyes.

The powder began to tickle my eyelids. "I put it thicker on the outside corners," she said. "When I'm done, if you smudge it with your fingers, it will look very nice and it will last longer." She kept working until she leaned back to admire her work. She gave me a warm smile as she took in her handiwork. She then retrieved a small hand mirror, holding it up for me to see. "Take a look."

I appeared a different person, more grown-up. She showed me how to smudge it to make my eyes smoky and exotic. She made me feel so peaceful here, applying makeup together. I liked her.

"Can I buy some of your *chooris*?" I pointed at the bangles on her arms. She nodded and dug into her bag again, pulling out a few and handing them to me.

"You must be very careful because they are made of glass."

I held them in my palm. They seemed too small for my wrist.

"You're very young, and your bones are flexible," she said, noticing my reluctance. "You can get anything on your wrist if you do it correctly."

I stretched out my hand. She grabbed it and squeezed my fingers together, then worked the bangles over my knuckles and onto my wrist one at time. She didn't stop until my entire right arm was filled with colorful bangles. I lifted my wrist and jangled them in the air. I loved how they sounded.

"How do I get them off?"

"You have to break them," she said. "If you wait till you get to your destination, they will bring you luck along the way."

As she put her *surma* and *chooris* back in her bag, I noticed a scar on her forearm, a white spot on her olive skin, surrounded by pinkish wrinkled flesh. She followed my eyes to her arm, then ran an index finger over the spot.

"It's a scorpion sting," she said. "It never quite healed right. Have you been stung? They're everywhere around here."

It must have been so painful. I couldn't stop staring. "No, I haven't."

"Then take this." She reached in her bag and pulled out a jar half filled with liquid with a rusty lid. The glass was old and cloudy, yet the liquid was clear. "When you come across a scorpion, kill it and put it in here." She handed me the jar. "This will make a medicine that you can apply to the sting. Never drink it. It's not that kind of medicine. But put it on the sting itself. Do you understand?"

I nodded and thanked her, then gave her the five afghanis. All the way back to our camp, I held the jar out in front of me, trying to figure out what kind of special liquid was inside. I shook it hard, then watched it settle, imagining what it would look like with a scorpion inside. I wanted to start hunting them right then. The conversation made me wistful, and a sudden longing came over my heart for Mommy.

When I showed the jar to Laila and the others, they just shrugged. Scorpions weren't that interesting to them. Not even to Zia. Masood seemed amused. He said he'd heard of the cure before and seemed glad I had purchased it. Laila perked up when I showed her my bangles, shaking them in front of her. She thought of buying some for herself but decided she couldn't part with her money.

We rested at the camp for several more days, but everyone kept to themselves, and no one had talked to the Kuchi but me since we had arrived. I'd heard my whole life from Mommy and others that they would only steal from you, rob you of everything you had if you turned your backs on them for a moment. Yet the way that young Kuchi mother played with her children and loved them, I couldn't believe for one moment that this woman was as cruel as people in the camp made her out to be. She made me think of how Mommy had cared for us, and I began to wonder about reaching our destination. Would she be there waiting for us, to hold out her hands in warm greeting when she saw me? Or would she turn away like she had that day in the driveway. I lingered on this thought as we waited to move on.

When we left a few days later, the woman waved to me. My bangles jangled in the air as I waved at her in return.

———

We climbed higher every day, working our way along the rocky trails, passing more villages where more families were burying their fathers, brothers, and sons. In every village we passed, many of them nothing but huts and a few animals, we saw only old men, women, and children. Even the boys Zia's age, in their early teens, had disappeared into the mountains.

At one village, Masood bought each of us a knife with a beige leather sheath. Mine had a handmade woven belt with a buckle that I fastened around my waist. He told us not to play with them because they were sharp, and we'd get hurt. To just use them if we needed to defend ourselves or to kill a snake or a scorpion. I couldn't wait to try mine out. I felt ready to defend myself and eager to use it on a dreaded scorpion.

Several other travelers had already been stung by scorpions, and I was determined not to go through that agony. Some became so sick that they couldn't travel. I hoped I could help some of them with the medicine. With my knife and my jar of secret liquid as protection, I looked everywhere for them as we hiked along the mountain trails. Every time we stopped to rest, I went off to hunt scorpions. One day I sat on a rock resting, and I saw one close by, sunning itself on a flat rock. I slowly unsheathed my knife. I didn't want to spook the critter and have it come at me. I held my knife in the stabbing position, blade down, firmly gripping the handle. At first I couldn't bring myself to stab it. Then I took a breath and slashed at it, the blade crushing into its back. It swished its tail, trying to sting me. I lifted it and dropped it into the open jar, and then quickly screwed on the lid.

I held the jar up and watched it scrambling to rise out of the liquid. It fought a losing battle valiantly before steadily sinking into the fluid and drowning. My heart raced with victory. I had done it. Every fear I'd ever had of scorpions disappeared in that moment.

We spent several days on the road while Masood tried to find a village that could offer us hospitality. Every one we passed through was crowded with fleeing refugees. Every day on the road, I stalked scorpions whenever we stopped to rest. I learned to stay clear of their tails after I cut them off because they kept moving and could still sting. Before we reached the next village to rest, I had seven scorpions in my jar.

Now if someone got stung, I was confident I could help them. I had every reason to believe the medicine would heal a scorpion wound. At night I kept the jar right by my side. Often scorpions would crawl into the blankets of travelers sleeping on the ground. When someone was stung, their cries would wake us.

I dreamt often that my captured scorpions escaped and crawled all over me, stinging and causing me pain. When I awoke, I knew it was all a dream because the scorpions in the jar were dead.

Finally we reached a typical village of mud huts that was crowded with travelers. A villager told us about an event that troubled all of us: several months before, a young girl had been raped and killed. They had never caught the man who did it, and the village elder who told us about it was certain it wasn't one of the residents, because they all knew each other very well. So many refugees fleeing the country had passed through over the last year that the man who did it could easily have slipped away in the night, unnoticed. He told us to watch out for ourselves.

This was very troubling. It made me think of Mina's father, a supposed Muslim, selling his own daughter to another man to become a wife and slave. But Islam teaches that a man must not touch a woman without her consent. Mina didn't consent to be a wife. None of this made any sense to me, the more I thought about it.

I talked to Shakila, and she told me that rape and murder are sins in Islam. I understood that well, but still everything I'd seen with my own eyes, the way Mina was treated, filled me with doubts. The way Islam was practiced in the countryside was very different than my father's religion.

———

That night, my sisters and I hardly slept. We whispered to each other about the rapist. Every noise outside our hut became a potential danger. I began to wish I were a boy. Zulaikha and Laila were older, and so they were more of a target, and I became afraid for them, watching them every moment.

"Can you imagine," I said under my breath to my sisters. "If he came, and I turned into a wolf. I would tear him to pieces." We all laughed.

Masood must have known our fears, because soon afterward he began to teach us how to fire a gun. He'd purchased a BB gun from a villager and took us outside the mud walls to practice. He showed Zia first how to load and fire it. Zia did okay, hitting the target most of the time. Then he handed it to me. I loved the feel of the weapon in my hand. Zia set up some targets to hit in the distance. I sighted the barrel the way Masood had shown me, then squeezed off round after round—tat-tat-tat—I plunked all the rock piles he'd set up.

Shooting was exhilarating. Masood had a surprised look on his face. "You are a natural-born shooter," he said. I glowed. Zia and I rose every morning, eager to begin our practice. Masood wouldn't give us any more BBs to shoot, so we used chickpeas. We made targets out of mud and let them dry overnight so they'd be hard. We both got very good at hitting the bull's-eye.

One day Zia asked me to hold up a matchbox. He convinced me he could shoot it out of my hand from a distance without touching me. He was good with the gun. I had seen it with my own eyes. Besides, a chickpea wouldn't hurt if he hit me. So I grabbed the matchbox and held it up high over my head. He ran back and then turned to me, raised the gun and aimed it and fired.

The pain began with a spot of heat on my palm, then it radiated out into my fingers in a fiery sensation in flares of shooting pain. I bent over, holding my hand, trying to quench the sharp darts prickling my palm; tears of agony streamed down my face.

"Why'd you move?" he yelled.

"I didn't," I screamed, nearly breathless.

We didn't return until the pain subsided a bit. I decided to tell Masood that I'd hurt my palm when I fell and scraped it. He looked at my wound closely but didn't say anything more. I didn't want him to take away Zia's shooting privileges. It didn't really matter anyway, because Zia didn't want to do any more shooting after that. The black dot on my palm persisted for a long time. I went back to collecting scorpions, filling my jar until it was packed with them. I wanted to be ready to help the next time someone awoke in the night screaming.

The entire village was quiet, and only the sounds of the nearby war in the mountains interrupted my sleep. I thrashed awake from a deep slumber with a piercing pain, like I'd been shot with a bullet in my calf. Then I felt something scaly, like an insect crawling up the back of my leg. I flipped over and jumped up, pulled my pants away from my skin, and shook the scorpion off.

I went to Zia where he slept on a *charpai*—a handmade wooden frame with rope stretched across its width to form a tight mesh that worked as a mattress—on the other side of the hut. I didn't want to wake everyone else, because it would make my sisters go crazy with fear. "Zia, I got bit."

He wrestled awake and looked around for a moment. When he realized what I'd said, he leapt up. He grabbed a scarf and tied off my leg above the wound to stop the poison from traveling up my leg and to my heart. By this time, it felt as if someone had shot a needle into my calf. The stinging persisted and grew from intense to white-hot in seconds. Zia hurried to find my backpack and retrieved the jar. I slumped on his bed, doing everything I could not to yell out in pain. He knelt by me and unscrewed the top of the jar.

"Cut me," I said. I began to shiver from pain.

"No, you do it," he said.

I don't know what he was thinking. Was he afraid, or didn't he believe this would work? He handed me my knife. The shooting pain had coalesced into a chill that crept steadily up my leg. I had to do this, but I was shivering with either fear or cold, I couldn't decide. I steadied myself with a breath and quickly made a small cut over the sting. He then poured the solution over the open wound.

In an instant, my leg went numb, though the wound itself stung. I didn't know if this was supposed to happen, but it was as if my leg was dying. I didn't know what to do. The nomad lady didn't tell me what would happen once I used the solution. She hadn't warned me about this. I hadn't thought to ask. I gritted my teeth and squeezed my eyes shut, hoping the stinging would pass soon.

"Enjeela, do you remember when Padar brought home your first bicycle?" Zia asked. I held back tears, but still my eyes were watering. I wanted to cry, but I didn't want to wake my sisters or else there would be a lot of crying and blaming, Laila telling me what I should have done. "Do you remember when I was going to teach you to ride it?"

He spent the next half hour reminding me of how he would hold my bike by the seat to keep it steady. He would tell me to keep pedaling, and I remember my little feet turning the crank with all my might, then he flung me forward, and I pedaled on my own. A few seconds later I dived headfirst into a neighbor's bush.

I laughed at the memory and he laughed too. The laughing made the pain ease a little. So we kept talking—about chasing kites together, jumping over the neighbor's fence, running and playing and getting so dirty that we had to take extra-long baths to rid us of all the grime. We played soccer with our friends, and he even taught me to shoot a slingshot. We climbed trees, and whenever I got in trouble, we were always together. Zulaikha and Laila were older and more concerned with school and girlie activities. Zia and I were constant companions, and I became a tomboy. He taught me to be tough.

We talked for a while, and I began to relax. The sensations in my leg subsided to the point that I could hobble back to my bed and lie down. I eventually even went to sleep. I stayed in bed for several days. I lost my appetite and kept myself covered up. I told Laila and Zulaikha and Masood about the scorpion sting, and Masood looked at it carefully. I didn't want to show it to my sisters, particularly Zulaikha, who was squeamish and sickened easily, so I kept it covered up. I didn't tell anyone I'd used the Kuchi medicine except Masood. He was glad I had. He had heard of others using it and getting better.

Despite the medicine, I wasn't doing very well. I was listless and weak and hardly ate anything. My heart raced all day, and the swelling around the wound on my calf itched painfully. The half-inch incision I had cut had turned all red. Through the night, my leg kept twitching and it wouldn't stop. I kept covered up all day and lay as still as possible, trying to breathe slowly. Even Fatima, who kept to herself with her own sicknesses, noticed I wasn't doing well, and she sent Shakila to check on me.

"Is there anything we can do for you?" she asked. I always turned down her offers for help. I didn't want her to go out of her way to do things for me. She had her own worries, but it did make me feel much better that she was thinking of me. We weren't just strangers thrown together on the road anymore. I knew she cared about me, and it made me believe we'd overcome our differences.

Lying in my bed for all those days gave me time to think about how much I missed the Afghanistan of my childhood. I was still a child, of course, but since we had left Kabul, the strenuousness of the journey had sharpened my wits. There had been so much walking and anxiety in the past six months. I had nearly forgotten what living on Shura Street had been like. It had been safe and private and filled with fun and love. I wasn't much older, but I didn't feel the same. I had no home; I moved from place to place like the nomads. I hunted and killed scorpions for fun. I'd seen enough death to last me a lifetime. I had found a *shama*, a place of peace and tranquility that war didn't reach; maybe I could find another, a place to rest. I wished I could stay in this bed, pull the covers up over me, and just forget all the walking. I had no idea what lay ahead for us, over the mountain Masood said we must cross soon to make our way out of all this chaos.

Over the next week, the pain subsided enough so I could rise from bed and hobble around. I had to walk slowly at first until I gathered my strength. Masood came by often, offering words of encouragement.

"If you think more about where you're going, to Pakistan to meet your father," he said one day, sitting beside my bed on the ground, "it will be easier to heal."

That's the day I began to think of Peshawar, where Padar had promised to meet us. Masood kept saying it wasn't too far now, just ahead, over one more mountain.

13

A People at War

Masood led us up a series of rugged trails that ascended farther into the Hindu Kush. This mountain range runs for five hundred miles along the eastern border between central Afghanistan and northern Pakistan. It is notorious for its difficulty to cross, with treacherous roads, narrow passes, and many summits that are snowcapped year-round. We took one of the many dirt tracks edged by craggy cliffs that overhung the narrow paths as we zigged and zagged up deep crevices that had formed into natural passes. The air grew chilly as summer waned. We tromped silently along, concentrating to step carefully over the ruts and debris that had slid down the steep slopes. This was no time to fall and twist an ankle, or worse.

The rapid fire of machine guns echoed across the hills and rippled along the canyons, soon followed by the boom of cannons and bombs. The gunfire and thud of shells hitting the ground seemed part of nature. It was part of the life we were living that even as the din grew louder, as if it were in the adjacent canyon, we didn't stop to wait it out. The battle noise didn't cause dread in me like it used to. It was evident that Masood had climbed these mountains many times before. He had kept us a couple of steps from the pitched battles for months now. No one, not even Laila, questioned where he was leading us.

After nearly a week of trekking upward, the road dipped down into one of the many high mountain valleys. In the center lay a small village. It was smaller than the others, with just a few huts crudely constructed with sunbaked mud bricks and timbers bunched around a patch of barren earth. We gathered in the square by a hut for a breather to drink some water and eat a piece of fruit. On the other side of the hard-packed dirt yard, a group of women in long chadors stood around a body wrapped in white cloth. A few of them sat on the ground by the body. A spot of red, like a badge, blotched the body's chest. It had to be a man—a son or father—killed in the war. The women's crying and singing a sad lament of loss cast a bitterness over our fatigue. There were no words between us. What was there to say? The men of my country were being slaughtered, and there was nothing we could do but escape it. We ate quickly and kept to ourselves and then rose and shouldered our packs. The sooner we scaled the last mountain, the farther we would be from seeing any more death and destruction.

I don't know what the others were thinking as we trudged deeper into the mountains. The path was so rugged, each of us had to watch where we placed our feet. Masood had warned us not to twist an ankle or fall. Injuries would slow us down, and we had to get past the war to a safe village. The rat-a-tat-tat of machine guns echoing down the canyon walls was monotonous. We seemed to be moving toward the sound of an intense battle, but by this time we knew Masood would not go on if it wasn't safe. I kept my head down and watched each step, and like the others, blocked out the war, the death, the blood.

As the day dragged on, my footsteps became heavier. Hunger bit into my thoughts. I lost myself in thinking of our next resting place. Oh, what a treat fresh food and water would be.

I kept right behind Masood, watching where he stepped, imagining myself taking a hot shower when we reached Peshawar. We filed along a narrow path hemmed in by sheer cliffs that rose on both sides of us. Masood had told us that we would be meeting Padar at a hotel there, and while the thought of reuniting with Padar was what I was most excited about, the anticipation of soap and clean sheets and eating with a fork was almost equally as exciting. We followed Masood along a winding path as the clatter and thump of warfare vibrated off the walls all around us. The angry bursts at times sounded as if they were behind us, then overhead or out in front. It was impossible to know how close we were to the actual fighting. As close as the war sounded, we all kept our heads down, watching our every step on the uneven path. I had gotten so used to the gunfire and thumping of the big guns and explosions, I just kept putting one foot in front of the other. Then we turned on a sharp bend in the path that opened into a wide spot. A sharp burst of an automatic rifle exploded from a pile of rocks above us. I jerked to a stop in fright, and even Masood in front of me stood rock still in surprise. He reached out his burly arm and flattened me against the wall. The others behind me did the same, forcing themselves flat against the rough edge of the mountain.

From the cliff above us, something fired in a puff of smoke and hit an army tank hidden in the rocks at the farthest edge of the clearing. The tank exploded in a fireball, sending a plume of gunpowder and dust into the air. Khaki-uniformed Soviet soldiers in their distinctive steel helmets fired back, aiming high to the cliffs and at a cluster of rocks along the canyon wall, where a line of mujahideen were firing at them with automatic rifles. I pulled up my shirt to shield my nose; the odor of burning machines was so pungent. Jets screamed overhead and unleashed bombs that twirled as they burst into the mountainside. Huge plumes of dirt rained more dust and debris on us. The concussions slapped hard against my eardrums and shook the earth beneath me. I wanted to run, but the smell and shock of the bombs stunned me into a frozen terror. Above us and all around us, freedom fighters fired down on the Soviets until the face of the mountain filled with flashes of flame and smoke. Russian soldiers scrambled for cover, running, shouting, and shooting. Their tanks were on fire. The dead and dying were everywhere. One soldier nearby had his leg blown off, and blood pooled on the ground. I watched in revulsion as the life oozed from the man as he writhed in agony.

Dread filled my arms and legs. Death here would be nothing more than a stray bullet. This was war. Chaos, blood, and smoke. I tried to run, but my feet wouldn't move.

"Get to a cave," Masood shouted. He grabbed my arm and yanked me away. "Run, run." He waved toward the side of the road. As he dragged me along, I couldn't take my eyes off the war. This was different from watching tanks and soldiers drive around Kabul. Men were shouting and firing at each other. Soldiers were on the ground bleeding and dying. Smoke and dust and a hazy pall floated over the road.

Masood yanked on my arm so hard I thought he'd pull it off. I ran alongside the hill, behind him. We passed men in peran tumbans standing in the open, Kalashnikovs gripped in their hands. They swept a tight arc, aiming their fire at Russian soldiers crouched behind a truck. Screams of pain were everywhere. These men had no fear on their faces, just pure concentration.

"I have children here!" Masood called out over and over. All of that cool calm in his voice he'd had every day since we first met evaporated. "I have women and children."

We ran right past the freedom fighters, who stood in the open, firing, their eyes glazed with the rage of warfare.

"I have children. Don't shoot, don't shoot."

One bearded man wearing a *pakol* cap and brandishing a rifle yelled at us from the rocks above. He waved for us to come toward him. Masood led us through the rocks to an opening. He pushed us inside as we passed him.

The cave wasn't very deep, so we pressed back as far as we could, hiding behind rocks or bundled up on the ground. I squatted against the hard rock wall, breathing rapidly, trying to slow down my speeding heart. My forehead was damp from sweat, and my legs weak and tired. My body ached from the fear. I labored to breathe normally.

"Masood," I whispered after a while, "are we safe?"

He only held a finger to his lips. The fighting went on outside for most of the day. We didn't move until well after the shooting had stopped. Then only Masood went out to speak to the freedom fighters. From the mouth of the cave, I overheard their conversation. They told him the country would be destroyed unless the Afghan army joined the fight against the Russians. We were all warriors, they said, and we must all fight to protect our country. I remembered Padar telling me how important it was to fight for our country. These countrymen had a difficult time understanding why the Afghan army wasn't helping their fight. I had seen firsthand in Kabul that the Afghan and Russian armies were on the same side. The defense of the true Afghanistan had been left to civilians.

We stayed with the freedom fighters for several weeks in the caves. A few other families settled down near us. A couple of mothers with young children, and old women bent over with years, carried their meager belongings in baskets and in cloth bundles slung over their backs. The rest of their belongings had been lost in the bombing of their homes. The stories that filtered in with the refugees were of constant dangers and destruction. "The Russians are bombing the villages," one mother said in a matter-of-fact way. "They don't know about these caves, so we're safe here."

"Our whole village is gone," one of the women said. She told me about her young son, barely Zia's age, who went off to the war with the other men in her village. She hadn't seen him in months.

"They are fighting like these men," an old woman told me, as she tended a small fire built with twigs and roots she'd scrounged from the ground.

Other mothers told the same stories. Their sons and husbands were off at war, probably hiding in another cave somewhere else in these barren mountains, cold, tired, but determined to expel these foreign soldiers. The sadness on their faces, the droops in their shoulders, as they went about their duties, caring for the children and cooking, appeared to be too deep to overcome. But they carried on, dwelling on stories of hope. "We will return and build our homes again when these men go away," a young mother said.

"And what about you?" another woman asked me. "Will you return to Kabul?"

We had risked everything to escape. Yet I had no idea what my life would be like if we didn't return. "Someday. I think we will." Even as I spoke those words, I had the sense that I had spoken more wish than fact. Families all over the country were splintered.

My family was hardly the only one fractured by war—Mommy and my sisters were in New Delhi, Padar still in Kabul, and here we four were in an unlit mountain cave, eating over a crude cook fire, steps away from the horror of death. My family's strife was but a drop in the flood of countrymen fleeing for their lives.

In another place and time, I would have wept at the staggering loss all around me. But weeping was of no use here. In these caves, the women's only goal was to survive so they could rebuild their lives. Crying got no one closer to that end.

"There are many brave Afghans," a wizened old man told me one night around the campfire, "who have already died." His rifle leaned against the rock wall beside him. "I don't know how long we can hold out against this army with tanks and jet bombers."

"As long as there is one Afghan in this country," said another old man at the campfire, "there will be an Afghanistan." My padar had said that same thing so many times. When we didn't have any electricity in Kabul or we sat around by candlelight, and he read to us or recited poetry, he'd always end the session by saying that to us. As if he were trying to give us some hope that our country and our people would survive these troubling times. And now sitting up here in this rocky cave, a village man in traditional dress, with a full beard and rustic ways, said the same thing. It was more than a saying but a deep belief that lived everywhere in this rugged country. If I were a boy, if I were older, I would not hesitate to defend my country.

At night, the freedom fighters snuck out and gathered food for all of us. Masood paid them, but I believed they would have brought us food regardless of our money. When they came back, they told us they had buried dead fighters and villagers. I often stood in the mouth of the cave, watching the beams of their flashlights, marveling at how brave and determined they were. Not one of them was willing to back down in the face of overwhelming odds that they would not win this war. Their adversaries had jet fighters, helicopters that spit bullets, and tanks and machine guns. These men had their rifles, RPG launchers, and their skill in living in the mountains. And their courage. It didn't seem like enough.

One night I stood at the entrance watching them file out, and one of the bearded men stopped and patted me on the head. He must have seen the questions in my eyes. "I hope for the freedom of Afghanistan," he said. "I am not afraid, even to die." I watched them march single file into the night. They went willingly into the darkness with only the hope that their sacrifice would mean something more than spilled blood alone—freedom for their children and for me.

———

Like a bad storm on the other side of the mountains, we could hear the sounds of bombing and gunfire move away from us. One day Masood said it was time to leave. We packed and went back on the road. Men from the village helped us with some donkeys but would only allow us to take them to the next village. The donkeys knew the trails well, and we moved quickly along the rocky trails to the village.

I sat behind Zia, holding on to him tight as we made our way over the bumpy and rutted road. It took all of my energy to not fall off the donkey's swaying back as it made its way up the treacherous path.

After a long climb, we reached another village. Masood spoke to one of the men, who said we were very close to Pakistan. The man advised us to stay there for the night as we still had a long climb ahead of us. I was excited about the thought of finally getting away from the fighting and death and seeing Padar. Yet I was also sad at what I would leave behind—my country, my home.

On the last night in Afghanistan, we were all asleep in a small camp of escaping refugees. Masood had us huddle together in a tight circle with our belongings beside us. I awoke to the rustling of a rucksack. I propped myself up on my elbows, peering into the darkness, wondering if someone was sick or hurt. The silhouette of someone leaning over Zulaikha's belongings, wearing a *pakol* cap and a tunic, made my heart bang against my ribs. Someone was robbing us. I reached over as quietly as I could and just nudged Masood without saying a word.

He leapt up from his blankets, his machine gun already in his hand. He pointed the gun right at the man's head. "Get out of here!" he shouted at the man.

The man froze, then raised his hands in the air to show his harmlessness. He slowly rose to his feet and backed away. Then he turned and ran out of the camp. Everyone in the camp woke up. Someone asked, "What happened?" Another man close to us called out, "There's a robber around." People startled awake and began checking their things.

"I've seen him stealing for the past two nights while we were in the caves," Laila said. I was furious she hadn't said anything. A few men arose and began searching for the thief, but Masood did not move from standing over us, his hand on his machine gun, his eyes searching the camp. Conversation rose in the camp. Men stoked the campfires and sat around sharing their experiences with robberies, break-ins, and the trouble they'd had on the road, and even though the stories were tragic, the talk itself among the community became a safe haven in the dark. Some sat around talking, others lay in their blankets, too exhausted to move. Masood stood over us, vigilant and alert. I tried to follow the conversation, but I was so fatigued, my limbs so heavy. I just wanted to surrender to the night. I lay back down. So did Zia and my sisters.

Our guide finally sat on his blanket, but he didn't lie down. "Tomorrow we climb the biggest mountain. Get some sleep."

I stared at the stars. They gleamed back at me, spread across the blackness in uncountable numbers, the earth and sky connected in pinpoints of light. This would be my last night sleeping in dirt. The ground was hard, but somehow even its hardness had become comfortable. I remembered owning a bed of feathers and springs, but I didn't remember what that comfort was like. Now I had only a backpack as a pillow and the stars for my ceiling. They were luminous enough that I could have read a book by their light. I gathered my shawl over me to keep warm. The air had a crystal clarity to it; I could see forever into the sky. I let my thoughts roam to the happy moments when my whole family had been together. The words of "Within the Circle" came to mind:

> And the pregnant belly curved and shaped by ex-
> cellence of its kind by the soul within
> And the plants and the round surface of the uni-
> verse and Mother Earth itself
>
> I have gotten the creator's hint
> There is something within the circle the creator loves
> Within the circle of a perfect one

God created the circle the same way he created the stars and the planets. It seemed so simple. If that were true, then I was part of his great cosmic plan, and someday I'd return here.

We rose before daylight to prepare for our day. There was an excitement in our group as we packed. "Today we climb the last mountain into Pakistan," Masood said cheerfully. When we set out, Zia told me to stay close to him, that he would help me up. Fatima walked with such a heavy step, I wondered how she would make it up. We would have no donkeys.

These were the highest parts of the Hindu Kush, and the trails up the steep sides were narrow and treacherous, often strewn with boulders, and ran right along cliffs. Since I was the youngest in our group, I knew they were all concerned with how I was going to make it up this last mountain that separated the two nations. Once we reached the peak and crossed over the other side, we'd be in Pakistan. No more sleeping on the ground. No more eating with our hands. No more dodging bullets.

All during that day of hiking, I took the trail so easily, with a different step than when we had begun so many months before. Spring had just arrived in Kabul when Padar woke us in the middle of the night and set us off, and now the air had grown chilly. Ramadan had passed, so the summer was well over and fall was setting in. We had been on the road nearly six months. Everything about me had changed during that time, as if my very DNA had been rearranged.

I believed my pleasant life would last forever. I now knew the error of that thinking. Life could change in an instant.

———

In the cool of the early day, we reached the base of the last mountain. We had been climbing for about a week through the Hindu Kush to reach this mountain. We were already several thousand feet high, but this mountain went even higher. It was by far the tallest one we'd seen. It was also the steepest one we'd encountered. But on the other side of it lay Pakistan and freedom. We all stood at the bottom gazing upward at the thin, well-trodden dirt path etched in the side of the mountain. It zigzagged up the rocky face until it disappeared into a wispy line as thin as a piece of string. Masood began up the trail, but the rest of us stood there, looking up the face of the mountain. No one said anything; it was impossible not to be intimidated. But I'd come this far. I'd faced down soldiers, a wolf, and a scorpion, and I refused to let this mountain get in the way of my reunion with Padar and comfort.

I turned to Laila, Zulaikha, and Zia behind me. "Let's run up it."

"You're crazy." Laila shook her head in disgust. "We can't run up it. We'll be lucky if we can walk up!"

Even Zia looked awed by the trail. I smiled at them, turned, and took off. I caught up with Masood, then I sprinted out in front. I wanted to blaze the trail. If I found something that would block our way, I could go back and warn them. Every step upward, it became a little more difficult to breathe, but I was a lion, I would not give up. Soon I was so far ahead of them, they had disappeared from view. I ran up the trail for hours. When I finally reached the summit, I collapsed on the ground, panting for breath. After I recuperated, I stood and took in the view. I could see across both sides of the mountain. Afghanistan to the west was a series of mountains and valleys that went on and on. To the east I could see the buildings of Peshawar. I was straddling the border, one foot in each country. One of Padar's proverbs came to mind: "One cannot exist with a heart torn in half between two loves, two decisions, or two worlds, because it will eventually break in two."

I didn't want to leave Afghanistan, but I stood there gazing into Pakistan. I must leave one to reach the other.

Alone on the mountaintop for several hours, I ran through in my mind what I was leaving, possibly to never return. The memories of the happy times had already faded. I turned toward the new country, Pakistan, and wondered what lay ahead. By the time the others arrived, sadness over leaving Afghanistan had mutated into anticipation for the future. We rested there for a while before beginning to descend. When it was time to go, I couldn't wait to get into Pakistan, so I ran all the way down the mountain. I could hardly contain my enthusiasm until I reached the bottom. I was alone and out of breath, but I felt hopeful for the first time since the Kuchi woman had sold me the bangles and the scorpion jar.

A long line of soldiers with rifles stood along the border post, blocking our way. I looked back up the trail at our group, and all I could see was a row of dots descending the mountain. I waited, smiled at the soldiers, trying to get their attention, and when the group finally reached me, they were dusty, tired, and thirsty. I pointed to the soldiers in front of us. Masood told us to wait together and went up to speak to them. One of the soldiers glanced over at me, and I pleaded with my eyes: *Please don't hurt us. Just let us pass. We've come so far and been through so much to get here.* The soldiers talked among themselves, then told Masood something. He wasn't smiling when he turned from them.

Masood came slowly back and bent on one knee to speak to us. "They will let you and Fatima through, but I can't go."

We all stared at him.

"You will be fine," he said, his voice as authoritative as ever. He pointed to something beyond the border post. "That's a bus stop over there. Wait there for the bus, and it will take you directly into Peshawar."

He gave each of us a brief hug. I tried to hold on to him. "I have to go, little lion." He pulled me from him. He stood and gave us a stern look as we gathered around him. "You are all very brave. You have come a long way, and now you are here at your destination." He reminded Laila of where we were to meet Padar.

She nodded. "I have the address, yes."

"Then you are ready to go." He pulled his tunic around him. "I will bring your father to you. So wait for him, no matter what." With that, he turned and left us. With his shoulders straight, he hiked back the way he had come.

"He's not coming with us," Zulaikha said, her voice incredulous. We were all thinking the same things as we watched in silent shock as he began climbing the path up the mountain, returning the way he had come. He was one of the bravest men I'd ever met, and I learned so much from him. None of us said a word as he disappeared up the path, into the heights.

14

Angels along the Way

True to their word, the guards let us pass over the border into Pakistan. After crossing over, we waited with a group of other travelers for a bus at the stop Masood had told us about. We looked around, getting our bearings; it was strange to not have Masood with us. I spotted a vendor down the street from us selling sodas. It had been months since we'd had one. We quickly ran to the stand and each bought one. We stood around in a circle, tipping the sodas into our mouths. The sweet drink on my tongue tasted of the simplest pleasure. It hardly washed away the taste of river water and weak tea we'd lived on for the past six months. None of us spoke as we drank. My sisters and Zia all had smiles—something I hadn't seen much of on our journey. I could feel myself smiling too, despite how dirty we were. With dust in our hair, mouths, and ears and over every part of our bodies, we were a mess. We had been wearing the same clothes for so long. But here we were, standing in Pakistan, and the sounds and grief of war were so far away, we couldn't hear them. All of us must have sensed this at the same moment as we drank our sodas and began to relax.

It was an old bus, brightly painted and jammed with riders. It was apparent we were in Pakistan from the dress of the passengers. The Pakistanis we saw were darker skinned, like Indians, and wore traditional clothes: the men wore *shalwar kameez* and *jinnah* caps, and the women wore *dupattas* and *shalwar kameez* also. Most Afghan men wore Western dress, jeans and sport shirts, and women, scarves over long tunics. After I found a seat, I finished drinking my ice-cold soda slowly, enjoying its coldness.

The bus wound through Peshawar's noisy streets, picking up and dropping off, until it made its way outside the city limits and crossed into a dusty refugee camp. We stared at the clusters of tents and the dirt streets, each filled with Afghan refugees, mostly women and children. We had all been forced out of our country by war; orphaned by our country, forced to live on the road, in camps, anywhere we could find to lie down and sleep simply to survive. Fatima leaned over the seat and touched my arm. "Their husbands are all fighting, I'm sure." I kept my eyes glued on them until the last of the tents passed out of sight.

I started to dream of a warm shower and soft bed as the bus made its way through the labyrinth of streets. Fatima had a brother and sister who lived on the outskirts of Peshawar. She insisted we stay with them for a few days to rest before moving on to the hotel where we were to meet Padar. We could rest and refresh ourselves from a long journey.

Tired, thirsty, and hungry, we arrived at the door to Fatima's brother's house on the far side of Peshawar. Her brother and sister met us at the door of their home that fronted a narrow street busy with people, pushcarts, and motorcycles. He stood in the doorway, taking in the four small strangers with his sister and her daughter.

"Who are they?" His manner was gruff. Her sister was even less inviting, standing behind him in the doorway shaking her head. They looked us up and down. We'd worn the same clothes for weeks. Once, before we had entered the mountains, we'd washed our clothes in the river. But now they were caked with dirt. Our faces were grimy with mountain dust. We hadn't a chance to wash since coming off the mountain. We must have been a sight; four impoverished children would take up space and require food. Still this was not at all what we expected after having been so graciously received into the huts of the most poverty-stricken villagers.

Fatima told him about our journey across the mountains and that we were alone and waiting for our father to join us from Afghanistan.

"In this town, everyone works for their own food and water," he said, nearly growling. "We can't take care of these kids."

"Brother!" she said, but he cut her off with a hard glare.

"They have to go." He waved his hand toward the street. "Go."

Fatima froze for a moment trying to take in her brother's words. "We've walked all day, across the mountains, at least give them some water."

He shook his head. "Go, go." He waved us off. For the first time since leaving Kabul, I felt like a beggar. And Masood, who would have had something to say to these selfish people, wasn't here to speak for us. When her brother ushered Fatima and her daughter through the door and slammed it behind them, we four stood staring at the wooden door closed to us, weary and alone. No more adults to guide us. I could feel the blood pulse in my temple. I started to bang on the rough wood door with my fist. They couldn't just leave us in the middle of the street like this. They had to help us. But Zia took my arm and led me away. We wandered up the side street, still dazed at being rejected by Fatima's brother, and our unceremonious parting with her and Shakila. It was like more family members disappearing right in front of me.

We turned onto a busy road, a hard-packed dirt thoroughfare filled with beeping cars, bicyclists zipping by, motorcyclists weaving among the trucks, jitneys, and food vendors who pushed their wooden carts past us, calling out the prices of their wares. We blended into the crowd of women in burkas and chadors making their way in and out of the storefronts. The aroma of rice and chicken and spices cooking in one of the shops reminded me how hungry I was. We were little ants that had been absorbed into a maze of unfamiliar streets and scents. It was nearing dusk; the late-afternoon shadows crept across the road as we huddled together outside a food vendor, gaping at the meats hanging from the ceiling of the stall. We had eaten such small portions for the past six months, and now, to see so much meat all in one place made us realize how close to starving we had been on our journey.

We must have been staring like lost urchins, because a man approached us.

"Did you children just arrive from Kabul?" he asked. He was dressed like many of the men on the street, in a sand-colored shalwar kameez and a jinnah cap, with a genuine smile. At first none of us spoke. I didn't know what to think.

"Yes," Zia said.

"Where are you staying?"

Laila showed him the piece of paper with the address we were look-ing for. "Do you know how we can get to this hotel?"

"Oh, this is very far," the man said. "I'll take you to a nearby motel for the night, and tomorrow you can get on the early bus. That will take you where you need to go."

He took us to a motel and helped us sign in. He even paid for our stay. He told us to stay in the room and that he would be back. Thirty minutes later he showed up with food—fried potatoes, naan, and rice. We were all very grateful—and very hungry.

"This place, the city, is not safe at night," he reminded us as he stood by the door. "Stay in your room until it's time to catch the early bus tomorrow morning." He turned and closed the door behind him. We never saw him again, but he probably saved our lives.

The next morning we woke early, washed as best we could, and made our way to the bus stop. Laila kept a tight grip on the scrap of paper with the address of the hotel. We boarded the bus and were finally going to our meeting place. The bus ride gave me a strange feeling; a fear haunted me. None of us spoke of Padar, but we all must have harbored a silent hope he would eventually show up to meet us. But each of us had our own suspicions. He had rarely been sober for the last year. The night he woke us to send us on our journey, he'd been clear-eyed and solemn—the Padar I loved more than anything. But we all silently worried that he might have fallen back into drinking once he was alone. There were so many reasons to doubt I would ever see him again.

The sun blazed at high noon by the time we reached a train station, which the driver had told us was next door to the hotel. He pointed to a tall beige building on the other side of the station. We stepped off the bus into a crowd of people who had just disembarked an arriving train. One final obstacle to wade through before reaching our journey's endpoint. Hesitating outside the wooden double doors we stared up at the building. It stood at least ten stories tall and it appeared quite old, but we were so excited finally to have reached our destination.

Inside the lobby, the hotel appeared even older and very traditional. To the right of the lobby was a small lounge full of chairs with pink, orange, and red pillows. Worn Persian carpets covered the floors, and dark tapestries covered the lobby walls. We all followed Zia to the front desk, where a plate of incense burned; it smelled like roses. There were two gentlemen behind the counter wearing shalwar kameez. One was younger, maybe in his thirties, and the other was an older man who seemed no longer able to smile.

"We need to rent a room," Laila said, like she'd done this a hundred times before.

The older gentleman looked us up and down. "Is it just the four of you?"

"Yes," Laila replied.

He shook his head. "Sorry, there must be an adult with you. We cannot rent you a room."

Zulaikha shrank back; Zia glanced around as if searching for an answer. I sidled up to Laila at the front desk.

"There will be an adult with us soon," Laila protested firmly but politely. "My dad is on the way. He's coming from Afghanistan. He instructed us to stay here at this hotel. He'll meet us here in a couple of days. So we have to be here."

The older man continued to scrutinize us with darkened eyes as if he knew us to be the biggest liars. The young man bent down over the counter and looked at me directly. "What type of room would you like?"

"The cheapest one you got," I replied, looking him right in the eye to show him—and the old man—that I wasn't intimidated.

"We have money," Laila added quickly. "But we'd still like the cheapest room because we don't know when our dad will get here exactly, and we need what we have to last us awhile."

The younger man smiled at us and nodded his head. He seemed sympathetic and understanding and continued to give us looks of reassurance that we would be okay as he checked us into a room.

The older man grumbled and fussed around the front desk before he reluctantly took us on a tour of the hotel and showed us to our room. It was close to the lobby, and the window opened onto the back alley. The walls at one time had been white but now were a putrid gray. A weird stench permeated the air, probably from the trash bins below the window that were piled high with garbage. As disgusting as it was, we were excited to have a room with a toilet, a shower, and beds with mattresses. No more bathing in rivers or relieving ourselves behind trees and in bushes and sleeping in our clothes on the hard dirt.

With two full-size beds in the room, there was plenty of sleeping space, but Zia wanted his own bed, so we asked for a third bed for him. The young man told us no extra beds were available at the time. Zia said he would sleep on the floor, but the rest of us wouldn't have it. We decided to take turns for however long we had to stay.

That first night, we sat around the room. Laila wanted to count our money to see how long we could stay in the room. She pulled the money out of her backpack. She wanted us to pool our money to see how much we had together. I gave her all of mine. So did Zulaikha and Zia.

"We have plenty of money," Zia said.

"Yes, if we are only here a week or two," Laila responded as she stacked the cash on the bed.

"It won't take him long to get here," Zia said.

"How do you know?" Laila snapped back. "You heard what that man said last night. The streets here are dangerous. If we have to live on the streets, who knows what will happen to us."

"What if he gets so drunk he never makes it at all?" Zulaikha said.

"He'll come," I said, not sure where my optimism came from. "You'll see." Just then I wouldn't allow myself to think differently. "Let's go out and eat one big dinner tonight, some rice and kabobs and tea," I said.

"We have to be prepared to survive for as long as possible." Laila stuffed all of the money in the backpack. "We have enough to stay here for about six months." Laila scowled. "We'll go to the market and try to make the food we buy last us."

For the first month, we spent each day in the hotel lobby, watching all sorts of interesting people come and go. We wanted to be the first to recognize Padar when he came through the large double doors into the lobby.

When they grew tired of watching people come and go with no sign of Padar, my sisters and brother would go upstairs and play cards with a deck that Salman, the owner of the hotel, had given to us. But I would stay late in the lobby until I couldn't keep my eyes open. I wanted to be the first to greet Padar. And every night, when I could no longer keep my eyes open, the man behind the desk would tell me to go up to my room.

To further save money, we bought milk and bread at a corner bakery. We ate that for breakfast, lunch, and dinner. We drank water from the bathroom faucet. When we got tired of that and complained too much, Laila purchased a bit of sugar. We would stir it into our milk, then chop up the bread and soak the pieces in the sugar milk. It was pretty tasty. Sometimes I shared my ration of bread with Zulaikha. I liked the crust and she liked the insides, so we would split it that way. She often cut the crusts off so closely that I was left with meager strips of hard bread, while she ate the inside of the bread. After a while her habits began to bother me.

Once in a while, Laila would let us order food from the restaurant in the hotel. Normally she let us eat only enough to stave off our hunger, but every now and then, she knew she would have to give us special treats to keep us from rebelling against her iron hold on the money.

———

After another month of waiting, we couldn't stand to sit inside anymore. We decided to do some sightseeing. We all agreed to stay together so as not to get lost in a foreign city. On one trip we found a big bazaar, and we walked around, smelling the restaurant food and running our fingers along the clothes and other goods the vendors were selling. The stalls were crowded with people and colorful merchandise piled high on tables and hanging from the awnings: fabrics and dolls, clothing and clocks, decorations for the home. This place seemed to have everything, and we walked around in awe.

One day I saw a young mother holding a little girl's hand as the two worked their way around the bazaar. It made me think of Mommy and the times we used to shop for fabric in the bazaar in Kabul. I tried to remember what it was like to have her arms around me or what my father's voice sounded like. I could vaguely remember her touch and the timbre of his voice. These shreds of family life tamped down the fears that he would never show up. That he had grown so drunk he'd been killed in a car wreck or taken away by the secret police. Other than Padar, no one had any idea where we were. Not even Mommy.

———

Three months went by, and still no sight of or word from Padar. One night as we lay on one of the beds playing fis kut, all of our angst seemed to come to a head.

"I don't think he's coming," Zulaikha blurted out.

"The Russians could have put him in jail," Zia said.

"I don't think so," I said, truly terrified that we were all thinking the same thing. Yet I didn't know what would happen to us if he never showed up. I forced myself not to entertain the idea we would be all alone—forever. "He will come," I said. "He wouldn't just leave us like this!"

Laila bit her bottom lip like she had something to say but held it back. Finally, she spoke up. "We have to have a plan if he doesn't come."

"What do you mean?" Zulaikha said. "We could never survive on our own."

"*You* probably won't," Zia said, a bit sarcastically. "But I'm sure the rest of us will do fine."

Zulaikha gave him an angry glare. "Look at you! Skinny as a stick. How are you going to live without anything to eat?"

"At least I don't eat all of Enjeela's bread and leave her nothing but the crusts," Zia said.

"What?" Zulaikha looked at me.

"It's true," I said. "You hardly leave me anything."

Zulaikha raised her arms in exasperation.

"Don't worry about it," I said, fearing this would escalate the argument.

"Hey, we have to stick together," Laila said. "I was just saying we should think about what we're going to do if Padar doesn't come."

Zulaikha hung her head, and Zia scooped up the deck of cards and shuffled them. As soon as Zia began dealing the cards again, everyone calmed. Concentrating on the game always helped us avoid thinking about the next problem we faced. Laila laid down the first trick, and a new round of play began, as if nothing disturbed our world.

We played fis kut in silence the rest of the night.

Well into the third month, I grew bored of playing cards and roaming the city streets, especially with no money to spend. I began to pass time in the lobby talking to Salman. He taught me to speak Urdu so we were able to communicate better. Each morning I couldn't wait to wash up and run downstairs to practice my Urdu with him. He made me feel safe in the hotel, that if we'd been abandoned, I would have a place to live and someone to care for me.

Each day Salman was excited to see me. He referred to me as his little girl. I kept him company behind the counter every day as he checked in the hotel guests, and sometimes he even let me hand over the room keys. He would have me call his girlfriend's house to ask for her. Since she wasn't supposed to be dating anyone, she wouldn't be summoned to the phone if a man had called. Once I heard her voice, I would hand the receiver to him, and they would talk for a long while.

This was my new life, and I grew accustomed to it. My hope that Padar would come and take us to join Mommy began fading away; I began to think that it would be better to stay here in the hotel with Salman forever.

When I mentioned this to Salman, he tried to sound upbeat. "If I had a daughter like you, I would do everything in my power to get you back."

———

We had been in the hotel for more than five months when one day Salman turned to me. "I want you to do something."

I leaned close to him. "What?"

"Go buy something different to wear. You've had these same clothes on since you got here."

He didn't sound angry, but I could clearly see the disapproval on his face. I looked down at what I was wearing: I had lived in these clothes night and day for nearly a year. I felt so utterly embarrassed. Still they were all I owned. The other clothes I'd brought had become so worn out, I'd discarded them along the way. I'd almost forgotten that changing outfits was something people did.

I ran back to the room and grabbed some of our money out of the backpack where we kept it. No one was there to see me take it or argue. I headed to a nearby bazaar. I strolled through the busy streets past shops with tables displaying their food, toiletries, toys; they seemed to sell everything there. I was single-minded, searching for a clothing store. When I found one, I went inside and let a salesgirl help me pick out a dress and chador. They were beautiful, so clean and new—no tears, no stains, not even a wrinkle. I couldn't wait to get back to the hotel to put them on and show Salman.

With my purchase wrapped up under my arm, I made my way to the end of the bazaar, where the taxis and vendors all lined up along the busy street. I looked up and down the street that was choked with traffic and people. I tried to recognize a landmark or a building, anything that would give me a clue which direction I had come from. I had been so excited about buying a new dress, I had run from the hotel to the bazaar not even paying attention to the route I'd taken.

I turned down street after street, scouring the buildings for something recognizable—a storefront or the train station or a bus stop, anything. After a while I stopped in the middle of the street. I bowed my head and began to cry. Eventually a boy approached me and asked me a question in English. He was a teenager, maybe about sixteen years old.

"Where do you live?" he asked. I didn't speak or understand English then, so I simply shrugged at him.

"Hotel," I said in Urdu. Miraculously it seemed as if he understood. I tried to describe the train, hoping he'd understand that the hotel was next to the station. But no matter how hard I tried, he couldn't understand me, and I began to cry harder in frustration.

He asked me, "Do you sing a song?"

I didn't comprehend what he said, so I just shook my head.

"Let's sing a song," he said. "Sing a song . . . ding-dong . . ." It was a sweet little tune, and he told me to repeat after him, so I did. Soon I forgot about being lost, and I was no longer scared, just having fun. We strode through the streets, and he pointed at buildings, expecting me to recognize one. When I shook my head, we moved on. Eventually we found the hotel, and he walked me right into the lobby.

"Salman!" I cried. He sat in his usual place behind the front desk. "I went out by myself, and I got lost." I turned and pointed at the young man. "He helped me find my way back."

Salman smiled warmly at him. Then slowly, he stood up, put his palm to his chest, and bowed slightly—a sign of gratitude. "Thank you," he said, his voice low and sincere.

I thanked the boy profusely too. As I ran around the counter to give Salman a hug, the young man simply left. I turned to thank him again, but he had disappeared. I felt truly blessed.

"I bought an outfit!" I told Salman. "I'm going to take a shower and put it on." I went upstairs, where my brother and sisters were so busy playing cards they hadn't even noticed I'd gone out. They thought I was downstairs as usual. When I stormed excitedly into the room, none of them even looked up. I could have been lost in the city for days before they would probably have even noticed I was missing.

With my new clothes, I finally felt like I had something to look forward to. I showered and changed, then ran downstairs before any of them saw my new dress. In the lobby, I showed off to Salman.

"You look beautiful!" he said, and his eyes lit up. He seemed truly proud of me for the attention I had shown myself.

One month later, our money was running dangerously low. I knew we were running low, because Laila was giving each of us less bread and smaller portions of milk each day. When I told Salman that we were low on funds and eating just pieces of bread sopped in milk, he sent food up to our room. It was very kind of him, but none of us thought he'd do it for very long.

When Zia or Zulaikha would complain, Laila would tell them to shut up. We'd all fallen into a jaded state. It was becoming more of a reality that one day we would run completely out of money, and Padar still wouldn't have shown up. We didn't talk to each other much about anything, especially not about Padar. We just did things to make the time pass. We sat around and played cards. When that got boring, we'd stare out the window into the alley.

"Seems like we've been waiting for years," Zulaikha said one day.

"It's been six months," Laila said, not taking her eyes off her cards.

"That's a long time," I said.

"We only have enough for rent for one more week," Laila said. "That will leave us with no money for food."

We stared at each other, letting the shock of what had finally come to pass sink in. Six months we'd lived in this tiny room together, and now we wouldn't even have this small bit of security.

"We can't go back to Kabul," Zulaikha said. "Where do we go?"

We didn't know a soul except for Salman in Peshawar. No one mentioned Padar.

"Maybe we can find work?" Zia said. "I think I could get a job."

"How much could you earn?" Zulaikha asked. "Would it be enough to feed us? And for how long?"

"I'll pay the rent," Laila said. "If Zia can find some work, we can buy some bread at least."

"Do you think Salman would put us on the street?" Zia asked.

They all looked at me since I was so friendly with Salman, the kind owner. He'd been sending food to us a couple of times a week lately. Maybe he would let us pay for our extra stay when Padar showed up. I didn't think Salman would force us to live on the streets, but I had heard him ask other customers to leave the hotel when they could no longer cover the room.

That Saturday, Laila gave Salman the rent. She didn't tell him that was the last of the money we had. We would have a roof over our heads only until the next weekend.

On Wednesday, we sat on the floor playing cards and talked more about finding work. Zia had gone out into the city each day for a few hours, looking for work. He didn't appear enthusiastic about his prospects when he returned. I wouldn't have minded working. At least it would give me something to do all day. Yet I doubted I could find anyone who would hire a little girl. I had no idea how I would go about even finding a job.

"Have you found a job yet?" Zulaikha asked Zia.

"It's hard—" Zia began to say, but his sentence was interrupted by a knock on the door. We never had visitors, only the room-service staff if they brought us food. But we had eaten hours ago. We all glanced at one another for a good minute, too scared to get up and see who it was.

"Did you tell Salman we don't have any more money?" Zulaikha asked, staring darts at me, then at Laila.

"I didn't say anything to him," Laila said.

"I didn't say anything," I said, trying to remember what we had talked about. He was always asking me about what we ate and drank. I did tell him we were very low, almost out of money. But he had never said anything more about it.

"What if he sent that creepy old man up here to kick us out?" Zulaikha said.

"What did you say to him?" Laila hissed at me.

There was another knock at the door. This time it was more urgent.

None of them moved, so I slowly pushed myself up and went to the door. I opened it just a crack and peeked through. It wasn't Salman. This man had a scraggily beard, longish hair, and dusty peran tumban. He looked like he'd just walked a thousand miles across the mountains and deserts of Afghanistan. His face under that thick beard appeared vaguely familiar. He smiled at me and held out his hands in a warm greeting. Then I knew. I swung the door wide open for all of them to see.

"Look!" I said, then my throat was choked by a sob. Standing in the doorway of our room was Padar.

15
Days of Waiting

Though Padar stood in the doorway a few feet from me, I dared not touch him, fearing his image would fade and evaporate like a mirage. I had wished nearly every moment since we had arrived at this hotel that he would appear just like this. Behind me, my sisters and Zia were silent, so maybe I *was* dreaming. A cruel trick of my overwrought imagination.

He knelt on one knee so we were eye to eye. "Enjeela, it's me." His familiar voice was warm and comforting. Even from behind his shaggy beard, his smile was unmistakable. He wrapped his arms around me in a warm hug. Flesh and bone. I held on to him so tight I could have choked him. Once I had embraced him, Zia and Zulaikha and Laila all ran to him, each hugging and shouting in exultation and relief. We were all crying, and he let us mob him as he worked his way into the room.

"I told you he would come for us!" I shouted over the din of the tearful reunion. We were all so glad and truly surprised; he arrived just as he had promised.

After we had finished jumping around, shaking off all of the anxiety and fear of the moment before I opened the door, he sat on the edge of one of the beds and looked us over, appraising each of us. "I am so sorry it took so long to get here. What have you been eating?" he asked.

Laila showed him the dried bread crusts and empty milk bottle.

He took the milk bottle from her hand, and he reached out to her with the other. "Children, children!" His voice was sad, and we all ran to him. He gave each of us a brief hug; I could see that he wanted to linger over us, but he could not allow himself to show too much emotion. It just was not his custom, even though I could see he felt deeply about our condition. "You must be hungry."

"Yes!" we all shouted. *Hungry.* I had lived so long with a gnawing pain in my stomach, it had begun to feel normal. None of us even complained anymore about how little we ate. Bits of food had become extravagances, so the thought of eating a full meal again made us all excited.

"Where do you want to go?"

We all shouted different places—everyone had their own ideas of a celebration. But my voice rang out above the others: "There's a restaurant next door that smells really good."

He clapped his hands, then started for the door. "Let's go!"

The five of us ran downstairs, laughing and still crying. In the lobby I saw Salman. I ran over to tell him that Padar had arrived. He nodded at me with a smile, reminding me that he'd been telling me all along that my father wouldn't leave me behind. His smile seemed to take on a sad tinge even as he congratulated me on the happy news. Now that Padar had arrived, it meant that we would be leaving soon.

At the restaurant, my dad ordered every type of rice they had—green, red, yellow, white—a feast of color and flavors. He told the waiter to fill the table with food. I had never felt so full in my life. When we went back to the hotel, I curled up in one of the beds next to Padar. A comfortable feeling came over me that we were together again, and finally at peace.

I stayed at my father's side all that week as he made the arrangements for the next leg of our trip—he told us that we would be moving on to Islamabad, where we would visit a friend he had worked with at the American embassy in Kabul. I thought this would be another long journey, but Laila showed me on a map that Islamabad was a day's ride east by car from Peshawar.

Padar took us shopping for new clothes to get ready for our journey. One night that week, at dinner in a restaurant by our hotel, Laila asked him why we had to go to Islamabad.

"Can't we just get on an airplane and fly to India, where Mommy is?"

He ate slowly as if considering his words. He had trimmed his beard and purchased some new clothes but still wore the traditional shalwar kameez like so many did in Peshawar. He looked refreshed, with his black hair neatly trimmed, much like his old self.

"We can't leave Pakistan just yet."

"Why not?" Zia asked.

"We left Afghanistan without passports or the proper paperwork and identification to get passports. No other country will let us enter without them."

"Pakistan let us in," I said, thinking I could clarify the issue of simply walking across the border past a few guards.

"Yes," Padar said, "they let all of us in with refugee status." He went on to explain how as refugees, we had no legal status, so we couldn't work and had none of the rights of citizens. We had no rights to travel to any other country, and the Pakistani government could force us back into Afghanistan anytime it wanted.

"They won't do that, will they?" Zulaikha said.

"It's not likely," he said. "But with so many Afghan refugees flooding the country, anything can happen. We have to get passports to travel to India so we can join your mother." He explained that he had wanted us to carry our birth certificates with us in our backpacks, but Masood had warned him not to do that. If we'd been searched by soldiers, it could have gotten us in a lot of trouble, even killed. He had wanted to mail the birth certificates to India, but since the Soviets had been watching everything he did, particularly what he mailed, it was too risky.

Before he left, the Russians had been accusing him of trying to spy for the Americans. They had been watching him constantly.

"I had to leave with nothing."

"Do you think we'll ever go home?" I asked him.

His dark eyes grew sad for a moment. "If the war ends soon, we can return. But who knows how long it will go on. First, we have to travel to New Delhi to join your mother and Shapairi, Ahmad Shah, and Vida. Then we can decide what to do from there."

"Are we going to live in India if we can't go home?" Laila asked.

"No," he said, very emphatically. "We will go to America."

We were all silently shocked, staring at each other in surprise.

"America!" Laila said, smiling broadly. We'd heard of America from all of Padar's friends from the American embassy. Many American diplomats and businessmen had visited our home on Shura Street. We thought of America as a paradise, a place with freedom and safety to be yourself. A model of what Afghanistan could have become if the democratic reforms had not been stopped by the Parcham.

"That's why we're going to Islamabad," he said. "My friend there works for the American embassy. I know he'll be able to help us."

We ate with renewed excitement, hardly tasting the food because we were chattering so much about leaving Peshawar and getting back on the road. *America.* The idea kept rolling around in my mind. It didn't seem real to me; neither did seeing Mommy. Padar spoke of going to New Delhi to see her as a matter of fact—it was not a hope or a dream, but a certainty. That night, I sat on the bed considering what it would be like seeing Mommy after so many years. Padar moved around the room, agile and sober and ever so helpful as we packed our clothes for the trip to see his friend. The room was filled with joy, but I could not see Mommy's face. I had this creeping fear that as warm and caring as Padar had been toward us the last few days, Mommy would be his exact opposite—cold, uncaring, and not interested in my life.

We rose well before dawn and dressed in our new clothes. Salman stood behind the desk as we checked out. He had been so nice to me, helping me through a dark time of my life. I wanted to go behind the desk like usual, give him a hug, and thank him for looking after me. My real father had shown up and taken the place Salman had filled so wonderfully for months. He had been a surrogate father, helping me to endure my loneliness, encouraging me to believe my future would be brighter than the dreary moments I lived through in his hotel. I felt like I was cheating him out of a daughter's love by walking out of the hotel with my real padar. I wanted to embrace him one last time and thank him. I was grateful for his kindness but afraid of offending Padar. Just before we left the lobby, holding tightly on to Padar's hand, I turned and waved at him. He smiled in return. Regretfully, I didn't leave him with any words of thanks, only my eternal gratitude for his willingness to befriend a hapless and nearly orphaned child.

———

The train ride to Islamabad was mostly quiet. Padar didn't ask us too much about our journey. I wanted to tell him about Mina and the scorpions and so much more, but I felt he didn't want to hear it. None of us talked much about what we'd been through, but we made sure Padar knew Masood had taken very good care of us the entire way.

About halfway there, he relaxed and leaned back. "I had planned on leaving sooner, but they had me under constant surveillance." He had been followed night and day, after work, and watched at night. They had suspected he wanted to leave, so they had warned him against it. "The war now is everywhere. It's getting much more difficult to escape."

In the weeks leading up to his leaving, he had been under constant pressure. The Russians had tried to intimidate him to cooperate with their spying schemes. He had to escape Kabul through a complicated route to finally meet up with Masood. Once outside Kabul, he'd followed the same route we had, but he'd been delayed in one village for quite a long time when the fighting caught up with him. He had many close calls with the army along the way.

As soon as we disembarked in Islamabad with our luggage, his friend Dawar was waiting for us on the station platform. He and Padar hugged, kissing cheeks as close friends did. We all greeted him with a polite salaam, our hands folded prayerfully, heads bowed in respect.

He drove us to his home—a beautiful, white, two-story house on a lovely, tree-lined street. His elegant Pakistani wife made us dinner, and we sat around his large table to eat. It reminded me so much of home in Afghanistan, but I was not comforted. The beautiful table with all the lavish food made me feel odd. Eating such delicious food when there were so many people with so little to eat, people I knew by name, whose faces I could see clearly in my mind, seemed wrong. I set my fork down; my discomfort was so overwhelming. My body was here, sitting at this beautiful dining table, but my soul couldn't forget the country we had just traversed. I couldn't get thoughts of Mina out of my mind, and the freedom fighters struggling for their lives in the freezing mountains.

We stayed at Padar's friend's home for several months while Padar worked on obtaining our passports. He went to the American embassy nearly every day to meet with different people. Many days he came home quite frustrated that he wasn't getting the help he needed to obtain identity documents and passports. But he stayed determined to do what he needed to do so we could travel. While he was gone, we kept busy. Since Dawar and his wife had no children, we took over the large living room, playing fis kut and eating lavish meals. The house reminded me of our home in Kabul: warm, loving, and plenty of food.

Though we were living in the diplomatic section of the Pakistani capital, Padar did not want us to go outside. Only after Laila and I kept questioning, he told us that he was probably being watched. He feared the Russians knew where he was, and as soon as he went to the Embassy of Afghanistan to apply for a passport, they would know for certain. His friends in the American embassy were trying to assist him, but he had run into bureaucratic roadblocks. One night in the living room of the gracious home, he unburdened himself after a particularly disappointing day. All four of us sat on the sofa while he took a chair across from us.

"They keep a list," he said, referring to the Afghan administration of Babrak Karmal, the new president the Russians had installed to lead the puppet government. "Enemies of the state are kidnapped and sent back or just killed."

"Why would they want you back in Afghanistan?" Laila asked.

"They think I know how the Americans are planning to help the mujahideen," he said.

"Do you?" I asked.

He clenched his jaw. "Even if I knew what President Reagan was thinking at this very moment"—he punched his index finger on the coffee table—"I would not tell them anything. But I'm sure they think I know things that are important to them, so they pursue me still."

Each day after that, when he left, one of us would stand in the large windows of the living room and watch the kids pedaling up and down the street and playing soccer. We wanted to know if someone was following us.

After several months, Padar rented an apartment for us. It was in a nice section of town not far from the diplomatic neighborhood. It had two bedrooms, a living room, a kitchen, and a small balcony. It came completely furnished, with sofas, chairs, a table, and beds that were well used. We were comfortable there. While it wasn't the home I'd known, we were together as a family in our own home. We were no longer guests in a hotel room or in someone else's house, and compared to how we had lived during our stays in the villages, this small apartment was luxurious.

I'd never seen Padar cook before, but he took over as the family chef. He organized the kitchen, took us to the markets to purchase food, and planned the meals. I wanted to learn to cook, and so I asked Padar to teach me. We spent hours in the kitchen together, and he taught me how to cut the beef for the kebabs and to steam the rice just right and season it till it was flavored the way we enjoyed it best. For the first time in our lives, we cooked and ate together and quickly fell into routines old and new. At night Padar would read to us as we all lay on the floor cuddled up with one another. During those days of waiting for our documents, he wrote poetry and read the poems to us in the evenings. He was an amazing poet. His recitations kept all of us in rapture, the way he spoke with such passion and feeling.

We had reading sessions like during our days in Kabul, but now Padar wasn't drinking. These sessions weren't about helping him maintain his sanity but more about him exploring his life, his soul, and how he'd been thrust out of everything he loved and had worked for. He seemed on a search for meaning. The words of the ancient and magnificent poets acted as his guides.

He encouraged all of us to recite for him, not only to exercise our memories, but as a form of meditation. We all worked to memorize his poems. I found poetry fascinating. The words that came to me as he read them gave me a way to understand my experiences, just as he searched his own emotions. I sat at his feet as he read from his favorite poets—Hafiz Shirazi and Rumi. It didn't seem to matter what the poem was about, the words always came around to describing a way out of my fears—always through love and faith in God.

I had witnessed up close how rude and violent men were determined to force their version of love and safety on others using guns and blood. It didn't matter what the men called it, political order or religious fervor, it was all from the same place—the hellish dark side of man that is motivated by hate.

Mina's parents called selling their daughter into sexual slavery part of their tradition, and Mina's husband treated her according to the dictates of his religion, but it was all the same. Their actions were motivated by hate. Hate is not from God. People who use religion to hate can't love God. It is impossible.

The Parcham embraced communism as the superior social order, but they could only enforce their rule with bullets and armor. Their revolution stole from my father the fruits of his hard work and toil that had made my country a better place to live for so many people. Those dreary days in Kabul before we escaped, I witnessed Padar being stripped of more than his possessions: his deepest dignity. It was no excuse for his drinking, but I understood better now how he had let those demons take over.

An even deeper mystery I wrestled with was that I believed we existed in the hands of God. He evidently carries us with a light touch. He does not clench his fist around us and force any of us to hate or love—these are choices.

During the long days when he went off to the embassy, Padar demanded that we stay inside, even going to the extreme of locking the apartment door from the outside. The most we could do was stand on the small balcony and watch the kids on the streets. In those quiet days, I also began writing my own poems. Words just gushed up from somewhere; I wrote about the moon, the sun, the ocean, the flowers, the birds, and the mountains—and how, with the kiss of God, they all came to life. Padar read all of it, smiling as he went over each word, nodding in satisfaction, rocking gently in his chair as I sat at his feet.

"Everything that surrounds you, all this beauty, is the work of Allah," he said one day, handing my sheet of poems back to me. There was a new gentleness to his voice. He seemed to have come to terms with his losses, and he truly enjoyed teaching me about poetry and writing. Sitting on the floor during those days, and writing poems and listening to him recite his poems brought relief and hope to each of us. I could see it on everyone's faces. We didn't live in the large and spacious home of Kabul, with servants and great luxury, but it was possible, maybe for the first time, to see true beauty, even in the devastation and sadness that surrounded us.

One day Padar took us to visit an old friend who had recently arrived. He lived in a very poor section of Islamabad, where many Afghan refugees were settling. Padar spotted his friend, Ali, standing outside a shabby apartment building in a section of Islamabad that looked worse than any part of Kabul. The streets were made of dirt; the buildings were run down, with paint peeling off in giant flakes as if they were shedding their skin. The cars on the street were beat up and noisy. Smoke from cooking fires straggled up into the atmosphere above the neighborhood. The smoke hovered in a cloud of despair that I could feel. Most of the people here had lost all their wealth or were forced to leave everything behind in order to escape to Pakistan. With scant money or few assets, they were forced to live in these deplorable conditions. It was harrowing to see my fellow countrymen being treated this way.

Padar and Ali greeted each other warmly. As they talked, I watched the kids playing in the streets. Every one of them was dirty; they looked the way we had after reaching the summit of the Hindu Kush. Many of them had tattered clothes. I could tell from the tone of Padar's voice that he was saddened his friend had to live here.

"The refugee camps are far worse," Ali said to him, as if reading my thoughts. "People have to live in tents. They're sick all the time, and there is little medicine to go around. Many are dying."

"Why?" Padar said, concern in his voice. "Even in the villages at home, people have access to medicines."

Ali shook his head that it wasn't so here.

"I must go and see this." Padar spoke with determination that he wanted Ali to take him to the camp to see what could be done to help them.

Ali purchased food from a shop on the street. Padar hailed a cab, and all of us piled inside for a ride to the camp. When we arrived,

I walked with Padar and Ali down the long row of tents. They were pitched in long lines with narrow streets that filled with swarms of kids playing with sticks and rocks. Rubbish was piled high, and the heat of the day must have made the canvas tents bake like ovens. The kids had a wild look to them, as if anything they determined to do, they could get away with. As we walked deeper into the camp, misery oozed from behind every tent flap. Most of the floors were dirt. Some had canvas or blankets laid over the ground, and possessions were strewn everywhere.

Ali began to hand out the food he had bought. Children gathered like metal flakes to a magnet until the crowd was dense, hands reaching and pleading for something, anything, to eat. His supplies vanished within a few minutes. They clamored for more, but the two men held their hands up to say that was all they had.

We went back to the camp every day. Padar always brought bread, fruit, and clothes to give to those in need. He had always been a charitable man, but he wasn't working now, and I was nervous about money—residual feelings from our days in the Peshawar hotel, no doubt. I assumed we were living off money he had managed to bring with him. It wasn't difficult to remember those days we spent cooped up in that hotel room in Peshawar waiting for him, each day our money running lower and lower. We could easily have been forced to live in these tents if he hadn't shown up. But he had, and he had taken care of us so far, so I decided to trust that he knew what he was doing.

In the camps, I often ran with the kids, envious of the fun they had playing with other children their age. I made a friend with Youssef, whose whole family had died when a bomb exploded on his house. He was the only survivor. Another friend, Muzghan, had come with her family. They were farmers, and the war had destroyed all their crops and animals. With nothing left, they had decided to come and start a new life in Pakistan.

Another one of my friends was Sophia, from Kabul. She asked me if I had ever visited Paghman, a beautiful park outside Kabul where everyone went for picnics on Fridays.

"My parents often took us there to fly kites and to play," I said. "I love that place."

"I used to enjoy it the most of all," she said. "I hope to see it again one day."

"So do I." I thought of all the other places I wanted to see again. Glancing up and down the dirt lanes of the camp, I felt so far from the carefully manicured Paghman Gardens.

Our little group grew to be good friends. Even though I pretended to be one of them, they all knew I was just a visitor. I always came with clean clothes and didn't have to wear the same outfit week after week. They didn't seem to care, but it bothered me that I wasn't one of them. Because of my family, I'd escaped not only the war but the destitution so many others experienced every day. I had a nice warm bed and a shower whenever I wanted one and plenty to eat, thanks to Padar. I had no answers why I should be so blessed, but I thanked God for it.

I wished there were a way for my friends to escape that camp.

There was an epidemic of hopelessness that ran rampant up and down each lane of tents, behind every canvas flap, in and out of endless food lines. Under the stale odors of cooking oil and overflowing latrines, these refugees were homeless. They had no idea where they would go next to start a new life. I began to wonder if the people of Afghanistan had been cursed.

16

INHALE AND EXHALE

One night after dinner, we didn't go to the camp. Padar had us all sit down in the living room of our small apartment for a talk.

"We cannot get passports here in Islamabad," he said. Disappointment dripped from his voice.

We all tried to speak at one time, asking him why.

"It's very complicated with the embassy. The Afghan embassy here doesn't want to help because of my work with the Americans. They say I must return to Kabul to apply through the proper channels for a visa. The Americans say they can't help get a visa without identity papers. As refugees, we are supposed to get special exceptions, but they say it will take a long time. There are so many refugees applying."

"How long?" Zia asked. We'd already been in Islamabad nearly five months.

"It could take a few years."

We were all silent. The hope that I would finally see Mommy began to drain out of me. I had not received a letter, heard her voice, or seen her face in nearly three years.

"Are we going to be stuck here forever?" Zulaikha said, truly frantic at the idea.

Padar shook his head. "I'm not returning to Kabul for any reason. The government will put me in jail, and you will become orphans." He rubbed his short beard, thinking. "We can't wait a year. It's too dangerous for us to stay here much longer, but I have another plan that will get us to India much sooner." He folded his hands and gave us a confident smile.

"What? What?" we all stammered to find out what he had figured out.

"I have a very good friend in Karachi. We will stay with him for a while. He's very influential in the city. He'll help us get our identity papers, then we'll go to India." He smiled in that rueful way he did when he wasn't giving us the full story. Maybe it was all those years working in the American embassy, where he learned not to talk about the things he knew. He'd gotten good at keeping secrets. As much as I believed him when he said we would get identity papers in Karachi, I felt a deep disappointment that we couldn't leave for India from here.

The other day, Laila had taken out a map she had purchased in Peshawar when we were trying to figure out how many miles we had walked out of Afghanistan. I had traced a finger along a route from Islamabad to New Delhi, where Mommy lived. Laila said it would take only a day to drive that far. We could take a taxi or a bus or a train and be there tomorrow if we had passports. Instead, we were going to Karachi, which was way south, almost to the sea.

"Are we going to spend another year in Karachi waiting around?" Zulaikha asked with a tone of disbelief.

He laughed; his smile warmed the room. "You'll see. Don't worry, it won't be anything like you've experienced so far. Karachi will be very nice."

"Have you heard from Mommy? Is she well?" I asked, my excitement growing.

"I haven't talked to her since leaving Kabul. The last time I spoke to her, she was recovering from her heart surgery." His face grew grave. "It was a very long operation."

His words had that neutral tone, as if he were speaking about the weather or the crops from his land. He wouldn't talk any more about her. I didn't want to think of not having a mother when I reached the end of this journey. So I didn't.

We were on our way to see her, even if we had to travel to every city in Pakistan to get our papers. I believed this was happening because I kept positive thoughts even when it was difficult to do so.

On my next trip to the refugee camp, I told all my friends the news. I hoped they would be happy for me, but all I saw was sadness. I realized I should not have told them. They were so naïve, like my friend Mina.

Later that day, when I began to pack my new clothes, I felt selfish. I had so much, and my friends in the camp had so little. I packed most of the clothes in a bag to take to the camp.

"Who are you taking these to?" Zia asked, nudging the bag with his toe.

"To the kids!" I replied. "You should donate some of your clothes to Youssef. You have way more than you need."

Zia shook his head. "Youssef is too young. He won't fit into my clothes."

"He'll grow into them!"

Zia finally gave me some of his clothes, and Laila gave me some of hers too to take when I went to say my final goodbyes.

On my last trip to the camp, I was excited to give my friends these gifts, and they were happy to receive them. Yet it was a very difficult goodbye for all of us. We hugged and cried for a long time. I knew I wouldn't see them again.

When I went home, the rest of my packing was easy—I'd kept only two outfits. When Padar found this out, he beamed. I could tell he was proud of us. If I could have, I would have given my friends all of my belongings. I was on my way to see Mommy. I had everything I needed.

We rose in the early morning while the city was quiet and hauled our luggage from our apartment to the curb, where a cabbie waited to take us to the train station. It took an entire day and night and into the next morning to reach central Karachi. We ate and slept on the train as it rattled south, making innumerable stops along the way. When our taxi finally pulled into the driveway of a beautiful three-story home with big wooden doors, my exhaustion vanished. Every window was lit up like they were waiting for us. Padar jumped out, strode up to the front door, and rang the bell. We all piled out of the back seat, glad to stretch our legs, and followed him. A gentleman dressed in all white answered with his two daughters behind him. The two men hugged, then ushered us all into the warm light of the home. The man in white with a wide smile and neatly combed black hair leaned toward me. "Hello, little one, my name is Abbas."

He asked each of us our names, and we each said salaam in greeting. His daughters, Habibah and Daliyah, greeted us as honored guests. Habibah was in her twenties, and Daliyah was around eighteen. They both had long brown hair worn in a single braid, tan skin, and hospitable brown eyes. They took us on a tour of the house, which was huge and colorful, like it had come right out of an Indian movie. The first things I noticed were the windows: they were made of stained glass in blue, pink, and green, and they were tall, like in a church, with flowing, gold curtains. One big room had windows all over, and they were all open, so I felt like I was in a room with no walls. Another room downstairs had a swing set hanging from the ceiling. Over the weeks we stayed here, I spent a lot of time swinging.

In the backyard was another room: a building, separate from the house, that wasn't on our tour. We knew they wanted us to stay away. My hosts were so pleasant and kind, I decided to rein in my inquisitiveness.

Each morning four servants served us a breakfast of eggs, bread, potatoes, and tea. Each evening we had an elaborate dinner with many
courses: lamb, beef, chicken, and vegetables and rice, rich with spices—
turmeric, brown and green cardamom, cinnamon, and black pepper—
all served by the well-dressed servants, who could have been waiting on
kings and queens. We were pampered, fed, clothed, and looked after
like we were part of the family. Habibah and Daliyah were particularly
warm and caring, very much like their father, who radiated peace and
kindness.

In the afternoons, I spent time in the room with the swing, relaxing
and reading and talking with my sisters and Zia. Padar spent his days
with Abbas. They seemed to have a lot to talk about, because those two
were always together.

One afternoon the two sisters called in their driver to take us four
kids to a bazaar. It was very different from the one I'd seen in Peshawar—
this was more like a big outlet mall. They bought us Pakistani dresses
called Punjabi with bangles and earrings to match. We were in heaven.
The second we arrived home, I ran to the room I shared with Laila to
try them on. Then Habibah drew on my palms with henna. I floated in
a world of ease filled with simple pleasures.

I was being treated like a princess, but Youssef, Muzghan, and
Sophia from the refugee camp were never far from my thoughts. Their
laughter, playful shouts, grimy faces, and their aspirations to escape
from the muddy, smelly life in tents all mingled in my thoughts while
Habibah drew on my palm, the soft, warm strokes of the brush sending
chills of comfort through me. This dream, for I knew it as one, couldn't
last. For nearly a year, I had run with my friends through the muddy
lanes of a rambling tent city and lived on crusts of bread and milk
with my sisters and Zia in a tiny hotel room, always teetering on the
very edge of a fierce hunger. That seemed to be the world most people
lived in every day of their lives. Abbas's daughters' care and solicitude
couldn't guarantee it wouldn't happen again, that my life wouldn't turn

from this sunny way of living into one of sleeping on cold dirt with nothing but a chador to cover me. I tried to push the real world out of my thoughts and enjoy this pristine house of servants and bright colors every minute I could.

———

One morning I rose early, before even my hosts, and padded downstairs. The dawn twilight slowly merged into a new day. Through the large window of the family room, I spotted the white one-story house in the large backyard. Several men I hadn't seen before walked up a stone path and disappeared inside.

My curiosity overcame me. Even though I knew I shouldn't go, I stole outside and followed the stone path to the wide-open door of the building. The room was large and filled with people silently seated on prayer mats. In the middle of the room, an old man sat cross-legged on several cushions, his eyes closed as if he were meditating. The men and women surrounding him were deep in prayer. Among them, I noticed Padar. He sat in the front, next to the old man, praying. I waited by the door, taking in what they were doing. Soon they stirred to leave, and many of them approached the old man in the center and kissed his hand before turning to the door.

I'd never seen so many people, even in the great mosque of Kabul where we had gone to pray, pay one man so much respect. I knew this man must be holy. There was a sense of peace and love in the room. They had all touched something higher, apprehended something peculiar that drove my curiosity. Questions fired through my mind. As I watched the people with contented glows on their faces stream by me, I felt a firm hand on my shoulder. I turned to see the gentle smile of Abbas's wife.

"You shouldn't be here," she said. "This is for adults who come here to ask for their sins to be forgiven. That is Jaleel, a very holy man, and he prays for them." She took my hand and led me back into the house.

All day I wondered what sins Padar had asked forgiveness for. Maybe he felt bad about his drinking and his fighting with Mother and the stress his behavior had had on all of us. The sight of Padar reverently approaching Jaleel made me wonder what made the man so holy.

I wanted to discuss this more with Padar, but it seemed every day when I tried to find him, he was either meeting with Abbas and Jaleel or they had left the house. We all knew he was working hard to find a way to get our passports. With so much at stake, whether we would be able to travel to India, it didn't seem right that we spent all day swinging in the indoor play room, reading, playing games, and eating lavish meals, but there wasn't much else to do but to enjoy myself. Besides, Padar had not given any of us one shred of doubt that he would get the documents we needed. Week blended into week, and it seemed like we were going to stay here forever.

One night after dinner, Padar sat with us in the large living room, where my sisters and Zia were gathered to read poetry. We behaved as if we had moved in. "Aren't they tired of us yet?" I asked.

Padar crossed his legs and brushed back a shock of black hair. "In our culture we never tell our guests to leave. Our religion requires we take care of the less fortunate. These people are my good friends, and this is what friends do—we take care of one another when we are in need. Abbas knows I would do the same for him and his family any day if he were in my shoes."

I asked him, "What do you mean if he wore your shoes?" I couldn't imagine Abbas wearing Padar's shoes.

He laughed. "No, no, nothing to do with shoes. I meant that if Abbas was in the same situation we are in, and I could help him, I would."

I had to let that sink in, but I thought I understood it.

Not too long after that conversation, he invited all of us to sit with him when Jaleel spoke. The holy man talked about spirituality from morning till night, and people would come so they could hear his words of wisdom. I liked what he said, and I attended almost every day.

"We are all God's children, and we are all connected somehow." This made me think about Mina. She'd been like a sister to me, but our lives had been so different. Had she been less fortunate? She had never been able to attend school like I had. Nor had she had a personal guide, as we did, who took her step-by-step out of the war. She had no one to protect her from her husband and his other wife. Nor did she have parents who would never sell her for any amount of money. Padar had taken care of us, made our way of escape, then risked his life to reach us, and now worked hard to take us to the next step on our journey. I considered us fortunate, despite what Padar had said about our situation.

In the early-morning sessions, Jaleel spoke and then read poetry. His poems always spoke of how we were all in the hands of Allah. That he was all around us and knew each of our steps. This brought great joy to me and peace, knowing God watched over our family. When he finished, everyone unrolled their prayer rugs and did *namaz*. These daily prayers became a time of meditation, and a sense grew in me that our journey would be a great success. That I was going to see Mommy at last. I believed it with every inhale and exhale as I offered my prayers to Allah.

Every night as I lay in bed, I had so many questions about why the world was the way it was. Why things happened to certain people. I wanted to talk to Jaleel some morning after everyone left. He often met with Padar. Being here in this house, listening to Jaleel's talks and watching Padar and Abbas together discussing poetry and Allah, I couldn't help but imagine these men were closer to God than any I'd ever met. I felt I was closing in on something. Something far too big to touch or even understand in great detail.

One bright morning, with sunshine gleaming through stained-glass dining room windows, as we sat around another sumptuous breakfast, Padar said he had an announcement to make.

"We are leaving in a few days, so pack your clothes," he said.

"We got our passports?" Zia said. The excitement ran through us.

I jumped up from my chair. "We're going to Mommy!"

"We're going to India at last," Zulaikha said, a tone of relief in her voice.

"Hold on, everyone," he said. "We're not going directly, but we are going to India."

We peppered him with questions, but he didn't tell us too much, except that we were flying to Dhaka, then taking the train into New Delhi.

That night in the room I shared with Laila, we spread out her map on her bed. The flight from Karachi to Dhaka, Bangladesh, traveled clear across the entire nation of India. The route was thousands of miles long. And the plane would go right over New Delhi.

"Why would we do this?" I asked. "Why can't we land here?" I pointed to the capital of India on the map.

Laila shrugged as she traced a route on the map with her finger. "He's got his reasons, but he's not going to tell us."

"He must have gotten our passports, didn't he?"

"Don't be stupid. We wouldn't be flying on an airplane if he didn't."

Yes, of course. We had been in this home for months. He must have the proper documents for him to decide it was time to leave. I lay back on my bed, imagining for a minute that when he handed me my passport, I would guard it with my life. Someone would have to steal my soul before I let it go. I would tie it to my body with a belt and wear all my clothes over it. That little paper book was all that kept me, my sisters, Zia, and Padar from being with Mommy. From being a whole family again. That night as I sloughed off into sleep, my thoughts ran wild, imagining what it was going to be like to see Mommy again, to look into her eyes, and tell her everything that had happened in the last three years.

Our days of waiting were coming to an end.

17

Karachi to Dhaka

The black glass windows of Jinnah International Airport's main terminal gleamed in the early-morning sunlight as we rolled toward it in Abbas's big black car. At the curb of the busy terminal, the driver hopped out and opened doors, unlocked the trunk, and shuffled out our luggage while I stood on the sidewalk, taking in the scene. Men in colorful shalwar kameez and women in bright Punjabis were busy hefting luggage and hurrying to catch their flights. My sisters and I wore our new Punjabis, with bangles and earrings to match, and new shoes. We soaked in the excitement of traveling as we followed Padar and Abbas into the terminal.

Padar strode with such confidence as he and Abbas led us to the counter. We checked our luggage and took only our backpacks on board. Abbas escorted us down the long terminal concourse; its polished tile floor sparkled under the lights. There was a long line at the gate for our flight to Dhaka. I had never heard of Bangladesh before Laila had showed it to me on a map the other night. It was a new nation, formerly part of Pakistan. Padar had never explained why we had to fly across the whole of India instead of traveling directly to New Delhi, but if there was anyone we could trust to get us to Mommy, it was him.

The four of us kids stood in the waiting area trying to contain our excitement. Abbas and Padar moved up to the counter to speak to the attendant. They had a quick conversation, and the man looked directly at us, and Abbas and Padar nodded. They must have announced our flight, because people rose from their seats in the waiting area, taking up luggage and bundles and corralling children. A worker opened the door to the stairs leading to the plane. The two men continued to speak to the attendant off to the side, then turned and headed toward us. Padar had a tight smile on his face, as if he were pleased with his conversation but concerns lingered in his clenched jaw.

The two men embraced, a final goodbye. Abbas touched each of our heads and wished us well. After he left, Padar said to us, "Let's go." We picked up our backpacks and followed him.

He strode up to the desk of Pakistan International Airlines, where two men clad in blue uniforms worked behind the counter. A long line of passengers stood in front of one attendant, who took proffered tickets. Padar held all of our tickets, which were stuffed into their paper jackets. With a furtive glance of his dark eyes, the other man behind the counter scanned the crowd lined up in front of the attendant next to him before Padar handed over the thick packets. He lowered them out of sight to his desk.

This was the first time I had ever flown on an airplane, and all the things that went on were a bit mysterious and intriguing. Years before, Mommy had left with Vida and Shapairi on an airplane. Before they left, they went for photos for their passports. I'd never seen a passport before, and I didn't remember sitting for any photos, so I wondered what ours looked like. I nudged away from beside Padar, who intently watched the man with our tickets. I slipped around the side of the counter, which was a couple of inches taller than me, until I could see the counter in front of where the man stood, shifting his weight from foot to foot as if marshaling his energy. The packets were stuffed with rupees, the same Pakistani bills that Abbas's daughters had used to pay for our clothes and treats when they took us shopping.

The man turned his dark eyes on me, his face contorted in silent rage. He began cursing at me in Urdu, waving with his hand for me to leave. Padar reached around the side of the desk and yanked me by the hand to him. Once beside him, he froze me with a reproachful glare. He held me close by him as the attendant finished his work. The man handed the packets back to Padar. He led us through the door, down the stairs to the tarmac, and across to the stairs leading to the plane. Padar clutched my hand all the way, lest I get away from him. He showed a flight attendant, dressed in a crisp blue skirt and jacket, our tickets. She smiled and motioned us up the stairs and into the plane.

We were on our way to see Mommy.

The plane ride took most of the day. Padar seemed distant, preoccupied, the whole trip. Zia and I sat behind him, Zulaikha and Laila across the aisle from us. Zia allowed me to have the window so I could watch everything. When the plane finally lifted off the ground, I felt a lightness in my thoughts even as I was gently pushed back into my seat as the big steel machine rose higher and higher into the blue sky. Soon we were skimming along among the clouds, wispy strands of cotton that swirled around us as we sped on our way. I had dreamt of this day. The day we would finally stop being guests in others' houses or living in hotel rooms, and settle down into a home of our own, like we had had in Kabul, all of us together in one large family. Even as Zia and I played cards and laughed and ate the chicken meal and drank the sodas the very nice attendants set on our seat trays, I couldn't help but wonder if Mommy would even remember me. Some nights when I closed my eyes, all I saw until I drifted off was the back of her perfectly coiffed head of hair through the rear window of the car as she pulled out of the driveway for her plane ride to India. She had never turned to wave goodbye.

We landed at Hazrat Shahjalal International Airport late in the afternoon. I glimpsed the city of Dhaka in the distance as the plane floated in for a landing. It looked endless, with tall buildings and warrens of streets jammed with cars. They moved like ants, millions of ants.

We deplaned and strolled through the spacious, modern concourse among women in bright saris and shalwar kameez of every color, men in jeans and *lungis* and bright shirts, and a few in suits. Padar insisted we stop at one of the shops that sold snacks. We loaded up on little pastries, fruit, candy, and soft drinks. The train ride to New Delhi would be long, and we'd have to change trains often, and we wouldn't always stop to eat. We each stuffed food and drink in our packs and headed down the concourse. Our heels clacked on the shiny tiles of the new terminal, past restaurants and duty-free shops selling everything from clothes to books.

Padar steered us toward the baggage carousels at the far end of the airport. With our luggage in hand, we headed toward passport control. He told us as we gathered around him that the train station was not too far from the airport. Once we were outside, we would catch a bus to the station. My excitement rose as we approached men in uniforms who were checking each passenger's paperwork as they passed through to the exit. I could see through the glass doors on the other side of them. Outside, where passengers waited for rides. Some boarded buses; others were bundling their things into taxis and vans and autos—everyone was leaving, and we'd be leaving soon too, on our way to India.

At first I didn't recognize where the voices were coming from, I just knew they grew louder as I watched people streaming out the doors toward their destinations.

"No, no, no, you cannot enter with these," the guard said to a smiling Padar, who stood, holding the ticket packets out to him. The guard towered over him. With an angry glare, he pushed the packets back hard into Padar's chest. He acted as if he'd been insulted, the way he glared at Padar and then at us behind him. "Where are your passports? Where are they?" he shouted in Urdu.

The guard's voice was so agitated that others rushed over. The men spoke among themselves in a language I didn't understand, with animated hands. Padar interjected once in a while, gesturing to the packets in his hand as if saying these were enough. They all disagreed, shaking their heads; one wagged his finger at Padar as if he were a child and should know better. Another shouted insults in his face in a manner that was clear and precise in any language. Padar, with his normal calmness, in a warm, soothing voice, implored them to take a look at the packets. "Just take the packets, please do us this kindness. This would be best for the children, to let us leave and be on our way. We are simple refugees trying to return to our family," Padar pleaded.

As nice and pleasant as my father was, it only set the loud, tall guard on fire. With his head shaking, his eyes pulsing with the passion of an injured soul, he began pushing Padar backward, toward us, ranting of all the infamous things he would do to us for trying to break the law. Padar tried to hold his ground, but the big man shoved him out of line, and the other guards took us by the arms. One ugly, gap-toothed, dark-faced border guard gripped my arm as if I were a murderer finally captured after a long hunt. We were dragged out of line; our own shouting, mingled with the angry threats of the guards, created a world of noise and chaos that enveloped us until we landed on the cold floor of a windowless room. Our luggage crashed to the floor beside us. The door slammed, and a latch caught on the other side. The sudden silence and coldness of the dirty tile shot through me all at once. I pushed myself to my knees.

I forced myself not to cry. "What happened?" I asked. "What are they talking about, breaking the law?"

Padar didn't answer. He brushed off his clothes and straightened his shirt. He helped each of us up and had us crowd together on the small bench. The stench of the dingy room caught up to me as I wiped my face with the sleeve of my dress. The room once had been painted white, but now the walls were scuffed and bruised as if a thousand brawls had taken place here—people bashed against the walls as punishment for what, I couldn't imagine.

Padar paced the length of the tight room a few times, turning after a few steps, pinching his lips together, as if trying to frame the words to explain to us what had just happened.

He paused, and with one hand on his hip, he faced us. "We have no passports."

Laila sighed. Zulaikha caught a breath.

"Why didn't we get them in Karachi?" Zia asked.

Padar only shook his head, as if thinking hard about his question. "It was impossible to get our passports in Pakistan. I tried very hard." He stared down at the floor. "So many others from Afghanistan had passed through this way, I thought we could too."

"How are we going to get to India?" Zulaikha asked.

He finally looked up at us. The strain and fatigue began to pass from his face. "Don't worry. I believe this is the way for us. We will succeed in reaching New Delhi."

He stood there in front of us with a half smile on his face. This was like a giant game to him, a chess match of international wits. A test of his faith in Allah or the power of poetry to overcome all odds.

He went back to pacing. We sat in silence. Still I shivered at being treated like criminals. Freedom had been so close; I could have reached out to the glass doors that led outside and touched them, but now . . .

"Is that why we couldn't fly directly to New Delhi?" Laila asked.

He nodded. "I was told this was the easiest route across the border. Many others have entered India through Dhaka . . ." He started to say more but fell back into pacing.

We huddled together for warmth while he worked the floor on the other side of the room.

"What's going to happen to us?" I whispered to Laila. She seemed too shocked to answer. She shook her head; she didn't know. We sat hunched together for what seemed like hours, until someone fumbled with the latch on the other side of the door. Padar ceased pacing. I froze into a tight band of muscle, ready to fight back if they tried to beat me. Zulaikha, on the other side of me, clutched my arm.

The door swung open, and a Bangladeshi policeman stepped into the room, an aide behind him. He was definitely the man in charge. Thin, with a tight-fitting blue uniform, perfectly pressed, and a breast full of colorful badges, he glanced over us with an imperious air. Two gold diamonds and a golden leaf gleamed on his epaulets. He had a wispy black mustache on his dark olive skin. A blue beret with a gold medallion was cinched down over his short black hair. Despite his stern demeanor, he had the softest dark eyes. I wondered if he had any children of his own.

He stood erect, as if he were born that way.

He held a document in his hand and one of the ticket packets Padar had tried to pass to the border guards. "Are you Abdullah Ahmadi of Kabul?" he asked. His voice had an official tautness to it.

"Yes, I am," Padar said from across the room. "And these are my children." He spread out his hands toward us. "Zia, Laila, Enjeela, and Zulaikha. We are on our way to New Delhi to be reunited with my wife."

"And you expected to pass through customs without passports," the policeman said, holding up one of the packets stuffed with rupees. The bills hung out of the ticket folder like wilted lettuce.

"We have been deprived of our rights by the Afghan government to emigrate legally. We have come here as political refugees," he said, speaking confidently.

"I have spoken to the Afghan embassy. I was told that's not the case. That if you had applied through proper channels in Kabul, you would have been given every consideration as any Afghan citizen."

"I would have been jailed by the Soviet puppet government if I had applied to emigrate. You well know that."

"I know nothing of the sort. The Afghan ambassador is adamant that you return to Kabul, Mr. Ahmadi." He folded the bills back into the packet and handed it to his aide. "Apparently you have some unfinished business there. Once that is complete, I'm sure you will be allowed to emigrate as you wish."

"We are political refugees," Padar protested.

"You mock us with your conduct, Mr. Ahmadi. We have no such status for those who would bribe their way past our customs." He held out his hand. "Please give me the other packets you offered the guards."

He dug them out of his coat pocket. The officer checked each one. "We will purchase one-way tickets for you and your family's return to Kabul. You can apply for your passport and exit visa through proper channels. Then you can return to our beautiful country at your leisure, as a treasured guest."

I shot up from my seat. "You're sending us back!"

"Enjeela, please," Padar said, reaching toward me.

"You can't send us back," I yelled. "You can't."

"Please, little girl," the officer said. "You must understand—"

"We have to get to India," I shouted at him. "We've traveled for nearly two years to get here."

"That is no concern—"

"You can't stop us from going to India."

His grin became more resolute. He folded his arms over his chest, and for the first time, his eyes hardened. "There is a flight tomorrow that will take you to Islamabad. You will be met—"

"No, no, you can't send us back." I couldn't hold back my tears. I felt a warm hand on my shoulder.

"Enjeela . . ."

I shrugged it off. "If you send us back, they will put us in jail. They will beat us like they've done to so many others, they will kill us!"

He shook his head. "That is none of my concern. You can't come here illegally and expect to be greeted with open arms."

"Please, please, please," I pleaded. All I could think of was all the grief we'd been through to reach Mommy, and I couldn't accept this decision in silence. "You have to let us through so we can see our mother." I reached out for his sleeve, but he fended me off.

"You can stay the night here. Be ready to travel in the morning."

I fell to my knees and began screaming. I couldn't control my voice, the words, the tears, the anguish; they poured out of me. "You have to let us go. You have to. You have to. We can't return to Kabul. They'll kill us. They'll murder Padar."

I was so weak I couldn't lift my head. I don't know how long I pleaded with him, but he stood over me in silence while I stooped on my knees, wailing with every bit of strength in my being. When I fell into convulsive weeping, he turned to the door and closed it hard behind him. The latch fastened on the other side. I remained on that floor for hours before my sisters and Padar were able to console me enough to get up onto the wooden bench. I laid my head in Padar's lap, and I finally drifted off into a hazy sleep.

18

INSHALLAH

Sometime in the night, a guard opened the door, and Padar helped me to the restroom on the concourse. I went in with Laila and Zulaikha. We relieved ourselves, then washed our faces, and cleaned ourselves as best we could. My face had streaks from crying so hard. My dress was dirty from kneeling on that filthy floor. I rearranged my clothes the best I could to be presentable. Followed closely by the airport police, Padar led us to a restaurant that was open, and he purchased some rice and chicken. A guard stationed himself outside the restaurant.

I ate slowly, thinking of what it would be like arriving in Kabul. I could muster few feelings about returning. My crying had drained everything out of me. I felt like melting right through the plastic bench.

"How can they do this to us?" Laila finally asked, breaking the silence. None of us wanted to bring up the dismal subject of our deportation.

Padar ate rather languidly, not at all in a hurry. "There are always reasons to hope for the best to happen, children. Remember that. We are in the hands of Allah."

Hands of Allah. Mina is also in the hands of Allah.

"Do you remember the poem by Hafiz?" he said.

Laila rolled her eyes. "Which one. You've told us hundreds."

"Ah." He smiled. "It's called 'Out of This Mess.'"

We all shook our heads. I could not recall it. Here in this cold café in the airport concourse, he lifted our spirits, reciting with his deep and resonant voice. He recited a poem about being humble and asking God for guidance and help. It gave me a sense of security.

My sisters and Zia laughed. I didn't understand why they were laughing; maybe because we'd been through so much already. I felt stiff inside, and trying to laugh felt like peeling the scab off a fresh wound.

"I don't see how being humble is going to get us out of this mess," Zulaikha said.

"One never knows," he said.

I admired that he always seemed, in these difficult moments, to keep things in perspective. His strength in God gave me strength to believe, even though at times I had grave doubts, that I was in the palm of my maker, and he was holding me there. My fatigue had not lifted, and my body struggled between sleep and panic. But the fear of being forced to return to Kabul had lifted. I had no way of knowing what would happen, but there had to be a way out of this mess.

After we finished, a guard escorted us to the gate of the Pakistan International Airlines flight that would take us back to Islamabad. We tried to make ourselves comfortable in the hard plastic seats of the waiting area. I must have dozed off for a few hours, because when Laila shook me awake with a yank of my arm, the room was flooded with early-morning light.

I rubbed my eyes. The sky outside the large windows overlooking the tarmac had brightened with a new day. Padar seemed optimistic this morning. As if help would show up from somewhere.

"Enjeela, look." Laila tugged on my arm again.

A few feet away, near the row of seats adjacent to the concourse, the polished policeman who had spoken to us in that room stood talking to Padar.

"Come on." I rose, and we sidled up next to Padar. I slipped my hand into his, and he clenched his warm palm around mine.

The policeman held a fistful of plane tickets. He tried to hand them to Padar, but Padar held his free hand up, palm out, not willing to take them.

"Listen, Officer, we are Muslim, and we need to pray. My family always attends morning prayers. You must let us go to the mosque."

For the first time, the put-together policeman appeared a little confused about what to do. He looked down at me but wouldn't meet my eyes.

"It's not right that you refuse us. I have taught my children always to pray, and here we come to your country—"

"I have not refused you," he said with a crisp tone. He glared at Padar. "I have not said what I will do." He glanced up the concourse and turned half away from us with his arms folded tight against his chest, as if he looked for an answer from somewhere. "You want to pray, then you shall pray. But I insist you take these." He handed the tickets over, and Padar took them. Then he handed over some bills. "This was left over from your purchase. I am expecting you and your family to be on that flight today at noon." He turned to Padar. "There will be people expecting to greet you in Kabul. Do you understand me, Mr. Ahmadi?"

"Perfectly."

"I will escort you to the taxi stand. The Baitul Mukarram mosque is a few miles from here. It is a most magnificent complex of buildings, one that often swallows people whole who do not know it well. But I'm certain a man of your intelligence will find his way around." His stiffness seemed bred into him. He turned and marched away.

"Quick, gather your things," Padar said to us. "Hurry, hurry." We all ran to our things. I hoisted up my small suitcase and hitched up my backpack, slipping into the straps.

"Hold hands," he commanded. He took mine, Zulaikha clasped my other one, and we descended an escalator, turned to the luggage area, and headed toward the glass doors leading to the street. The police colonel waited for us at passport control, at the very same booth of the big guard who had assaulted us so viciously yesterday afternoon.

When the officer appeared, the guards snapped up, standing at attention. He waved us to the front of the short line. We came up behind him.

"They are leaving," he said, a stout look on his face. "They are going to Baitul Mukarram for morning prayers."

"Yes, Colonel." The guard stood aside to let us through. Padar stationed himself across from him, and we passed between the two men, who never ceased eyeing each other.

Before Padar passed through, the colonel spoke, his dark eyes set on us. "You will return for the flight, Mr. Ahmadi, inshallah."

"Yes, Colonel, inshallah."

After Padar stepped a few feet beyond the customs booth, he turned back, held his hand over his heart, and said, "As-salaam alaikum."

"Wa alaikum as-salaam." The police colonel pivoted briskly and headed back up the concourse. We hustled out the glass doors into the golden sunlight. The morning air smelled of exhaust from the idling taxis and buses, with a noticeable tinge of freedom around the fringes of the cool air.

The Baitul Mukarram mosque was a white slab of marble that rose prominently from the earth and shimmered in the morning light. It was one of the largest mosques in the world, and it sat in the middle of a teeming Dhaka. Padar explained that it was constructed as a cube to mimic the famous Kaaba in Mecca. As our taxi from the airport wended its way through the dense traffic of exhaust-spewing trucks, endless cars, rickshaws, and numerous oxen carts, the white cube continued to rise above all of the other buildings and loomed dominant in the sky as the taxi drove up to the massive east entrance. It was one of the most beautiful mosques I'd ever seen.

My sisters and I retrieved our chadors from our backpacks and covered ourselves. The driver stopped far down the curb where a space opened up, and we climbed out. Padar paid the fare, and we all lugged our suitcases up the walkway. A wide marble courtyard sprawled out from the entry arches and led to the interior prayer spaces.

We were soon enveloped in a crowd heading into prayer. Men and women mostly wore shalwar kameez and all the women wore chadors, even the children. The cube itself was nine or ten stories high, and the entrance arches were halfway up the face of the stone edifice. An attendant pointed to where we could leave our luggage. The women streamed to one side, the men to the other.

"Meet me right back here at the pillar by your luggage when prayers are over," he said, pointing out the spot. "Don't leave the mosque without me." He stared right at me. I promised him I wouldn't. "It doesn't matter how long you have to wait for me, don't move. We're safe inside here. No one will bother us. Not even the police. Do you understand?" We all answered yes. He let us go, and my sisters and I headed off with the other women to pray.

We spread our prayer mats behind rows of women reciting their prayers. I knew mine by heart and went through them quickly. As I prayed, I remembered a Hafiz poem Padar always recited.

Pray
Somewhere in this world—
Something good will happen.

I recited this poem in my head all the way through the service. Soon women rose to their feet and began rolling up their prayer mats to leave. Working our way through the stiff crowd, holding hands, we found the pillar, where we waited for Zia and Padar.

Worshippers poured through the exits to the east, the north, and the south. Padar and Zia emerged, and we followed Padar out onto the large marble veranda that swept around the building. People lounged around in groups, talking and waiting. He led us to gardens made of wide lawns and roses and bushes of every kind, meticulously trimmed and maintained. We strolled along the paths until we found a stone bench by a fountain, where I sat with my sisters. Zia and Padar sat cross-legged on the grass in front of the pool of water at the fountain's edge, and we ate the snacks we'd stowed in our backpacks the night before. The trilling water hitting the stone soothed us. I felt myself unwind a bit. The tranquility of the moment belied the agony I had felt just hours before.

"The colonel wanted us to return, didn't he?" I asked.

"Yes, he did," Padar said. We all looked up as a knowing smile crept across his face. "Inshallah—if Allah wills it. God often puts these choices before us. I don't believe for a moment that it is the will of Allah we return to Kabul to be handed over to godless murderers."

"If we change our mind, we change our life," I said, repeating something that he had recited to us many times.

"Bravo, my little poet," he said, smiling at me.

The only sound in the garden was a gurgle that I could have sworn turned into laughter that spread across the entire area. The air suddenly became light and sweet-smelling.

"If you look for love and hope in this world, you will find it. Look around you. Look where we have ended up." He spread his hands out wide to indicate that we should take in the breadth of the garden, as if this ordeal was all part of some grand scheme designed so we could witness this patch of serene beauty. Always a silver lining in Allah's mysterious ways. That same hand that slaps down some, blesses others.

"Are you aware that gardens such as these are constructed in a certain pattern?"

"Like a poem," Laila said.

He nodded. "In a way. These gardens are said to resemble the pattern of heaven."

I took in the plants and trees and lawns with a more scrutinizing gaze. I didn't see any pattern that told me anything I could identify specifically as heaven, except the flowers smelled fresh, birds sang in the peaceful surroundings, and it was quiet and safe. If quiet and peace and a sense of safety was heaven, then this place resembled it in that familiar way. But it was Padar who had figured out how to get us here.

We rested there talking for a long while until he led us through the gardens, pointing out the different plants and trees, strolling by the many fountains that dotted the green lawns. Before long, the muezzin's call to prayer rang out over the grounds. We returned for afternoon prayers and then met up again at the same pillar.

"Do you think the police are looking for us?" Laila asked.

Padar shook his head. "I don't think they care to, really."

"I'm hungry," Laila said. We all agreed it was time for a regular meal. Padar led us out to the veranda again to an elevator. As it went below the mosque, the doors opened up into a shopping mall. We were barely out of the elevator when we were hit with the strong aroma of curry. We found a restaurant and feasted on fish curry with eggplant and apple; and spicy chicken, black rice, and fried vegetables; and *khejur gur*, a sweet dessert made from date-palm sugar. After eating, we all sat back and let out a sigh of pleasure. We strolled the underground mall full of shops selling every type of clothing, cookware, electronics, bicycles, jewelry, and more. It made me homesick, but in a pleasant way. In some imperceptible way, we were journeying closer to what we all wanted, and here were shops full of reminders of good things to come.

The call to evening prayers was broadcast throughout the mall, and we followed the crowd upstairs to pray. Afterward we met Padar and Zia again near the same pillar, and this time Padar guided us toward the north exit, on the other side of the huge mosque. We mingled with the crowd flowing out of the mosque, and once near the curb outside,

Padar hailed a taxi, and we all climbed in. No one had followed us. We were free to travel. Padar was right again that it was not Allah's will we return to Kabul. Inshallah.

The driver took us across the city to a hotel, where we dragged our luggage into the lobby and waited while Padar checked us in. Upstairs, the three girls had our own room, and the men had an adjoining room.

In the hall by our doors, Padar handed over a key to Laila. "Let's get cleaned up. I'll order some food in about an hour."

It was after seven that evening when we all met in Padar and Zia's room. Padar slouched in a chair by the window overlooking the city, which had turned to a sea of sparkling lights—red, white, green, and flashing neon of every shade.

I sat on the bed, eating from a plate of rice and chicken. We had just eaten a few hours before, but the tension must have made us all ravenous. Padar flipped through a small address book. He puffed on his pipe as he worked through his book.

"What're you looking for?" I asked him.

"The number of an old friend. I'm pretty sure he lives here now, or somewhere around here."

"Who?" Laila asked.

He rested the small book on his lap. "You may remember him. He came to some of the embassy parties I used to host at our home. Ram Ispahani."

There had been so many diplomats and businessmen and politicians that visited our home over the years. I didn't remember anyone by the name of Ram. With a name like that, he had to be Indian or Bangladeshi.

"Was he a diplomat from the Indian embassy?" I asked.

"No, he was a pilot."

"Did he work with Saleem?" Laila asked. "I think I remember him, the tall, handsome man with a mustache? He used to fly Indira

Gandhi to Kabul. He would come to our house while Gandhi attended meetings."

"That describes a lot of men," Zulaikha said.

We all laughed because it was true.

"Is he going to fly us somewhere?" Laila asked.

"Not likely. But he can drive us in his car," Padar said as he rose and went to the phone on the small desk and dialed a number. He spoke to the man that answered in the most genial way, catching up. They talked like long-lost friends or brothers. We watched TV for a while, then he had us go next door and get ready for bed. I dragged myself through changing and washing up. None of us had slept much at the airport, and the day had wrung all the energy out of us.

Sleepy and ready to climb into bed, I heard a knock on the adjoining door between the rooms. "Girls," Padar called. "Come in here a minute. I want you to meet someone."

Dressed in our nightgowns, we slipped into robes, and Laila opened the door. In the next room we met Ram Ispahani. He was a strikingly handsome Indian man, dark-skinned and tall, with a bushy, gray-flecked mustache. His salt-and-pepper hair was trimmed short, and he wore jeans and a sport shirt. He had the brightest dark eyes—they were intelligent, alert with a glint of humor. He sat on the edge of one of the beds.

"Salaam," he said to us. We each greeted him, and he gave us the warmest smile. He then turned to Padar, who slumped in the chair by the window. "Of course I will help," he said. "We will leave in the morning, early. I know just the place we can cross. I'll have you on the train to New Delhi by lunchtime."

A short while later, back in our room, we snuggled under clean, warm blankets and crisp sheets. Through the closed door, we could hear them laughing and talking loudly. The men were deep into their plans or having a great time reminiscing, or both.

"I can't believe it. As soon as one plan falls apart, Padar just comes up with another one," I said.

"This one better work," Zulaikha said. "I hated getting nearly beat up by those airport guys. They were horrible."

"Freaks," Laila said.

"Gorillas," I said. We all started laughing.

As we quieted down, I murmured, "Tomorrow will be different." But I was speaking to myself. Both of my sisters were asleep. I closed my eyes. We were going to India. I whispered under my breath: "Inshallah."

———

Passing through the center of Dhaka even at an early hour was no easy task. Just after dawn, the sidewalks were filled with women in saris and men in jeans trudging off to work. The streets were jammed with rickshaws: two-wheeled carts pulled by boys on bicycles. All of them were decorated as stunning works of art, in bright luminescent reds, fluorescent greens, yellows, and blues. We turned down a street and were met with a horde of rickshaws. We moved slowly through the traffic, past glass-walled buildings, cement towers, apartment houses. The city went on forever.

We left the city to the west along route N5, a well-paved two-lane highway that passed through several smaller cities, each with elaborate temples and mosques, industrial buildings, office buildings, and power plants, before reaching the countryside where we would cross the two-mile-wide Padma River.

Ram planned on taking us to Kolkata, which was in West Bengal state, India. It was a long day's drive from Dhaka, and we should be there shortly after dinnertime. He thought we would easily blend in with the native Indians because of our dark skin. We'd be able to purchase train tickets for the ride to New Delhi. Ram talked so confidently; it seemed so simple.

As the day unfolded into a blazing morning, it became clear that Bangladesh was very different from Afghanistan. Everywhere, we passed green fields, stands of palm trees, and thick forests. We crossed small rivers and creeks, and ponds were everywhere. The fields of crops—corn, wheat, hay, alfalfa, rice—were in full bloom. Padar recognized all of them and pointed them out as we sped by. Cows roamed the fields, and Ram explained that in parts of Bangladesh, and more so in India, cows were sacred and were not to be eaten.

It must have been before noon that we turned off the main highway onto rough back roads. Some were no more than wheel tracks as we traveled deeper into the countryside. I was beginning to feel sick to my stomach. Ram stopped the car, and Padar had me sit up front with him. He held my head as I tried to hold back the nausea.

The two men chatted and bantered as we drove. Ram was full of stories about people I didn't know, dignitaries he had flown all over Asia and Europe.

We now passed farm houses and villages that were more primitive, simple mud huts with shaggy thatched roofs. When I couldn't hold back my nausea any longer, Ram pulled over and I threw up on the side of the road. Padar held on to me as I leaned over a grassy ditch.

When we were back to driving, Ram soon came to a crossroads. He turned left and far down, I could see a building in the middle of the road.

"There's the border crossing," Ram said. "It's very isolated. Once we're across here, we will join back up with the road to Kolkata."

He rolled the car slowly up to the gate and stopped a couple of yards from it. He turned off the ignition. Our car sat in the middle of the dusty road. In the silence, we stared out the window at the guard post. A border soldier in rumpled camouflage fatigues with a rifle slung over his shoulder sauntered into the sunshine to inspect our car.

"You kids stay here," Padar said. "We'll be right back."

"This won't take long," Ram said.

They both got out, closed the doors, and walked slowly up to the guard, who had now been joined by another one. Both of them had rifles. We rolled down the windows to listen. At first they simply talked, Ram gesturing with his hands, the guards shaking their heads. A third uniformed man came out of the building and stood with the men.

They asked Ram and Padar many questions and gestured toward the car. We watched through the window as the questioning became more intense, with one of the soldiers stepping close to Ram, who must have felt threatened, because he moved back. Padar spoke very little and only in reply to the guards' questions. Finally, Ram shouted something back at one of the men in uniform. The soldier struck Ram on the side of the head with his fist. Ram staggered back and fell to the ground.

"What are they doing?" Zia shouted. Laila told him to shush, and we all sat up, clenching the seat backs and each other, watching more intently through the windshield.

One of the guards began hitting Padar. I screamed, and we all jumped out, running toward the fight. By the time we reached him, he and the soldier were trading blows. I feared they were going to shoot him, he fought back so ferociously. Ram and Padar were both fighting with the soldier. Finally, an officer stepped forward and stopped the fight.

"That's enough. That's enough."

The fighting stopped, and they backed off. Padar and Ram stood their ground.

The soldier stood close by us. He waved his hand back toward Bangladesh. "Go back to where you came from. Don't try to enter India again, or we will arrest you all."

Ram and Padar turned to the car and motioned for us to follow them. Ram limped slowly, trying to catch his breath. Padar's nose was bloody, and red rivulets ran down his cheeks, over his lips, and down his chin.

Once we were all back in the car, I retrieved a cloth from my back-pack and gave it to Padar to clean his face. He held it to his bleeding nose. We sat in the silent heat for a few minutes until Ram had gathered himself enough to start the car. He turned it around and slowly headed back the way we had come. We settled into the back seat quietly; it wasn't the time to pepper Padar with questions.

We drove for a while. "I will find another way," Ram finally said, as if he had been thinking things over carefully. "Do you want to try again?"

"Of course," Padar said from beneath the cloth, without a moment's hesitation. "My children are survivors. One thing I can tell you, no one can stop them. If the whole world fell apart, there would be four survivors—my children. I'll give up before they do."

In the back seat, we glanced at each other in amazement. If he was disappointed or discouraged by the fight with the border guards, he didn't show it. He was more determined than ever to get to India. Somehow, someway, we were going to see Mommy. It was our destiny.

19

GARDEN OF DREAMS

We were parked outside a low-slung village market in the afternoon heat. After leaving the border, Ram had made his way off the dirt roads back to the main highway to a village with markets, mosques, and office buildings. We were beginning to sweat in the back seat as we waited for Padar and Ram to return. They had disappeared inside the market at least a half hour before to purchase some food and sodas. The street was busy with traffic and activity—small cars, trucks, and the occasional rickshaw with passengers. We'd been warned not to leave the car, so we bided our time watching the people pass by.

The two men came out carrying what they had gone in for. Back in their seats, they passed out cold sodas and a local flatbread sandwich, a chicken shawarma. We were famished.

While we ate, we listened to Ram and Padar discuss what they'd learned in the market. Evidently, they'd been asking the locals questions about the best way to cross the border.

"It's just not safe to cross here," Ram said. "Too much violence lately." We heard him retell what the shopkeeper had told him. Just last year, not far from the Bangladeshi border, over in West Bengal, the locals had risen up and massacred many illegal immigrants. Now the border guards stopped everyone to demand to see their papers, even farmers crossing their fields, since many of the farms ran right up to the border markers, and some lay on both sides of the boundary. Indians in West Bengal were angry at the flood of illegal immigrants, so intruders were often harshly sent back across the border, sometimes beaten, other times robbed, or worse.

"Someone inside the store said the Indian Border Security Force had shoot-to-kill orders," Ram said. "I have not heard of it, but it could be true."

"I'm not taking any risks with the kids," Padar said. "There has to be someplace safe to cross. The border is very long."

"There is. Don't worry, my brother, we will find it." Ram started the car and returned to the highway. At dusk we pulled into a city along the banks of the Padma River, the wide one we had crossed earlier that morning by ferry. The smell of the river was strong, of fish and dampness.

We stayed in a motel that night. Sisters in one room and Zia and the men in the other. We gathered in the men's room to eat, huddled on one of the two beds in the room. Ram sat at the small desk, speaking on the phone in hushed tones for quite some time. After he hung up, he and Padar went into the adjoining room and closed the door.

When they returned an hour later, Padar retrieved his backpack. He opened it on the bed and took out several bundles of bills that were tightly wrapped in rubber bands. He counted out thousands of rupees and handed all of it over to Ram, who stuffed the big rolls into his own backpack. Then Padar stood up as if he had an announcement.

"Gather around, children," he said to us.

We sat up straight, dinners on our laps.

"Ram is going to take us to Nepal."

"What?" Laila said.

"We've worked out a plan that will get us legally across the border into India, but we have to be in Nepal as tourists in order to cross over safely," Ram said.

"Where's Nepal?" Zulaikha said.

"This is the safest way," Padar said.

"But where's Nepal?" I asked. "Is it far from here?" I had heard of the country of high mountains, but I had no idea how we would get there or how far away it was. It seemed that every day, we got farther and farther away from India and Mommy. I sprang to my feet on the floor between the two beds; my dinner, which had been balanced in my lap, sprayed across the floor. "We're never going to see Mommy. Never! Never! Never!" I couldn't stop gushing out my angst. "We're going to get arrested. Deported. Or shot. They're going to kill us."

Two strong hands gripped my shoulders. "Enjeela! Enjeela! Stop this now." Padar knelt down in front of me. When I caught my breath, his dark-brown eyes were staring deep into mine.

"Listen to me right now," he said sternly. "We are going to your mommy. Do you understand me?" His voice was strong, reassuring, and certain. "I guarantee that with my life. We will get there."

We stared at each other for a long moment.

"Do you believe me?" he asked, his voice warm and urgent.

I bit my lip. His eyes pleaded with me to trust him. "Yes."

He pulled me to him in a hard embrace. He spoke into my ear in a soothing manner. "I promise you, we will reach her. It may take us a few more days. A few more weeks. But we will get there. Trust me, my love. Trust me."

My rigid body dissolved into his. I knew he meant every word of his promise.

I sat in the dark room at Padar's feet while he sat on the edge of one of the beds and puffed on his pipe. Zia snored lightly, sprawled out on the other bed beside us. My sisters were asleep in the adjoining room.

Ram had left to do some business surrounding our new plan to travel to Nepal.

Padar leaned forward, resting his elbows on his knees. He smelled of tobacco and aftershave.

"You know, during my escape, Masood often spoke of you, Enjeela."

Oh great. I was sure Masood had complained about me—a troublemaker, all over the place; at times, I didn't listen to him.

"He told me of your bravery. How you helped that man who was being beaten by the soldiers on the bus. He said he called you his little lion."

Something deep inside me began to warm; it flooded my stomach, my chest, and sent ripples of strength up my neck. Masood had said that to me often, and it had made me feel strong.

"You were always ready to fight to get to your destination."

My cheeks flushed.

"Yet you always doubt yourself. And that is not good. I've seen that in you since your mother left to have her surgeries." He leaned back and took a long pull from his pipe.

"She never said when she was returning."

He nodded, but I wondered if he truly understood. "Yet you wonder if you had done anything differently, if she wouldn't have left you."

"Sometimes, yes, I think that."

He nodded again, as if he were sifting my thoughts for some malady he could cure. "You want to know why we are here, and your mother, brother, and sisters are in India?"

"Don't you wonder that sometimes?"

He shook his head. "This situation, I know, is difficult to understand, but I believe it is as the poet says it is: 'This place where you are right now, God circled on a map for you.'"

"God means for us to be here, suffering?"

"He does not mean for people to do terrible things. Soldiers kill and murder and do harm because they are evil. But God knows we have come to this place, that we have things to learn so we can grow as human beings, as spiritual creatures. It's not enough to have all the things you wish for to make us comfortable. We must have much more."

God circled this village on the map and said I must come here—I didn't understand.

"You have a question for me, don't you?"

"Is she okay?"

"Do you mean did she survive her surgeries? Yes. She is recovering well. But it has been many months since we have spoken. Yet I'm certain she is okay." He took his pipe from his mouth, smoke curling upward. "You are afraid she might not love you anymore, aren't you? That when you see her, she might not remember you."

"I don't remember what she looks like anymore. Her face has faded from my memory. I remember Vida's and Shapairi's, but not hers. It's scary."

He pointed the mouthpiece of his pipe at me. "Have I ever taught you 'How Birds Fly'?"

I shook my head. He spoke most often to us in lines of poetry, but this felt different, as if he saved this one for me alone:

> Once in the past, I asked a bird
> "In what way do you fly
> in this gravity of wickedness?"
> She responded,
> "Love lifts my wings."

He puffed away for a long moment, staring at me with his dark eyes, waiting for a sign from me that I understood what he might be teaching me. Finally, he broke the silence in his softest voice. "You must observe nature carefully, Enjeela. Most people think birds fly because of the wind. What they don't see is that there is something more powerful than the wind that lifts them. That is what lifts us as people as well."

I wasn't certain of his meaning.

"Everything I do for you and the others is for love. Everything your mother does for her children is for love, even taking care of herself so she will be alive for all of us. It's this love that lifts us during dark times like this."

I wanted to nod my head that I understood, but I didn't have the certainty he did. I knew that he loved me, and if that was all I had, that would be enough.

———

The next day Ram drove us along the banks of the Padma River, which meandered west, then north. We were headed toward the far northern tip of Bangladesh, where the border with India and Nepal dissolved into a series of enclaves, and the border became fuzzy in places, according to Ram.

"The Padma River is called the Ganges once you cross the border in India." Ram nodded toward the wide, muddy green river that flowed by us as we headed north. Bangladesh was so lush, with well-watered fields and forests. He told us stories of how the Hindus came down every spring to the banks of the Ganges, a river they revered as holy, to wash in a ceremony that cleansed them of ten of their sins.

"What happens to the rest of their sins?" Zia asked.

"If God only forgave ten sins at a time, we would all be in trouble," Padar said.

We crossed over where two rivers met and followed the N5 north beside the Brahmaputra River. We wound through countryside of farms and ponds, across narrow bridges over streams, past more ponds and farms up into a finger of Bangladesh that pushed deep into a corridor of Indian territory. We stopped that night in a very tiny village. The crickets had come out, and the moon rose yellow and full over the distant trees as we made our way to our rooms. Our rooms were spare, with simple beds and a chair on a threadbare carpet that looked ancient. The walls had once been a bright blue but had now faded into a powder blue.

"We are near the border," Ram said, as he sat on a flimsy chair against the wall. All of us kids were together on the bed, eating a bland chicken-and-rice dish off paper plates. We washed it down with gulps from bottles of water.

"The border with Nepal?" Zia asked.

"Yes and no," said Padar.

We all turned to him, wondering how it could be both near and not so.

He chuckled lightly. "You see, the borders between Nepal and Bangladesh become very close in a few places, separated only by a small gap of India, so Nepal and Bangladesh are only a few miles apart."

"A gap?" Laila said, her voice rising in incredulity.

"Yes," Padar said. "It's a small gap of Indian land that's not guarded by their soldiers. So it will be easy for us to pass over it into Nepal."

"Do not worry," Ram said, as if he were discussing the possibility of rain. "It is not far."

"Just a few miles," Padar said. All of our eyes turned to him on the other side of the room. It was obvious that these two men weren't telling us everything. We were getting only the bits they thought we needed to know.

"Depending on the route we take," Ram said.

"What possible routes are there?" I said. "I climbed a mountain once to escape Afghanistan. It was one of the highest in the Hindu Kush."

"I've climbed that same mountain, young lady," Padar said, smiling. "This will be easier, I assure you."

"Does that mean we will be climbing a mountain?" Zia said.

Both men were concealing a smile. "It won't be easy, but it won't be too hard," Ram said. "You'll see. Now let's do something fun tonight."

"Let's have a poetry session," Padar said, his glee evident. Laila and Zulaikha groaned.

"Let's play fis kut," Zia said.

"I'll keep score," Ram said. "We have all night. We can sleep tomorrow."

All that night, we played cards while Ram kept score and Padar played his usual cagey game of outwitting us. Ram told one joke after another, and we laughed and played deep into the night. We were happy and warm and full of food, and we were healthy and ready for what was next. To reach India.

———

The next day we left our rooms after darkness had fallen. We carried only our backpacks. Padar had allowed us one change of clothes and a jacket. Our dress shoes and new dresses and bangles and earrings we had to leave behind. The rest of the space in our packs was for his stash of money. We all wore sneakers, just like we had when we escaped Afghanistan.

A man we'd never seen before pulled up in Ram's car. He was a local, whom Ram had hired to help us. Ram sat in the front while Padar squeezed into the back seat with us. The driver took us deep into the country along stark dirt roads, through rustic farms, along barbed-wire fences that, we were told, were guarded by Indian border patrol on the other side. We were tense, trying to not lean too hard into each other as the car jostled over potholed and rutted roads. We finally came to a wide space, where fields of grass straddled either side of the road. The driver stopped the car, shut off the ignition, and doused the lights.

Darkness blotted out the world until our eyes adjusted to the starlight streaming in through the windows. Not one light in any direction, except the glow of the moon that now hung low on the far horizon. The driver pointed across the field to our left.

Ram motioned for us to get out. We stood in the darkness in the middle of the road, jackets on, backpacks cinched onto our bodies. We lined up single file. First the guide, then Ram, followed by me, then my siblings, then Padar in the rear. I positioned myself right behind Ram. I wanted to see where we were headed. The guide didn't use a flashlight or an electric torch; he knew the path by memory.

He led us through the woods on the other side of the clearing. I tried to stay a few hand widths behind Ram; if I lagged or got distracted and fell off the pace, Laila, who was behind me, would run into me and push me ahead. I wanted desperately to see through the trees to where we were headed, but I stayed focused on Ram.

We straggled single file out of the woods into another glade that glinted under the moonlight. The scraping of Zia's jeans as he walked told me he wasn't far behind me somewhere in the dark. The grass bent under a mellow breeze. We marched through the damp grass over uneven ground. The guide hesitated. We all halted and looked up from our footing and found we were at the rear wall of a weathered barn. I could smell the cows and chickens. This place wasn't abandoned.

Ram crouched and waited for all of us to gather around him.

"The border is a ways away. We will go ahead to check the border post to make sure that it's clear," he said in a whisper, gesturing toward the guide. "You will wait for us inside the barn."

Ram and the guide led us into the barn. They showed us to a corner that was dry and filled with prickly hay. "Rest here. We'll be back."

The two men disappeared, leaving us with a few flashlights. Beyond the pale glow of our small lights, we could hear the animals but not see them.

"I hope we don't have to stay here too long," Laila said. "This place stinks."

I flashed my light down to the far end of the long barn. Several horses stamped on the hard earth in their stalls. Chickens strutted about, and the dark rafters seemed to creep with birds and critters.

Padar found some straw and laid it out for us. The smell was horrible, as if the barn had not been cleaned in months; I was sure there was a massive pile of manure stacked up somewhere deep in the dark recesses of this ancient building. The hay was dry, and we lay down and covered ourselves with our jackets and waited.

"We will only be here for a few hours," Padar said.

A few hours stretched into the entire night. Ram and the guide did not return until daybreak. We stirred from our cold sleep, rubbing our eyes and stretching our stiff limbs.

"The border is about a two-hour hike from here," Ram said, kneeling at the edge of the hay we had used for a bed. "I stayed there all night, waiting for the guards to leave. There's no permanent guard booth, so they park a jeep and sit and smoke in the woods. A couple of miles beyond the border is a tiny village we can hide in once we make it across."

Ram had brought food back with him. He told us it was important for us not to be seen outside during the day. Eating inside the barn was very difficult. The constant smell of manure stripped me of my appetite. It made us all grumpy at each other.

"Are we going to have to stay here again tonight?" Zia asked.

"We've come this far," Padar said, a real gentleness in his voice. "We must be patient."

When dusk came, we all rushed outside to relieve ourselves.

Zia and I stood in the dark shadow of the barn as Zulaikha and Laila went off behind a bush.

"You smell like shit," Zia said to me, not at all kidding.

"You smell like you've been rolling in horseshit your whole life."

He pushed me away from him with a laugh. Just then, Zulaikha and Laila returned across the field.

"Are you two fighting again?" Laila asked.

"He doesn't want to be near me," I said, "because I might make him smell better."

Zulaikha rested her hands on her hips. "You both smell like you've been rolling in horseshit."

The way she spoke so seriously, as if we weren't well aware of that very fact, made me laugh. Soon Laila and Zia joined in. Zulaikha always seemed like the last to get a joke.

Padar and Ram joined us from another part of the field they had disappeared to. "Children, keep your voices down," Ram said. "You'll spook the horses. It will give them gas, then we'll all smell like fertilizer forever!"

Soon we were all making too much noise, so Padar herded us back inside. The fresh air outside made us only more miserable when we stepped back into the barn. Ram left after dark with the guide to search out the border post again. If he was back before midnight, we would leave; otherwise we would stay. When he didn't return by twelve, we settled in.

This was our routine for several more days, with Ram and his guide friend returning in the early morning with food and the news that we might be able to leave with the coming dark. Padar had fashioned a table in the middle of the barn to make our life a little more comfortable. We distracted ourselves from the smell with games of fis kut, telling jokes, and making fun of each other to blind our noses to the reek while we ate breakfast, lunch, and dinner.

It was on the fifth night that an excited Ram woke us around midnight. "It's time to go. Gather your things."

I rose, fully awake in an instant. We threw on our coats, gathered our things, and headed outside. The weather had turned chilly, and with all the walking across fields covered in dew, we quickly became damp and cold.

In single file, under the moonlight, we silently marched along, keeping close to each other. I followed right behind Ram, who was out in front behind the guide. The local farmer who led us knew this path well. He took us between trees, along the edges of fields, and then across one sparse empty field that had been plowed but lay fallow. The pace was fast and tiring, but I didn't dare complain.

After a couple of hours, we reached a tall stone marker, as tall as the farmer who led us. He knelt by it in the grass, and we did the same. He pointed across to a small cluster of lights in the distance. Ram thanked him, as did Padar. The moon was high now in the night sky, and it lit our way with a soft yellow glow. We followed Ram in silence. It took us another couple of hours to reach the village, which was nothing but a cluster of thatched-roof huts around a courtyard with a well in the middle. The morning twilight steadily lifted as we trod between the huts.

We rested by the well in the early-morning chill. Fog hugged the ground, and we pulled our coats around us in an attempt to stay warm. Our clothes were damp from the fields, and there was nothing to do but squeeze in close to each other to gather some warmth.

Ram left to speak to some of the villagers. When he returned, he showed us to a hut where we could sit by a fire. Seated cross-legged on the ground by the flames, an old woman fed us, and the heat and warm food revived us.

"They have mules here," Ram said, sitting cross-legged next to us.

"I thought it wasn't far to Nepal," Zulaikha said.

"It's closer if we ride than if we walk."

Padar and Ram left to speak to the owner of the mules. A while later they came back with a string of animals, one for each of us. We had finished eating, and the woman drew some water for us to wash our faces and clean up.

A local farmer guided our train of mules. We set off as the early-morning gloom lifted and the sun peeked out from behind a distant snowcapped mountain. We traveled for seven or eight hours along slender paths, through fields, up hills, and down into a narrow valley that led to another village.

It wasn't as difficult a ride as the Hindu Kush climb months before. The terrain was uneven, strewn with rocks and fallen trees, but the mules seemed to know the path well. The day had grown warm, and the very tall mountains were still far north of us, but as it drew into the afternoon, the sun disappeared behind clouds and a chill returned.

At the next village, Ram found us a cabin to lodge in. It was rustic but warm, with a large stone fireplace along one side. Ram and Zia stoked the fire with fresh logs, and the one-room cabin quickly warmed up.

Cleaned up for dinner, we sat around the raging fire and ate our fresh vegetables and rice and drank warm tea that Padar had purchased in the village. We slept easily that night in small and spare but warm beds. Morning came too quickly.

———

"Today we will cross into Nepal," Ram told us as we mounted our mules.

"But we're in India now, why do we need to go to Nepal?" Laila asked.

"It's a much safer route if we go through Nepal," he said.

We set off in the morning mist. We had been traveling north, and the Mechi River was now fragmented from a wide and deep river to a series of rivulets. We rode all morning along a flat plain full of low trees and shrubs. The river itself was a series of streams that meandered across a sandy riverbed that in spring would fill to a great torrent with runoff from the Himalayas off to the far north.

We dismounted at the foot of the makeshift bridge that crossed one of the streams. We all stared at it. Narrow, not more than two feet wide, it was made from woven bamboo shoots, with a railing of bamboo stalks lashed together. It skimmed the surface of the sand banks, floated in the slow-moving streamlets, then back to a sand bank. It stretched like this far across the river to the other side: Nepal.

"It safe. It safe," the man leading the mules said in a language Ram understood. He urged us on with a motion of his hand. Padar and Ram thanked him, and he turned his string of mules and led them away.

"I'll go first," I said, not wanting to waste any more time standing here, worried that the border guards would suddenly show up.

Padar came up right behind me and we crossed together. When the bridge was on the sand, it was firm underfoot, but then once it crossed the water, the bamboo dipped under my weight. We decided it was better to not be close together so that the bridge would hold our weight better. There was no fear it would sink, but our shoes got so wet we may as well have just sloshed through the streams.

Once we were all on the other side, I looked back at our path. We had traveled to the farthest tip of Bangladesh, where a finger of land punched into India along a porous border, and then hiked the thirty to forty miles across fields and into Nepal. All because we wanted to be together as a family. Padar was going to great extremes to bring us together. I thought about his poem of the birds. He was doing all of this for love.

"Come on, let's go," Ram urged. "This is not time for looking back."

We moved along the path that soon came to a paved road. Padar said we needed to go south to the town of Kakarbhitta that straddled the East–West Highway to Kathmandu.

The foothills of the Himalayas were to our right, shrouded in a gray mist that moved along their rugged features; they rose in ranks until they disappeared in the haze. We hiked along a road bordered by green grasslands that riffled in the breeze. The air here smelled so pure, as if it had never been breathed before, and nothing had ever tainted it. Within a couple of hours walking, we reached the small village of Nakalbanda. The main road went right through town, where many of the townspeople rode about on bicycles. All the buildings were made of wood, with steep roofs for shedding snow. The sidewalks were narrow and covered in planks of wood. Ram stopped a man and asked for directions to a café. We entered a room with tables and chairs and a counter case of sweets and sandwiches. A nice lady served us sandwiches and Darjeeling tea from little cups. It was the sweetest, freshest tasting tea I'd ever had. Padar left to find a taxi, and soon we were bundled into an ancient van that had been garishly painted on the outside.

After a fifteen-minute drive, we checked into the Mechi Hotel next door to the main bus terminal in central Kakarbhitta.

We took turns taking showers and cleaning up the best we could, changing out of the clothes we'd slept in for the past week. Padar had us throw them away they were so smelly. At dinner that night, Padar laid out our plans. "From here on out, we are tourists. We do tourist things. I want us to think of this as a short vacation."

Laila laughed. "Are we going to visit all the monasteries?"

"Why not?" he said with a smile.

"What about shopping?" I asked. "Can we buy some clothes?"

"Of course," he said. "We must look like tourists when we pass into India."

"How are we going to get through passport control?" Laila asked.

"You'll see," Ram said. "We won't get into any more fights. I can promise you that."

That was a promise I wanted to hold him to.

———

The bus ride to Kathmandu took us along the East–West Highway that wound through mountain passes, gradually rising higher and higher until the road settled into a deep valley. The city of Kathmandu was laid out in colorful splendor before us, surrounded by hills. In the far distance against the bluest sky were the snowcapped peaks of the

Himalayas that stretched all along the horizon in both directions, one long, jagged ribbon. These were the tallest peaks in the world. It was said they touched the roof of the world, and from here it looked like they did exactly that.

It was late afternoon when we checked into our hotel, the Kathmandu Guest House in the Thamel district of the city. The rooms were neat and clean, painted in blues with yellow accents and bamboo floors, with very clean restrooms. One of our rooms had a kitchen with a stove and a refrigerator.

When we arose the next morning, Ram was gone.

"He went to India to take care of some business for us," Padar said at breakfast. We all peppered him with questions about their plan. He held his finger to his lips. "Quiet, children. You'll know soon enough."

He took us shopping for clothes in Kathmandu Durbar Square. The square was magnificent. The king's palace stood on one edge, shops full of clothes and pottery and artwork and jewelry on the other. Before we went into any of the stores, he warned us that these merchants always had two prices—one for the locals and another for the tourists. He helped me haggle for a good price on a beautiful Nepali sweater, hand-embroidered with colorful flowers.

Padar never carried a change of clothes, so he purchased himself some new pants and a shirt and shoes. My sisters and I each bought a new dress, and Zia bought new shoes.

We strolled the busy streets, taking in the sights like tourists, visiting temples that allowed non-Hindus to enter, running up the steep steps to Swayambhunath Stupa, with its gold-plated gods and multitude of spires. We toured a few palaces and visited the crowded market streets that teemed with shops and stalls. The streets were always crowded with cyclists and backpackers, bicycle rickshaws, and cars.

One afternoon Padar took us to the vegetable market, where he purchased everything he would need to make dinner. He bought some pots and pans, and that evening in the hotel, he cooked for us a dinner like we would have eaten in Kabul.

He taught me to cook chalow with kormas, and kofta, and lamb-chicken kabobs, and Kabuli pulao, and other dishes. We spent the days exploring and spent the evenings cooking and staying up late playing cards.

We had been there nearly a week, and Ram had still not returned. Padar said he would arrive when he was ready and not to worry. It was a rainy day, so we decided to stay in our room and play fis kut while Padar went out for some fresh fruit. It'd been raining all the previous night, and we felt cooped up for the first time since the barn as we sat in a circle on the floor holding our cards.

For the first hour, Zia won every hand, racking up points and ridiculing Zulaikha's play at every opportunity.

"You're cheating, that's why you win so much," she said, holding her hand to her chest so none of us could see her cards.

"I don't need to cheat to beat you." He threw down a trump, gaining more points. "All I have to do is wait for you to make a stupid move."

"Like that one," Laila said, picking up his discard and throwing down a three of a kind.

I laughed. Laila was right; Zia did make stupid moves at times. But I also knew that at one time or another over the last two years, each of us had cheated at this game.

"What are you laughing at?" Zia asked, his face turning a little red, thinking that I might be making fun of him too.

"You're a cheater," I said, pointing at Zia. "You're a cheater." I pointed at Zulaikha. "You're a cheater." I pointed at Laila.

Zia tapped his chest with indignation, his cheeks blanching. "Who, me? I never cheat."

That made me laugh even harder. Laila pushed me over on my back. "You're the biggest cheater of them all."

"And you're all stupid," I said through giggles, "because you don't even know all the ways I win at this game while you're not looking."

Zulaikha threw her cards at me. Then Zia did the same, and frustrated, Laila jumped on me, trying to pin my arms to the floor. "You wretched thing," she said. "I've had enough of you."

"You idiot," I said, trying to push her off me. Zulaikha grabbed one of my wrists so they could hold me down and start slapping me. "Help me, Zia. They're going to kill me." He grabbed Zulaikha's wrist, trying to pry it off me. I screamed when my wrist twisted; Zulaikha screamed; Zia shouted when someone pulled his hair.

Just then the door burst open. And we froze.

"What's going on here?" Padar said. "Get your hands off each other, before I slap them off."

Our wrestling ceased. Laila jumped off me. We all stood facing him.

"Haven't I taught you anything about how to treat one another?" He looked exasperated, disappointed. He set his bags of groceries on the table. He paced for about a minute, then stopped. "Get your coats. I want to show you something."

We gathered ourselves. I put on my new embroidered sweater with the colorful flowers. The rain had tapered off, and we each had an umbrella that kept the gentle sprinkle off us. We followed Padar through the narrow streets that were like canyons, the buildings were so tall. He walked quickly, turning into one plaza that fed into another, where we passed palaces, temples, and street vendors with their wares laid out on the bricks. Padar turned into a building that at first looked like so many of the others—white pillars across the front, steps leading up to a platform; the entrance was flanked by carved stone elephants, a favorite local deity.

"This is the Garden of Dreams," he said.

Up the front walk, it soon became evident this wasn't just another temple. The perfectly manicured lawns were bordered by low shrubs and colorful flowers, with slate walkways that were laid in perfect geometric patterns. This reminded me of the Paghman Gardens in Kabul, one of my favorite places. We entered through the archway at the top of the stone stairs and passed through an iron gate onto a broad walkway. Padar led us beside a lily pond, along a brick walk, past a set of half-circular steps that led down to a grassy amphitheater. A path of stones was set in a lawn that led to a brick-and-glass outdoor café, but we didn't stop for tea. We followed Padar deep into the garden, into an alcove surrounded by a decorative brick wall with coping painted white.

Trees hung over the walls, and neatly trimmed bushes grew along the edges, with a diamond-shaped fountain in the middle, water trickling soothingly out of its top into the placid pool below. It was a lush green oasis of privacy and charm.

Padar motioned for all of us to sit down on one of the white benches. It was hard and cold but none of us complained. He paced in front of us.

"What do you see here," he said, expecting that we would understand the lesson he was to teach us.

"It's quiet," Laila said.

"It's beautiful," Zulaikha said.

I could see that these weren't the answers he was expecting. "Look carefully, children." We each eagerly searched the garden, the peaceful surroundings. This was his way of teaching us about life, but his message was lost on me. "Look at the trees," he said.

"They touch each other," I said.

"Yes, that's right, Enjeela." He motioned toward the two large ones in front of us, where the branches were so close to each other as they reached over the wall, they intermingled. "Do you see them fighting?"

"How can they fight?" Zia said. "They can't even talk."

"They're like a poem, Zia," he said, raising his hand in the air toward them. "Their actions speak to us without words."

"They're symbols," Laila said.

"Of what?" Zulaikha asked.

"They can touch," he said. "Yet they don't fight. They get along."

"So we're supposed to behave like trees," Zia said.

"We're supposed to learn from the trees." He swept his arm around. "Look at the plants, how close they are to each other. Yet they give room for each other. They don't fight or complain. If you look close, you can see love everywhere."

"So we're supposed to just give way to each other," Laila said.

"Yes, that's it." He pointed at her with a genuine enthusiasm. "We're bone of bone of each other. Of all the people we are to trust, it's each other." He waved his hands back up toward the trees. "What you see is what love looks like. They can touch each other, yet they don't irritate or enrage each other. All throughout the world, love speaks to us, what it means to cherish and be kind and to respect each other. If we miss the message, we will get lost. We will lose out on what's important."

That all made sense. Even though we fought like dogs and cats sometimes, I had to think that there was not anyone I was closer to than Zia, Laila, and Zulaikha. It didn't matter that I hardly agreed with them about many things, but I did love them. We were blood. We were family. That was the meaning of this whole journey to India. To be a family. To be together. I saw for the first time the meaning of the trees touching and getting along.

It was dark by the time we made it back to the hotel and to Padar's room. He unlocked the door, and we all piled in. Laila was first, but she stopped cold, as if she'd seen something dangerous. Glancing around from behind her, I spotted across the room the faint glow of a cigarette. Someone puffed on it, making it pulse brighter in the dark. The tobacco smelled familiar.

Padar clicked on a lamp.

"Hello, brother," a smiling Ram said, puffing elegantly on his cigarette as if he'd been relaxing all day, waiting. "Hello, children."

"Ram," I yelled. "Where've you been?"

He nodded toward the table. "Taking care of business so you guys can go home."

On the table was a brown manila envelope. I went to snatch it up, but Padar beat me to it. He opened it and took out five tickets. One for each of us. I took one out of his hands. It was a round-trip train ticket, originating in New Delhi. Laila took one and scrutinized it.

"The ticket from New Delhi to Raxaul, India, was for three days ago," she said. Raxaul was just over the Nepal border.

"That's correct." He pointed at her, his cigarette curling smoke from between his fingers.

"The return tickets are for tomorrow," Padar said.

Ram smiled and took a deep drag. "What's for dinner? We better eat hearty because tomorrow we have a long bus ride to the border."

Zia gave a shout of joy. Laila cheered. Zulaikha smiled and laughed. Padar came over and shook Ram's hand. "Thank you, brother."

Ram's smile twinkled as he took another drag. I couldn't wait to cross over into India. We were family. God had circled this city on the map of my life. The trees got along; they gave way to each other. That's what love looked like. I saw it for myself in the Garden of Dreams.

20

THE ROAD HOME

It was midmorning when we rolled into the border city of Birgunj. From the window of our bus, the Shankaracharya Gate, leading into India, loomed large in front of us as we passed the Birgunj Customs Office, just a half mile from the border. The gate itself, with three-tiered pagodas extending from the top of each pillar, and from the center of the arch, another massive two-tiered pagoda, filled me with awe. Gold-leafed Hindu deities adorned the face of each pillar and the crown of the arch; the deities stared down at us. It was an impressive sight. A welcome sight. A beautiful entrance to the road to New Delhi.

The bus pulled into a dirt lot adjacent to the border. Padar and Ram had rehearsed with us what we were to do—act like tourists who were lined up at the border checkpoint. Our bus was filled with Indian nationals who had been vacationing and shopping in Kathmandu. With our validated round-trip train ticket to New Delhi, we would mingle with the many Indian citizens returning home after a vacation in the stunning mountains of Nepal.

Off the bus, I followed Ram, who surged to the middle of the pack of tourists as we strode toward the border checkpoint. A line of trucks, crossing into Nepal, trundled through the great arch of the Shankaracharya Gate. We headed in the opposite direction, past the arch, toward the border checkpoint. I couldn't help but remember the last time we had approached the Indian border, when Padar and Ram had been beaten by the soldiers. Everything inside me tightened into a knot. A line of tourists formed in front of us as our group advanced toward the guard station. We inched ahead, Laila and Zia right behind me, a step at a time. I peered around Ram, down the line ahead. A soldier leaned out a doorway, taking tickets from the hand of each person as they passed through to India. He would say something to them, return the ticket, and the line would move forward. My heart began to pound. The soldier would see in my face that I wasn't from India and he would stop me, ask me a question in Hindi, which I would know only if I were from New Delhi.

The line crept forward, closer to the guard post. Zia was jabbering about something behind me, but I blocked it all out, focusing on the shuffling of my feet across the hard-packed dirt. It seemed my whole past became one blurry clot of time—all I had thought about for the past four years was getting to India to Mommy. If this scheme that Ram and Padar had cooked up to fool the guards didn't work, I was certain Padar, if he didn't get beaten or jailed, would come up with another plan, one more daring, more audacious, more brazen, because these men in uniform with guns could not defeat our will to be a family again. I fortified myself with these thoughts as I approached the hand that stretched through the doorway, checking tickets.

With every inch forward, I realized that not one person had been turned down. The passage had been peaceful, and there were no nervous families waiting to the side for an uncertain fate. Everyone was being let through. No fighting, no arguing, no threats of going to prison. Still I began to jitter inside, thinking of all the possible things that could go wrong. Ram had told me to give the soldier a big smile, act like I was glad to be going home. To simply nod my head if they asked something. I couldn't help thinking of Padar's bloody nose just a few weeks ago.

Finally, Ram gave his ticket over. He hesitated a moment as the guard reached for it, scrutinized it, then waved him through.

One short stride ahead, and I raised my ticket to the man's outstretched hand. If I smiled, I don't remember consciously doing so. But I must have smiled, because the dark-eyed man simply touched my train pass with his finger, grinned back, and waved at me. I saw his lips move, but I didn't hear his words. I could hear nothing but a rushing sound. I swear I thought I heard the earth creaking on its axis. Zia shoved me from behind, and Ram took my hand and pulled me into India.

"Do you know what he said to you?" he asked me in his cheery way as we strolled away from the border.

I shook my head, too stunned to speak.

"He said, 'Welcome home.'"

———

The swift clacking of the wheels along the steel rails had a hypnotic rhythm that soothed me into a dreamy daze, but I refused to nod off. The lush Indian countryside zoomed by, field by field, village after village. Our roomy private sleeping car on the Raxaul train to New Delhi was luxurious, with soft, cushioned seats, a door that slid closed for privacy, racks above us for what little luggage we carried, and a porter who came around with regularity, selling everything from cigarettes to fresh oranges, pastries, and sandwiches. Padar loaded us up with snacks and fruit, which we devoured while he smoked and laughed. We all laughed, our mouths full, juices from the oranges dripping from our lips. There were no more obstacles in our path to New Delhi, and now we were clipping along toward Mommy. With every puff of his cigarette, Padar's shoulders grew rounder, his smile softer; the gleam in his eyes radiated relief as if a great battle had been won, and the troops who had lived on foreign soil for too long, battling implacable enemies, were finally on the road home.

It was just the five of us now. Ram had seen us to the train station in the town of Raxaul, which was a short bus ride from the border. We all said our goodbyes to him on the platform as we waited for our train to pull in. He was one of the warmest, kindest men I had ever met. He hugged each of us and wished us well and watched us as we boarded, giving us a big wave and smile as the window of our cabin rolled away from the station. I had known him for less than three weeks, but it had seemed much longer, a lifetime of friendship packed into my young memories.

As our car gently swayed west toward the capital, things pent up for so long in each of us unwound in a flight of craziness that we had been reluctant to indulge in since our days in Kabul.

"Did you know," I said to Padar, "that Laila made us drink milk for weeks at a time when we were in that hotel in Peshawar?"

"Weeks?" he said, leaning back jauntily in the corner of the seat. He pulled out his pipe and tapped a pinch of tobacco into the bowl, then lit it.

"She wouldn't give us any money to buy anything, not even a soda," Zia said.

"Hmm," he said, his pipe clacking in his mouth as he chewed on it and puffed. Clouds of sweet-smelling smoke filled the compartment as we went on and on about each other. Laila complained that I had not stopped jabbering the entire journey. That it didn't matter what time of night or day, if I was awake, I was talking. That I never listened to her and was always wandering off, like the time I ran into the forest by myself and they all were frantically looking for me, and Zulaikha had nearly been in a panic that I had gotten lost or kidnapped or even worse, killed by soldiers or wild animals.

We told him story after story as he puffed away on his pipe, taking it all in. He finally spoke up.

"Masood told me quite a bit about you guys," he said.

We all grew silent.

"He said you were vigilant for each other. He said you took good care of each other. Even when Enjeela was bitten by the scorpion, you all rallied around her to make sure she had what she needed. He told me about the little girl in the village—"

"Mina," I interjected.

He pointed the mouthpiece of his pipe at me. "Yes, I believe that was her name. He told me how much you all wanted to save her. It's a shame she didn't have a strong family like you guys do," he said as he rested the mouthpiece of the pipe back on his lips. "That wasn't her fault." He shook his head gently before taking another puff.

"Her family sold her," Zulaikha said. "Sold her!"

"You are very fortunate," he said, glancing at each of us. "Even when you had very little, you had each other."

"We still have each other," Zia said.

That was true. "You have all learned some important things," Padar said. "About yourselves and one another."

"Like what?" I said, always willing to stir the pot of controversy.

"That you can trust each other with your lives. That's why I have fought so hard for us to be together. All we really have in this world is each other."

The train wheels clicked loudly in the space of our silence as we considered this. Our family had been our strength through every difficulty and trial on the road, a sinuous, four-stranded cord that bound us together in strength and love—the whole, far stronger than each of us alone.

The rest of the ride into New Delhi, Padar told us stories, recited more poems, and regaled us with histories of India. It all sounded wonderful, and I wished Mina had been there to feel the comfort of Padar's voice.

―――――

We slept in the fold-out beds of our compartment as the train rumbled through the night. The last thing I remembered before nodding off was Zia snoring softly in the bunk above me. I awoke later in the early darkness, and the rhythmic swaying of the car tried to rock me back to sleep. But I couldn't stop thinking about finally seeing Mommy and the rest of my family.

What would New Delhi be like? What if I didn't like the new house? Or if Mommy just didn't want me around? We could band together and travel back to Afghanistan, couldn't we? We had done it once. Why not twice? The war wouldn't go on forever. My mind continued to run down these roads of speculation until the light of the sunrise streamed through the window, and Zia stepped on my leg as he jumped down from the top bunk.

"Ouch! Watch what you're doing," I said, trying not to wake the others. I pushed his foot off my leg. He leaned down so I could see his face.

"I thought that was the ladder the porter left," he said with his impish grin. "You do make a good stepping stool."

"Shut up."

"You're the one who's making noise," he teased. "You're always making noise, do you know that?" He tried to pinch my arm just to make his point.

"Stop it, you idiot. Leave me alone." I squealed, slapping his hand away and giggling.

"Shhhh," he said, holding a finger to his mouth. "You'll wake everyone." He couldn't hide his smile. He left the compartment to find the bathroom.

I rolled away from Zulaikha in the bed beside me and propped myself up on an elbow. Laila rubbed her eyes in the bed across from me while Padar snored in the bunk above her.

"Why are you so noisy?" Laila said.

"I'm just trying to wake you so you can be mad at me."

"Figures. It worked."

"Can't you be quiet?" Zulaikha said from behind me.

"Hey, Zia stepped on me and it hurt."

"He should have stepped on your mouth," Laila said, holding her hand over her eyes to keep in the darkness.

Zulaikha sniggered. Then I laughed too.

Another day together had begun. We'd soon be eating, then playing cards, telling jokes, and arguing over something minor.

Before lunch we changed trains. We made our way across a crowded platform to a train that would connect to New Delhi. We had seats that faced each other. They were comfortable and easy to doze in. The train made many stops, and as we drew closer to our destination, young people began to board. They played music. Some had brought cassette recorders that blared a wild, exciting sound. The young men all sang along to the bouncy music. One boy even got up in the aisle and danced.

"They are university students," Padar said.

"Did you sing like that when you went to university?" Laila asked.

He puffed on his pipe. A glint of joy came to his eyes as if he had a flash of good memories. He didn't say anything for a long moment, then pointed the tip of his pipe at us. "It's a great time, going to university. Every generation finds their way to have adventures. You'll each have your own experiences."

"Haven't we had enough adventure?" Zulaikha said. "I just want to sleep in one bed for more than a week at a time."

"Is that all you think about," Zia said.

She sneered at him. "If I had my own bedroom, I wouldn't have to listen to you snore."

Padar waved his hand in the air. "Okay, that's enough."

"Do you think we'll have our own bedrooms?" I asked him. He hadn't said much about where Mommy lived. What kind of house she had, or how big it was.

He shrugged. "I've never seen it." He reached into his shirt pocket and pulled out a square of paper with an address on it. "She told me some time ago that it would be large enough for all of us. This is as much an adventure for me as it is for you."

We all grew silent, just as the music and dancing grew louder. I could only think of the house in Kabul and Shura Street before the Soviet tanks occupied the city. Would there ever be a place as pleasant and happy and carefree?

The wheels clacked under our feet as we sped along. The raucous beat, the incessant clapping, and the energetic singing in the aisles created a driving impulse inside me to join in, to forget the fear and uncertainty that had been festering for so long. I remembered the shama, and the peaceful spirit I'd found there deep in the cave. And while this experience on the train was different in kind—joyous and raucous—it was of the same nature: people finding happiness in their lives. We had left so much happiness behind in Kabul, and today's train ride was a portent of gladness to come. I was excited, anticipating what my new life in India would open up to me.

Meanwhile, Padar chewed unconsciously on the stem of his pipe, making a clicking sound that told us all he was deep in thought. He fingered the scrap of paper with the address written on it as he stared out the window.

——

We pulled into the New Delhi Railway Station very late in the afternoon. We stepped off into a tangle of people calling, shouting, searching the crowd for familiar faces. Others hustled their bags or suitcases and packages, some with bundles under their arms, as they raced to make a connection. Children ran and jumped. I heard laughter and crying, and dogs scooted around, dashing between people's legs, hunting for food. Humanity jammed every square inch, so Padar held my hand as we wove through the surging crowd, up the stairs, and through long queues of people waiting for tickets, till we made it outdoors.

Cabs of all sorts—vans packed with people and belongings, brightly painted rickshaws of every configuration with bundles tied to roofs—lined the street. Teens with radios on their shoulders strolled by, music blaring. Padar hailed a green motorized rickshaw, and we all piled in. He showed the driver the address, and the little car lurched forward and merged into the dense traffic.

We drove through New Delhi, taking in the sights. The streets were jammed with cars and rickshaws and bicycles and people on the move. Shoppers darted in and out of stores along the street, carrying packages and bags. The sidewalks were full of displays of fruit and vegetables of every color and size, of clothes on racks, of electronics, toys, and so many people selling things from carts and stands. The city streets teemed with traffic—horns honked, cars sped by, and rickshaws weaved around traffic jams. With my head out the small window, it was easy to notice that not only was India a busy and colorful place, but it smelled different than any place we had been before; spicy curry filled the air. And music was everywhere. It seemed a nation possessed with it. A thrill shot through me remembering all the Bollywood movies I used to watch in the kitchen with Noor. The images of those dancers singing and dancing their way through their troubles came readily to mind. I wanted to jump out and grab some of the excitement.

We passed through neighborhoods full of small shops, clogged with pedestrians, and into sections with tall glass buildings and streets filled with expensive cars.

Padar grew pensive as we traveled the entire length of the city. I knew that when he grew quiet and serious, he was turning over something difficult in his mind. His unlit pipe still clacked around in his mouth. He hadn't seen or talked to Mommy in a few years, just like we hadn't.

After a long drive we turned into a neighborhood that reminded me of the diplomatic section of Islamabad only nicer. All down the wide, tree-lined street, we passed elaborate homes, two- and three-story, surrounded by fences and gates, with emerald-green lawns and colorful flowers. Many had expensive cars in the driveway.

The rickshaw driver stopped in front of an impressive two-story home that had large windows and was surrounded by a white fence. We piled out onto the sidewalk. After unloading our luggage, the driver took off, leaving us alone in the quiet of the peaceful street.

"Where are we?" Zulaikha asked.

"Greater Kailash," Padar said. He nodded at the house in front of us. "This is where your mother lives. It's beautiful, isn't it?"

In many ways it was nicer than our home in Kabul. It appeared to have a lot of bedrooms, with so many windows on the second floor. Padar gazed up at it. He had never told us he had any hesitations about finally seeing Mommy, but as he stood there rubbing his chin, taking in the fine home she lived in, there was a look of concern on his face.

While he stared up at the bright windows reflecting the afternoon light, I surveyed the neighborhood. Down a block, several kids were out in the street, kicking a ball and running, shouting at each other with carefree voices. I began to look around for a pear tree.

With a resigned shrug, Padar said, "All right, let's go." We followed him to the side of the house, where the driveway led up to a wrought-iron gate. Huddled together, we all peered through the iron bars.

Down the cement drive, along the side of the house, a tall, thin woman in an elegant housedress played with a child. My heart thudded at the sight of her wavy dark hair. It was Mommy. She looked healthy and was dressed so primly, just the way I remembered her from Kabul. With her was a lanky girl with straight black hair that swished around as she leapt to catch a big blue ball that the two bounced back and forth.

"Who is that girl?" I whispered to Padar.

"That's Vida," he said, his voice cracking a bit as if he was surprised at how much she had grown. I could hardly believe my eyes. She had been so small the last I had seen her, and now she was a vivacious little girl, so full of life and grown-up.

Just then the girl stopped bouncing the ball and turned toward all of us gathered by the gate as if we were waiting for permission to enter.

"Enjeela?" she cried, and began to run toward us. Mommy turned toward the gate and took us all in, cocking her head as if trying to figure out who this group of disheveled kids was standing at her gate. We had been wearing the same clothes awhile now, and our shoes were caked with dirt. We looked every bit like we'd had many days of hard traveling. She clasped a hand over her mouth, as if to keep herself from crying out.

Vida ran to us, her white dress rippling in the air. "Enjeela." She reached through the bars of the gate to take my hands. The moment our hands touched, every bit of love for her came tumbling back like we'd never been apart.

"Open the gate," I said. She unlatched it, and Padar swung it open. As Vida hugged me, Mommy made her way down the driveway, shuffling as fast as she could. Padar had told us of her heart surgeries, and while she looked healthy, she didn't move very quickly.

"My babies," she said, reaching out to each of us, touching each of us on the face. "My babies," she said again and again. "You're here. I can't believe you're here at last. We've been waiting for you for so long." Her voice, the expression on her face of relief, told me she was so happy to see us. I stood frozen at her words, not expecting anything more from her but wondering how much she remembered of me.

She came back to me and touched my cheek, placing her warm palm to my skin. "Enjeela," she whispered. "You've returned to me." Her touch was warm, comforting, welcoming. I fell into a moment of happiness, like melting inside. I closed my eyes, holding in tears, and held her hand to my cheek. She did remember me.

She brushed my hair down with her other hand, and she and I looked at each other. Her dark eyes glistened as she looked me over. "I've prayed for this, Enjeela. You're finally home."

21

Most Wanted Child

We all followed Mommy inside, where she immediately set to work in the large kitchen, preparing a meal for us all. I stood by, watching her go through cupboards, retrieving utensils and ingredients. I had no idea where anything was. This whole setup was so different from our kitchen in Kabul. I felt like a foreign child in a foreign home.

Ahmad Shah, who stood taller than I remembered, escorted us around the house, pointing out the bathrooms, where they kept the towels, the laundry room. As we strolled through, glancing into the rooms, I remembered Abbas's daughters, Daliyah and Habibah, touring us around their sumptuous home, and Habibah turning to us with her dark eyes and warm way, saying, "Please, make yourself at home." Now Ahmad Shah, with his sparkling black eyes, turned to me, and said those exact same words: "Make yourself at home." I couldn't shake the notion that I was a guest in a settled home life, an intruder in a well-ordered happiness.

Mommy laid out an authentic Indian meal for dinner: chicken masala, aromatic rice, and roti, an unleavened bread made from stone-ground flour. Every flavor was new to me: bright, warm, comforting, and deeply satisfying. We ate in silence, trying to extinguish our hunger built up from so much travel. I ate every bit on my plate and more.

Mommy sat on the other side of the table watching over us. She looked different. I tried to discern how, but I didn't want to stare. Abbas had fed us as lavishly till we felt like royalty, and like him, Mommy sat across from me now, smiling with broad satisfaction.

Soon the meal was finished and the plates cleared. Mommy stood and announced that it was time for us to shower. I'm certain we appeared and smelled the part of weary travelers. The thought of a hot shower and clean sheets in a warm bed was very inviting.

Upstairs, Mommy showed me to the bathroom. I was surprised when she insisted that she help me. This was so unlike her. In Kabul, Shapairi was the one assigned to keep Vida and me bathed and dressed in clean clothes. So now having Mommy help me undress, and then to have her wash my back as I let the warm water run over my body, made me a bit uncomfortable. I sat in the bath as she ran the soapy washcloth up and down my weary skin. She was treating me as a child.

"It's good to finally see you," I said as she scrubbed my back.

"It's been too long, Enjeela. Too long." Her voice faded into a soft lilt.

As much as I wanted to remonstrate and tell her that I had grown up in the years since I'd seen her, I closed my eyes and indulged the warm feeling; the soothing water penetrated to my weariness. Her touch over the cloth was nurturing in a motherly way. This is what I had missed all those years, and now she instinctively sensed it.

I wanted to tell her everything that had happened since that day she left Kabul: the days I spent huddled around coal stoves in freezing houses, with only the company of an emotionally depleted father and three frightened siblings. How we scraped by to survive. How we lived on the road; slept in the dirt, in the forest, on the side of the road, in mud huts; and ate like impoverished peasants. The memories strummed through me as she continued to scrub away—I wasn't the child she remembered. Yet the warmth of her touch kept me silent for a long while. I was her child. So I let her care for me.

Before I finished, Vida bounced into the room, a ball of sunshine and cheer, her hair flying about her face. "Enjeela," she shouted. "Move over. I need a shower too. I'll get in with you."

I laughed shyly, not wanting to hurt her feelings. We used to bathe together all the time, but I'd grown and matured. "Aren't we a little old for that?" I said as gently as I could.

With a look of disappointment, she stood in the middle of the bathroom in her underwear. "So I can't take a shower with you?"

"I'm almost done now anyway," I said, turning away from her. "Stay and talk to me while I finish up."

She shrugged and stepped back into her dress. But she was not one to stand still. So full of energy, she moved from foot to foot as if dancing and rattled off every possible thing we could do together.

"I can teach you Hindi," she said. She recited a list of phrases she knew well. She spoke them so fluently I was impressed. "I'm learning it in school, but I learned more just walking around and talking to people." Without taking a breath, she continued on. "Oh, and I'll take you to this market where we go—Mom, can we take her to the market? Please, please?"

Mommy had me lean back as she worked shampoo into a lather in my hair, kneading my scalp with her fingers. "Of course," she said. "Just not tonight, Vida. Enjeela needs her rest."

"Okay, tomorrow, then," she said, bouncing on her toes as if she were ready to take off and fly. "We'll go first thing in the morning. You'll love it, Enjeela. There's so much good food. So many nice things to buy. And I know everyone there. I speak to all the shop owners in Hindi. Oh, and we'll buy you a shalwar kameez. Oh, won't she look good in one, Mom? A pretty orange or a bright-yellow one."

Vida's rapid speech about every detail of the market, what we could buy and eat, was invigorating. Her energy seemed pent up, as if she had been saving all of these adorable descriptions just so she could shower them on me.

She kept talking as I toweled off, and she followed me into my room, talking away. There on the bed, new pajamas were laid out for me, and I climbed into them. I ran the soft cloth between my fingers. Mommy had made these herself, I could tell. They were my size and had been waiting for me to arrive. I felt so much less like a stranger, dressed in these pajamas from her own hands.

Mommy peeled back the covers of the bed, and I climbed in. Fatigue hit me as soon as she tucked the covers up to my chin. "We will get new clothes tomorrow," she said, "at the market." Finally, Vida stopped talking.

She bent over and kissed me on the forehead, a seal of her kindness to me. All those years of waiting welled up inside me; after so much travel and doubt, here I was in a warm bed, tucked in by Mommy. Her care brought moisture to my eyes as she pulled away.

"Sleep well, my child," she whispered. She brushed some hair off my forehead and gazed at me for an instant. I saw the tenderness in her eyes, as if she wanted to sew up everything that had been torn apart in our lives and mend every broken promise between us. I had so many things I wanted to say to her, but right then her touch was enough.

"Come, Vida," she said, turning away. "It's your turn for a bath."

Vida stood over me. I reached up and touched her soft cheek, so young and beautiful and full of life, so well cared for here in this home. She had grown into such a vivacious girl, it was hard to take in.

"It's good to be here, Vida." She leaned her cheek into my palm. "I'll see you in the morning."

"I'm glad you're here," she said. And as she bent over and kissed me, she said in her bubbly way, "I've waited so long for you to come home." Then she skipped back to Mommy. The light clicked off, the door closed, and I was alone in the darkness of my first night at my new home. A draft riffled the curtains through an open window. The night had turned the blazing-hot daytime temperature into a tolerable warm breeze. The gauzy fabric of my pajamas in my hand felt so good, like ones at the home I remembered from long ago. The glass bangles around my wrists clanked subtly as I shifted in bed. Sleep closed in on me as I let it take me away. But not before the smells of Mommy's cooking filled my thoughts, and the music in the streets as we rode through the city, and sights of the markets so full of fruit of every color and size. I was done being a Kuchi girl. I was home.

———

The sun hadn't been up very long before Vida bounced into my room, shook me awake, and took up exactly where she'd left off the night before. "We're going shopping today. Get ready, get ready." She had not lost one bit of her enthusiasm, and it made me jump out of bed. Yellow sunshine streamed in through the open window, and the freshness of the new day wafted in on a warm breeze. She sat on the edge of the bed as I went through the closet full of clothes Mommy had prepared for me. She had sewn dresses, slacks, blouses, and skirts. I chose a tan linen skirt and matching blouse. Glancing over all the clothes in the closet, I didn't think I needed much in the way of new clothes. She had been thinking of me, preparing for my arrival, from the looks of my closet. She had thought of everything—except for shoes.

Vida saw me staring down at my travel-worn shoes. "Looks like you need some new ones. We can get new ones today at the market," she chirped with a broad smile.

I held out my hand. She leapt off the bed, and we went downstairs, hand in hand, into a kitchen full of aromas of a delicious breakfast. The entire family was already seated around the table, eating heartily.

"Enjeela." Mommy greeted each of us with a kiss on the top of the head. I slid into a seat next to Padar, and Vida squeezed in between Zia and Zulaikha. Zia immediately began to tease her, and soon both of them were laughing.

"How did you sleep?" Padar asked me as he scooped out food onto my plate.

"Very good," I said. He filled my plate with slices of yellow mango, sweet banana, bright-orange papaya, dollops of yogurt, and what looked to me like a rolled-up omelet with musky-smelling spices and mushrooms. Though I'd eaten well the night before, I felt famished. I wondered if all those months of eating on the road had left me permanently hungry. I ate ravenously as Padar sipped his hot masala chai—a mixture of black tea and Indian spices and herbs.

"Do you eat like this every morning?" I asked Mommy as she sat with us.

She smiled warmly at me. "Some days, yes. Today is special. We are together after a long time."

"You better enjoy this," Ahmad Shah quipped. "Tomorrow you will get the usual, cornflakes and water."

Everyone laughed. I thought of the absurdity of my brother's humor: Mommy had prepared for our arrival—my new clothes, the beautiful house—and now that we were here, she nurtured us with her good cooking. The kitchen was filled with laughter and an abundance of satisfying aromas, and next to me, Padar sipped his chai contentedly, relaxed, as if a large burden had been lifted off him. Vida's constant laughing and chattering revived a memory of what it had been like those many years ago in Kabul, when we had lived together and shared our lives in those days of happiness. I glanced around and took it all in, so much at one time: it had been something like this moment.

─────

An hour later, a large black car pulled into the driveway, and a man dressed in black livery jumped out and opened the back door. He ushered the three of us into the back seat. Vida sat between Mommy and me, trying to contain her enthusiasm with a subdued squirming. On the way to the market, we passed little rickshaws, some motorized and others pulled by boys furiously pedaling bicycles. I wondered at how my fortune had changed so quickly, and now I was riding in the back of a chauffeured car. The sudden luxury felt a little odd to me, after so many days of riding buses and mules and carrying everything I owned in my backpack. But then Mommy had always demanded the best things in life, and here in India she didn't appear to lack for anything.

After a drive through bustling city streets, the car pulled to a curb. I stepped out into a vibrant market full of people on the move. The morning air was already hot and stifling. Cars, rickshaws, and carts pulled by animals jammed the street. Boys on motorcycles darted in between traffic in almost daredevil moves, and music filled the air. The kind of music, loud and lively, that made me want to dance. I found myself wanting to shimmy a bit on the sidewalk as I tried to take it all in. Right in front of us, down a long street filled with stores, merchants had piled their wares on the sidewalk, on tables and on racks, in front of their stores. The road was filled with shoppers in bright clothes, coming and going, inspecting goods, making purchases, and eating. The unmistakable smell of food was on the breeze—the sharp aroma of curry and earthy turmeric and delightful incense.

"Come on," Vida said, pulling me after her. Mommy was already making her way down the street. Catching up with her, I couldn't help but notice that she didn't move with the same vitality she had in Afghanistan. Her feet shuffled as if she couldn't take a full step, though she kept plugging forward. Her heart problems had taken a toll on her health, but she didn't let it spoil her desire to do things for her family. I followed her to the first shop, a fabric store with bolts of cloth leaning against the front window. So many colors, so many choices. I ran my hand down one—bright pink with embroidered gold flower blossoms.

"Do you like that one, Enjeela?"

I imagined myself in an outfit I'd seen so many other girls in the marketplace wearing: the shalwar kameez, with tapered pants and a long tunic with long sleeves. I'd seen some girls wearing them in Pakistan, but here everyone wore them.

"Yes, it's very nice," I said.

Mommy took the bolt inside to make a purchase while Vida and I chatted outside on the curb. I couldn't help but take in all the new sights as my sister rattled away about all the stores she wanted to visit and how many things she wanted to show me and buy me. Across the way from us, one store caught my attention. It had only one table in front of it, and it was piled high with green leaves. They were arranged in fans, like how one would spread out a deck of cards. An old man with wrinkled dark skin sat cross-legged on the ground next to the table. He wore baggy pants covered with stains, and his chest was bare. He held one of the leaves, which was rolled up, and stuffed it in his mouth, working his jaw hard to chew it. He noticed me staring and smiled. His mouth was nearly toothless, and dark-red juice dribbled down his chin. *He's bleeding,* I thought.

"Vida." I grabbed her arm to steady my shaking hands. "What's wrong with that man?"

Just then, Mommy came up beside me and must have seen the shock on my face and figured out what I was staring at. "That's *paan.*" She pointed to the tables. "See the leaves on the table? Those are betel leaves. They take those and stuff them with areca nuts and spices. It's not good—don't ever try it." Her voice was curt. She took my hand and led me away down the street. I couldn't help glancing back at the old man as he stuffed another rolled-up leaf in his mouth.

"What's wrong with *paan?*" I asked.

She fixed me with a glare. It was part warning that I should listen carefully and part exasperation that I was pushing the limits of her tolerance. "It's worse than cigarettes. It makes people crazy, and it gives them cancer. So stay away from it."

She didn't have to tell me twice.

We continued down the street, past shops and restaurants and tea shops, and turned into a clothing store. Vida helped me pick out a shalwar kameez. I couldn't wait to try it on. Both pieces, the tunic and slacks, were sky blue. After I tried them on, I spun around in the dressing room, letting the legs flare out. They were comfortable and fashionable, and I decided to wear them the rest of the day. I picked out a pair of new shoes, and before we left the shop, I tossed my old ones in the trash.

Farther down the road stood a large fruit and vegetable market. Mommy picked out what she planned to cook for dinner while Vida and I strolled among the colorful food stacked high on displays: yellow mangoes, green limes, red pomegranates, bunches of leafy greens that at first I didn't think were safe to touch because they looked so much like those dreaded *paan* leaves. Deep-purple eggplants were heaped up in large piles. We passed barrels of red rambutan with their greenish spikes, yellow breadfruit, and red guavas, which were sliced open to display the bright redness of their flesh. I touched all of them, relishing their textures; some were soft and pliable, others hard and cold. I hadn't seen a market so full of so many different fruits and vegetables at any time I could remember. I wanted to taste each one and savor the flavor in my mouth.

Vida gathered a few pieces of fruit, and we brought them to Mommy, who added them to her purchase. "There's so much here," I said. "Can we buy more?"

She smiled at me, almost in a consoling way. "Not today. We have plenty of time together. No one is going anywhere."

Her words were so tender and loving, I could feel tears welling in the corners of my eyes.

I reached up on the tips of my toes, put my arms around her shoulders, and kissed her cheek. "I missed you."

"I missed you too."

We looked at each other for a long moment. And I could tell from her face that she meant what she'd just said. In the middle of that crowded market, something good passed between us, an understanding that we had been apart from each other too long and it would never happen again.

Vida pulled me out of the moment, urging me to follow her into the street, where the music, which came from every direction, had grown louder. I shielded my eyes in the blazing sunlight that beat down on the crowded street. Vida clasped my hand and swung our arms with the beat and sang along with the lyrics. Shopping here was as much a celebration as anything else.

We followed Mommy from shop to shop, where she bought us little things—books, toys, sweets, inexpensive jewelry—just about anything we asked for. Money didn't seem to be a problem. After the frugal days we spent in Peshawar, her spending felt extravagant. Even though I hesitated to pick things out, Vida urged me on. I couldn't help but think about days in the mountains, when we ate bits of meat and cold bowls of vegetables, or the months in that Peshawar hotel, living on milk and soggy bread, and we wore the same clothes for months at a time. Now I was walking through this market, where every food was available at my fingertips. All the new clothes I could ever ask for and more. Many of the things I didn't think I would ever need, and here I was purchasing them. "You should get this," Vida would say, and suddenly I had a bracelet in my hands.

In a candy store, I stopped in front of a large glass bowl filled with wrapped candy: luminescent reds, greens, yellows, and oranges filled it to the brim. I touched the glass. If I wanted one, I didn't need to beg someone. I just needed to ask. All of those days of worry and meagerness were over. A load of fear and living on the edge of homelessness and hunger were over. A sense of relief came over me; life felt gladly lighter. I didn't need to carry all the concern about my future on my own. In that instant something had been returned to me, something I had lost in those days of war in Kabul, in the mountains of my country, something that lives only in the heart of a child. I turned at a familiar voice behind me.

"Half an hour till our driver returns," Mommy said, glancing at her watch. "Would you girls like a drink of tea before we leave?"

Vida bounced on her heels. Excitement radiated from her toes up through her face in an expression of perpetual fascination and fun.

"Yes." I nodded, taking her hand.

Mommy led us to a shop with a bright-red awning with "Tea Shop" painted on it in bright yellow. The interior was dark and hot, hotter than it was outside, and it had to be in the nineties in the street. Music blared in the darkness. It was lit only by a shaft of yellow coming through the open door. All the tables were full except one along the far wall. We reached it, and Vida went to the counter and carried back a tall glass full of steaming chai. She held it by the brim with her fingertips. Mommy carried two more glasses to the table.

"This is for you," she said. "I put extra milk in it." Steam floated in a thin stream off the glass. But she didn't hesitate to lift it and take several large gulps. With a satisfied moan, she set the empty glass on the table.

"It's a little different from the chai at home," Mommy said. "But I think you'll like it."

I leaned over my glass, inhaling deeper, and let the spicy aromas soak into my senses. The glass still steamed, but I laid my lips on the rim. I sipped the spicy tea—it was hot and sweet, creamy and soothing. It reminded me of how I used to feel sitting in the kitchen with Mommy years ago, basking in the warmth of our home. And now, here in this dingy shop, I had that same feeling. We were together. I tried to contain my smile.

"You like it?" Vida asked. She raised her eyebrows, expecting me to answer. She squiggled around to sit on her knees and leaned close to me. "Do you like it?"

I enjoyed making her wonder. So I took another sip, letting the warm liquid linger on my tongue. I suppressed a smile. Here we sat together, enjoying each other's company after years of thinking this would never happen. I had allowed too many suspicions to creep into my thoughts that when I met Mommy and Vida, neither of them would remember me. Or even care that I was around. But that hadn't happened. At this moment, I was a most wanted child and sister, and here in this shop, they both wanted me to enjoy this new land as much as they did. I stared into Vida's bubbly dark eyes. Eyes that said she could just pick up our life that had been suddenly interrupted. In that dank, cramped shop, I understood how much had been returned to me on this sweltering day in the marketplace. I couldn't hold it in any longer. "Yes, I love it. I love this chai shop. I love everything about India."

And I meant it with all my heart.

22

New Beginnings

Every morning, Vida woke me with her usual verve. She took it upon herself to coach me through my daily routine in Hindi till the words began to stick. Vida had little memory of her days in Kabul. When she left, she was but a toddler. India to her was home, and she had taken to the language, the food, and the way of life here with a natural enthusiasm. It oozed from her. She was reaching out to me with all of her heart to teach me about the beauty of this country, taking me to her favorite markets and to see her favorite movies. For years I had wanted to be here, but daily I found myself pining for somewhere else.

Padar and Mommy never talked of returning to Kabul. They discussed only news of the war, which had reached a terrifying pitch. It had turned even more murderous than when we had walked through the mountains and met the mujahideen fighting for their lives. The country was being destroyed, ripped apart, so that the Soviets could rework it in their own image. So many of my countrymen had been killed or maimed. It was hardly a place my parents wanted to raise their children.

In the fall they enrolled me in Vida's school. Dressed in the same skirts and blouses, we went off each morning together. I didn't know the language nearly as well as Vida did, who now spoke it like a native. Even though my classmates made a real effort to teach me what I needed to know so that I could play games with them at recess and lunch, I was a foreigner. A transplant. This was a land of bright colors in so many shades, and I felt like a dull shadow. Like the dun-colored mountains of my homeland.

When I was feeling particularly sorry for myself, if I couldn't remember a particular word in Hindi or was having trouble with school because I was behind in my lessons, I reminded myself of Mina. If she were alive, she would give anything to be with me here. There was plenty of food, nice clothes, and a beautiful house to live in. She would relish every second of this life. I had been given the blessing of an exciting opportunity—a new life. A life many of my countrymen would embrace without hesitation. I didn't know who to thank for my good fortune. But scowling over my misfortune didn't seem like the right thing to do.

In autumn, when the air cooled and the leaves of the trees turned into bronze torches of flaming color, families prepared for the Diwali festival. First they lit candles and small lanterns throughout their entire house and placed more candles and ghee lanterns in their yard. All up and down the street, the brisk fall evenings became a luminous pageantry of light. Families walked the neighborhood greeting each other. In front of the local temples, large bonfires roared, flames licking up into the night, peeling back the darkness. The brighter the night became, the greater the celebration. It was a time of cheerful fun, greeting one another, handing out sweets and small gifts—a celebration of the triumph of the light over the darkness, good over evil.

Mommy lit up our home and served sweet Indian treats to visitors when they came by to greet us. She had become friends with many of the neighbors, and the week of festivities was a time of renewing relationships with friends and family. In the joyful revelry of the moment, the festivities eased away memories of the holidays in Kabul. The brightness of the night made the darkness of the street safe for children to run up and down. The very fear of what might lurk in the darkness had been erased. So many times on my journey, I had cringed under my blankets, fearing what might attack us. But on this night, there was no fear, as if the possibility of evil had been chased away.

———

Mommy's friends, many of whom had children about the same age as Vida, visited often. They would sit around in the living room, chatting and sipping sweet tea while the children played outside. I often sat with them as they drank their chai and laughed as they talked about their lives, their children, their husbands. What struck me was the joyousness among them. The images of the mothers and daughters in the mountains of Afghanistan grieving the death of sons and husbands had soaked into my being. Tragedy was the only memory I had of so many women in Afghanistan. These visits delighted me, to see women enjoying their lives in a peaceful city. All of them had so much to look forward to. Life was different here, and I was beginning to enjoy being part of it.

Vida immersed me in her life. We continued going to her favorite markets, we played together after school, and on Saturdays we went to her favorite movie house not too far from our house. New Bollywood movies came out every week, and each of them had dancing and singing that mesmerized us. I remembered the Indian movie that Noor used to play in the kitchen while he worked on the family meals. How cheerful and upbeat it was. But here in India, music gave occasion for dancing, and dancing was a large part of the story in every movie.

At home, Vida would imitate the dance moves she had seen on the screen. She had been taking dance lessons for a few years now, and it was easy for her to pick up new routines; she was so lithe and coordinated. The whole family marveled at her skill.

At her dance school, she participated in every recital, and we attended them as a family, clapping and cheering for her as she danced.

She usually played the lead role, dancing with beauty and grace beyond her age.

Vida inspired me to take singing lessons. When I told her about my idea, she urged me on. My parents found a reputable teacher, and I went once a week after school. The lessons not only developed my voice but helped me overcome my fear of performing in front of people. When it came to recital time, my parents and Vida were always in the front row, clapping and carrying on. I had never imagined I would do such a thing in front of so many people, but afterward I felt like a millionaire because of all the attention.

One afternoon I went into the kitchen for a snack and found Padar leaning over a newspaper that lay spread out in front of him. He rested his head in his hands with his elbows propped on the table. He seemed to be studying the classified ads, but he only stared straight at the paper as if he were having difficulty reading the page. I knew he had been looking for work all the months we had been in New Delhi, without much success. His demeanor reminded me of days in Nepal when he had waited for Ram's return from India. He had become taciturn, withdrawn, unwilling to talk much about what worried him. When one of us tried to speak with him about it, he would brush us off.

We lived so well here, yet neither he nor Mommy worked. Before all the mess with the Soviets and having to leave Kabul, he had always worked. I didn't remember a time that he wasn't busy taking care of his properties or attending to business at the embassy, where he translated.

I'd often seen him in here in the evening with the paper spread out like this on the table. Now all he could do was stare at it, as if he were trying to figure out what to do. I stood by the refrigerator, wondering if opening it would disturb him. He was oblivious to my presence. I opened it and poured myself a glass of milk. He didn't move, so I cleared my throat.

"Enjeela," he said, glancing over at me with a half-hearted smile. "How was school today?"

Before I could answer, he began rubbing his chin with his knuckle, his eyes averted as if deep in thought. I went over and touched his hand, and this brought a smile to his lips. His frown lightened up, and he became instantly cheery, quizzing me about my day.

"Any luck finding a job?" I asked.

He patted my head. "Something good will turn up soon. There are many opportunities here. It's difficult to decide what to do." He spoke so positively, I wanted to believe not only his words but his intentions in giving me such a bright picture of our new world.

Later, after I went upstairs to get my books and begin my homework, I wondered why it was so difficult for him to find work. He spoke many languages and was the smartest man I knew. Surely something good would happen, like he had said. I knew he left the house every day, most days before Vida and I left for school. He kept very busy looking for just the right opportunity. I had no reason to believe his difficulties would last very long.

As the school year progressed, my Hindi became more fluent. I spoke it every chance I had, even practicing it at home with Padar. A new way of practicing my language skills began to take shape that year when I discovered boys. For the past five years, my brother had been my constant companion, and I had played with boys in the camps and villages, so it wasn't out of shyness that I didn't speak to them. No one would ever have accused me of being shy. I thought of boys like I thought about my brothers: they were a lot of help when you needed them and annoying inconveniences the rest of the time. I just wasn't that interested. Until I met Raj.

What I had not noticed about them before this was how charming and cute certain boys could be. Especially if they made me laugh.

Raj was tall with black hair, an attractive smile, and a beguiling sense of humor.

After school I often pedaled my bicycle, the one Padar had purchased for me, to one of the nearby parks. New Delhi is a city of parks. Everywhere you drive or walk, there is a carefully landscaped park, each one distinctive, with trees, flowers, lawns to play on, walkways, and more.

Raj and I would sit under one of the spreading oaks or ride our bikes along the path and simply talk. I enjoyed his friendship very much, and it was with his companionship that I realized boys were more than mere annoyances and could be very pleasant to have around. My new home was beginning to feel more comfortable in so many different ways.

———

Since the days of my sister Shahnaz's fairy-tale wedding to the very handsome Saleem, I had dreamt of having a wedding like hers. In my darkest moments, I had fantasized about finding a prince who would sweep me off my feet and free me from all the drudgery and insecurity of my travels. Until that episode with Mina in that scrap of a village she lived and died in. Since then, those dreams had faded. I hadn't thought much about the possibility of weddings and fairy tales until one of our neighbor's daughters became engaged.

A sense of anticipation rippled up and down the block. It became apparent to me that weddings in India were events the entire community looked forward to. A *shaadi*, or Indian wedding, is as much about uniting families as it is about the bride and groom's marriage. It's not unusual to have hundreds, even thousands of guests.

The ritual traditions were quite elaborate, and the family and friends were busy for days decorating the street outside the bride's home—the trees, gates, fences, cars, and even the homes were festooned with lights and flowers. Tents were set up along the sidewalks for guests. One large tent was set in front of the house, where the bride and her family would welcome the groom.

The day of the wedding, the street was blocked off to cars, and guests arrived early to greet the bride. Then they filtered outside to the tents. Some lounged on pillows under the tents, others around tables and chairs, visiting and relaxing. Singers strolled the street, and music was everywhere.

By the time we arrived, our neighbor's house was already full of relatives. Vida and I wore shimmering shalwar kameez of yellow and orange silk that Mommy had made just for the occasion. She had done our hair up in plaits and buns, and I wore brand-new sandals. The house was packed with guests, and the bride sat in the middle of the living room, where her mother and sisters decorated her hands and feet with *mehndi*. She wore an elegant red sari. Sparkling diamonds and brilliant gold jewelry decorated her head, arms, and neck, and every finger had several gold rings. Her mother and aunts doted on her, fastening bracelets, adjusting necklaces, making certain her hair was just so. Watching her, I felt magically transported to a time when love and happiness existed not as a dream but in real life.

Now I stood in the midst of a joyful celebration, and it kindled something inside me—maybe I could experience this one day.

Soon it was time for the wedding to begin, and we filed outside to wait for the groom to arrive. The groom, dressed in a yellow robe with a turban on his head, came into sight atop an elephant that lumbered slowly down the road. A cascade of velvety white flowers draped down from his turban, hiding his face. The beast was surrounded by the groom's family and friends, singing as they marched down the street. The huge animal had a painted face and was decorated with flowers. As it came near, I wanted to run over and touch it, but Mommy held me back.

The procession stopped in front of the house. The groom dismounted. And surrounded by family, he strode forward. The bride came out of the house accompanied by her father. When he presented her, and the young man took her hand, a lump caught in my throat. Even my normally stoic father seemed moved by the moment.

After the presentation, it was time to leave for the hall where the ceremony would take place. The bride and groom left, and the entire throng made their way to the reception hall. After everyone was seated, the bride was escorted to a chair under the *mandap*, an ornate canopy held up by pillars wrapped in flowers and garlands.

Their parents sat on each side of them, and the priest read them their marital responsibilities. The sacrificial altar was lit and the couple circled it seven times, each time reciting a promise to each other. Only after the circling was complete were they announced as husband and wife.

Once the celebration was over, the feasting began. They served naan with a variety of curries, samosas (savory pastries with spiced vegetable fillings), fragrant rice, pakoras (fritters), paneers (cheeses), nuts, sweet cakes. All of this was topped off with desserts of ice cream and fruit. I ate a bit of everything and watched the dancers, listening to the music late into the night. I went home full and happy and ready to attend another wedding. I wouldn't at all have minded having one of those for myself—someday.

Life for me in India became a fabric of events that fit well into my life. As the year progressed, I found it more difficult to sense the distinction between the old me, used to the old ways, and the new me, here in New Delhi. The colors and customs of this amazing country filled my imagination. I could see myself growing older here, finishing school, and maybe watching some handsome young man ride down the road atop an elephant to ask Padar for my hand. Why not? Everything seemed possible.

Padar continued to leave every morning looking for work, making calls, checking out opportunities to create a new life in New Delhi.

Mommy remained active, though her energy wasn't the same; some days she had to rest longer than usual. She kept us busy, making sure we were good students, that we stayed with our lessons—Vida with her dancing, and me with my singing. By the end of that first term, my Hindi became so fluid some began to think of me as a native speaker. The language even became part of my thoughts. Along with the food, the boys, the festivals and celebrations, which never ended.

Holi is the customary festival that celebrates the changing of the seasons from winter to spring. Vida and I embraced it with special enthusiasm. It's called the Festival of Colors, and that's exactly what it was. For weeks leading up to the day, stores sold packets of colored powder: fiery orange, ocean blue, hot pink, lemon yellow, deep purple, crimson red—all the colors of the rainbow in iridescent hues. Each time we went to our favorite markets, we would stand by the stalls that sold the powder from silver bowls you could purchase by the scoopful. We'd dip our fingers in the powder and smear it on each other's faces until the dissatisfied glares of the shop owners chased us away.

On the day of the festival itself, we dressed in white clothes and stood in groups out on the street, where the whole neighborhood was gathered. With our stash of packets, we commenced to pelt each other with the colored powder, creating a cloud of colors that enveloped everything. I heard laughter and shouting, but I couldn't see a thing. Not even Vida, who was beside me. When the dust settled, everyone was covered in a rainbow of hues, from our hair down to our feet. I recognized friends only by the white of their teeth that gleamed as they laughed.

Spring, Mommy explained, is a beginning, a time of growth, a time to sweep out the old and usher in the new. That night as I showered off the powder, the vigor of the day did make me feel renewed. I had washed off the refugee. I laughed at how much fun a change of season could be.

23
Moving Forward

It was July, and Vida and I sat outside the door of Mommy's doctor's office. Padar had asked us to wait in the hall while the physician discussed her latest exam, so we sat on a crowded, hard wooden bench inside the district hospital. The heat and humidity threatened to melt our clothes off. Mommy's breathing had become more labored the last couple of weeks, and her energy had flagged to the point of lethargy. We had been here many times before, and after we stepped into the hall, I had left the door open a crack so that Vida and I could lean forward on the bench and grab what we could of the conversation.

Heart attack. Options. Bypass. Life-threatening.

The doctor went on to say that she needed the surgery and that her life would be in danger if she didn't have it immediately. Vida and I looked at each other and held each other's hands for strength. I expected my parents to have solemn expressions on their faces when they came out of the office. But that wasn't the case. Mommy was as cheerful and positive as ever, and Padar possessed his usual poetic stoicism, as if everything that happened had been foretold in a verse of Hafiz or Rumi. I knew he went to his memory for comfort as he supported Mommy, who walked with a slight stoop and roll of her shoulders as she shuffled her feet down the hall toward the door.

A week later she lay on a gurney in a hospital room, wearing a blue surgical cap over her hair, covered in a white sheet. While a nurse hooked an IV up to her arm, the whole family gathered around her. She blew kisses and said not to worry, that she would see all of us soon. She kept a smile up even when they wheeled her out of the room.

I followed her down the hall.

"Mommy, Mommy," I whispered as I walked beside the gurney. I twined my fingers in her hand and held on until we approached the double doors of the operation theater.

Though her eyes were heavy with fatigue, she lifted her head a bit. "It will be all right, Enjeela. I will see you soon. Stay with your brothers and sisters." She squeezed my hand once, then let go. Padar took my hand and pulled me away. I watched as she disappeared into the room full of equipment and nurses and doctors until the doors swung shut.

We gathered in a small waiting room. The day was already hot and stinky with humidity when we arrived, but I felt suddenly chilled, slumped on the plastic chair. My brothers talked softly to each other about a game of cricket they were going to play with friends tomorrow. Shapairi stared off at a corner of the ceiling. Laila and Zulaikha sat on the floor, leaning against a wall. Padar sat next to me reading a book of poems. Shapairi asked if Laila had remembered to lock the front door this morning. Laila said she couldn't remember. That it would be okay. Zia said he had left his cricket bat in the living room. Somebody could steal it. Padar kept reading, burying himself in words. No one mentioned dying or death, only what we might cook for dinner or if it might rain. Each hour that passed, my stomach grew heavier, a weight falling into my legs. At dinnertime the doctor came into the room, still in his scrubs.

"It went very well," he said. "There were no complications." He told us it would be a few more hours before we could see her, though she wouldn't wake up for some time. We would be able to visit, but only briefly because she needed to be on a ventilator overnight.

After he left, I felt a weight lift. One of my brothers said he had known she would be fine. Padar patted my shoulder. Shapairi leaned back in her chair, smiling for the first time that day.

A couple of hours later, we were allowed into the recovery room. Mommy was hooked up to several monitoring machines and an IV. She was very groggy, and we were supposed to walk by her bed, then leave. I stood by the bed's railing, my hands clamped to the cold steel. A ventilator pumped air into her lungs in a steady rhythm, her chest rising and falling. The ventilator was only a precaution, the doctor had said. Yet to see her tethered to the machine made her seem less alive. Her eyes were closed, her lids tinged with red, as if her life lay on the surface of her skin.

"Enjeela. We must go," Padar whispered in my ear. He took my shoulder in a firm hold and led me away. He ushered us through the hospital to the entrance. He watched from the curb as we all climbed into a rickshaw. We left him alone, standing on the sidewalk in front of the hospital, his hand raised in a solitary wave to us. He would sleep in the room that night and see her through her most difficult hours. Just as he had done for us during our travels here.

The day had wrung every bit of energy out of me. As soon as we arrived home, everyone disappeared into their rooms. I dragged myself upstairs to bed. As I fell off to sleep, I couldn't get the last picture of Mommy out of my mind, wired up to those machines. So weak and helpless.

I awoke early the next morning, and all of us went through getting ready and eating in a meditative quiet. Even on the rickshaw ride to the hospital, we hardly spoke a word to each other. Zia wasn't his usual jocular self, and Vida sat beside me staring out the window, all the bounce and enthusiasm drained out of her.

My thoughts began to drift to the days in Kabul without Mommy. Chaos. Uncertainty. Restlessness.

A few months later, Mommy had convalesced well and was up and walking around, slowly working her way back into her routine as she gained strength. We all marveled at how she had recovered and were happy to see her energy and vitality return. One night at dinner, Padar arrived with a particularly bright glint in his eyes.

"I have an announcement." Padar leaned over his plate and glanced up and down the table. Mommy sat beside him, quietly touching her food with her fork. We all stared at him wide-eyed. It was so unlike him to tell us anything unless the situation was dire. Like when he sprang Masood on us in the middle of the night and said we had to leave right then. There was no discussion, just leave. I gripped my fork in one hand, knife in the other, wanting to hold on to something. "You all must know that we've been living on our savings for the last two years."

Yes, I thought. *That's what has us all worried.*

"We can't do that forever." He eyed each of us. Was he reprimanding us silently for how much we cost him? "But I don't want you to worry about money, because we aren't running low."

Across from me, Zulaikha let out a sigh. Zia smiled. Ahmad Shah still had a furrowed brow.

"But we will someday if I'm not able to find work. It's been impossible for me to find any opportunities here."

Everyone sat perfectly still.

"So your mother and I have come up with a plan." He put his arm around her shoulders. "One that will be good for all of us."

"Are we going to have to move?" Vida asked.

He smiled at her question and took a breath before he spoke. "Yes."

I squeezed my fingers so tight around the utensils I could feel the pain in my knuckles. Smiles turned to frowns. Zia sunk down in his chair.

"We are moving to America."

"America?" Ahmad Shah shouted. Forks and knives dropped to the plates with a clatter. "America!" he kept saying, as if a shock of electricity had shot through him. He clapped and hooted. Laila began jumping up and down, saying something about playing volleyball. Even demure Zulaikha had a grin on her face, as if she had secretly pined for America all along.

"Won't that be wonderful," Vida said, shaking my arm beside me. Her enthusiasm was electric. I found myself smiling and wanting to join in the euphoria of the moment, but I couldn't. My life was here in New Delhi. I would have to move away from my friends, my school, the boys I was coming to know, the festivals, the music, the dancing and singing. It would be leaving Kabul all over again. I couldn't imagine for one moment how America could be superior to the island of happiness I already had.

Ahmad Shah's carrying on became louder and louder over the idea of moving to "the land of opportunity." He kept talking about going to the beach and meeting girls with yellow hair. I didn't have any idea what he was talking about. A resentment boiled up inside till it must have shown on my face.

"Enjeela, aren't you happy about this?" Padar said, leaning toward me. "This is good news. Everything you could ever dream of is in America."

I wanted to tell him every bit of my feelings, but I dared not be disrespectful. "But I was just getting used to it here."

Padar patted my head, then smoothed down my hair. He moved a strand off my face, as if to reassure me. But I had moved enough in my life already, and in that moment I decided I didn't want to move any more.

"Can I be excused?"

Padar pursed his lips before nodding. I rose and dragged myself upstairs. I showered, then dressed for bed. I stood by the window, gazing out at the quiet street. This was my home now. Why should I leave?

Beside my bed, I knelt down and prayed. "Please, God. I don't want to go to America. I want to stay here with my friends and keep going to my school. I don't want to travel again. Ever again."

That night, visions of living through days of mud and starvation, wearing the same stinky clothes for weeks at a time, slogging through mud-caked villages of bearded men with anger in their eyes sifted through me in phantasmagoric scenes. Then there were the faces of family and friends that flashed on the wall of my mind—people I would most likely never see again, like Izmarai and Aunt Gul. The others were a swift-moving collage of smiles, laughs, and words swallowed in a chaotic mist, as if they knew they were leaving me forever, and it was okay.

I awoke tangled in my sheets, startled by the memories that fled from me. A soft light streamed through the open window. I was still safe at home, alone in my room. A new conviction welled up in me that I could never return to a country torn apart, and as much fun as India had become to me, it was not home. America seemed so far off, but Padar was right. America was a place of grand dreams where we could start fresh and build a future.

I understood how hard it would be to start a new life, how we would have to make sacrifices for one another to prosper in a new land with a new language, and I envisioned the things we could achieve if we worked hard, trusted and looked out for one another, and kept moving forward. That was all in my future, and my past had prepared me.

Acknowledgments

In the writing of this book, Enjeela Ahmadi-Miller worked with John DeSimone, who is the author of *Leonardo's Chair* and *The Road to Delano* and the coauthor with Raana Mahmood of *Courage to Say No*.

I would like to acknowledge a few other parties for their support and assistance in the creation of this book. They include my son, Alexander Miller, to whom this story is dedicated; my sister Vida Ahmadi; my best friend, Vivian Lombardi; Henry S. Miller; Brandon Rutledge; and my literary agent, Leticia Gomez. I would also like to acknowledge my editor, Erin Calligan Mooney, who showed interest in my story.

About the Author

Photo © 2018 Jason Ross Levy

Enjeela Ahmadi-Miller was born in 1975 in Kabul, Afghanistan, and is now a citizen of the United States. She also lived in Pakistan and India and speaks several languages, including Farsi, English, Hindi, and Urdu.

An entrepreneur since the age of eighteen, she has owned several businesses: a restaurant (Angelo's Pizza in Los Angeles); a cosmetics line (Ahmadi, sold in spas and salons in LA); retail stores (Bella Bella, Friction, and Milan, all in Dallas); and a clothing line (Henry III Generation, sold in Neiman Marcus and boutiques throughout the US). In 2004 she married prominent Dallas real estate guru Henry S. Miller III, and in 2005 their son, Alexander, was born. A dynamic mother who strives to be as open and giving as possible, she maintains a creative, passionate, artistic, and spiritual outlook on life.